For Dummies™
BESTSELLING
BOOK SERIES

Puppies For Dummies®

Core Commands

Teaching your dog commands helps him/her feel emotionally connected. Encourage anyone spending time with your dog to use the same commands. Keep this list on your refrigerator to encourage consistency.

Command	When to Use
Let's Go	When you're walking and want to encourage your dog to follow your lead.
Wait and Okay	Use Wait when you reach a threshold, curb, or stairway; release with Okay. (Also use these commands with food to encourage self-control and gentle mouth habits.)
Excuse Me	When your dog gets in your path (say "Excuse Me" with attitude as you shuffle through), ignores a command, or leans on you.
Name	Be positive when using your dog's name. Use it whenever you want to make a loving connection. Hearing it should help him trust you.
Sit	When you offer your dog something positive, such as a toy, treat, pat, or dinner.
Down	When you want your dog to sit quietly.
Stay	When you want your dog to be still for a period of time (say "Stay" in a serious tone).
Heel	When you need your dog to walk next to you (good for town or populated situations).
Settle	When you want your dog to quiet down for a time, such as during dinner, while doing homework, or while watching TV.
Stand	When you need to groom, bathe, or steady your dog in a crowd.
Off	When you want to discourage jumping and to get your dog off the furniture.
No Ma'am or No Sir	When you catch your dog considering the unacceptable: garbage grabbing, sock stealing, chasing, jumping, etc.
Kisses	Great for introductions. Encourage everyone to hold out their hand and say "Kisses."

Common Poisons

Dogs can mistakenly pierce a tightly closed container or knock low-placed plants to the ground. Prevent emergencies by keeping all toxic substances away from them. In case of an emergency, ask your vet how to induce vomiting.

Household Poisons	Common Plants	Outdoor Poisons
Acetone	Boxwood	Anti-freeze
Ammonia	Columbine	Carbon monoxide
Bleach	Foxglove	Charcoal lighter fluid
Chocolate	Hemlock	Gasoline
Deodorants	Ivy	Kerosene
Soap	Lily of the valley	Lead
Furniture polish	Lupine	Lime
Ibuprofen	Marijuana	Paint thinner
Insecticides	Morning glory	Phenol cleaners
Rubbing alcohol	Oleander	Rat poison
Tylenol	Poinsettia	Strychnine
	Yew	Turpentine

Puppy First Aid

This information is dedicated to Maison Gilman, a West Highland White Terrier who needed all of the first aid below to resuscitate her and who helped show me that these methods really do work. Bless her life.

Note: Regardless of the outcome, take your dog to your veterinarian immediately. The following emergencies cause internal stress, which requires professional attention.

Artificial respiration

For a dog who cannot breathe:

1. Open the mouth and pull the tongue aside to check for an obstruction.
2. Close the mouth securely and bring the neck to an outstretched position.
3. Bring the dog's lips down over the mouth and hold them securely under the chin to prevent air leakage.
4. Create an air funnel to the nose with your free hand or place your mouth directly over the dog's nose.
5. Exhale deeply into the nose every three seconds.

Heimlich Maneuver

For a dog who is choking:

1. Pull the tongue forward and check the mouth for obstructions. Align the head and neck.
2. Place your hands together just below your dog's rib cage.
3. Pull forward into your dog's abdomen.
4. Repeat five times vigorously.
5. Recheck the mouth, applying artificial respiration if breathing has stopped.

Doggie CPR

For a dog whose heart has stopped beating:

1. Lay a large dog on its side to perform CPR. Smaller dogs should be compressed on either side of the chest.
2. Place hands one on top of the other on the chest (two to four fingers below the elbow, depending on the size of the dog).
3. Press down and forward toward the head.
4. Repeat 15 times in 10 seconds.
5. Breathe into your dog's nose if his breathing has not resumed.

Hungry Minds™

Copyright © 2000 Sarah Hodgson
All rights reserved.

Cheat Sheet $2.95 value. Item 5255-4.

For more information about Hungry Minds, call 1-800-762-2974.

For Dummies: Bestselling Book Series for Beginners

TM

...FOR DUMMIES

References for the Rest of Us!®

BESTSELLING BOOK SERIES

Do you find that traditional reference books are overloaded with technical details and advice you'll never use? Do you postpone important life decisions because you just don't want to deal with them? Then our *For Dummies*® business and general reference book series is for you.

For Dummies business and general reference books are written for those frustrated and hard-working souls who know they aren't dumb, but find that the myriad of personal and business issues and the accompanying horror stories make them feel helpless. *For Dummies* books use a lighthearted approach, a down-to-earth style, and even cartoons and humorous icons to dispel fears and build confidence. Lighthearted but not lightweight, these books are perfect survival guides to solve your everyday personal and business problems.

"More than a publishing phenomenon, 'Dummies' is a sign of the times."

— The New York Times

"A world of detailed and authoritative information is packed into them..."

— U.S. News and World Report

"...you won't go wrong buying them."

— Walter Mossberg, Wall Street Journal, on For Dummies books

Already, millions of satisfied readers agree. They have made For Dummies the #1 introductory level computer book series and a best-selling business book series. They have written asking for more. So, if you're looking for the best and easiest way to learn about business and other general reference topics, look to *For Dummies* to give you a helping hand.

Hungry Minds™

1/01

Puppies

FOR

DUMMIES®

Puppies FOR DUMMIES®

by Sarah Hodgson

Hungry Minds™

Best-Selling Books • Digital Downloads • e-Books • Answer Networks • e-Newsletters • Branded Web Sites • e-Learning

New York, NY ◆ Cleveland, OH ◆ Indianapolis, IN

Puppies For Dummies®

Published by
Hungry Minds, Inc.
909 Third Avenue
New York, NY 10022
www.hungryminds.com
www.dummies.com

Library of Congress Control Number: 00-101104

ISBN: 0-7645-5255-4

Printed in the United States of America

10 9 8 7

1O/RQ/QZ/QR/IN

Distributed in the United States by Hungry Minds, Inc.

Distributed by CDG Books Canada Inc. for Canada; by Transworld Publishers Limited in the United Kingdom; by IDG Norge Books for Norway; by IDG Sweden Books for Sweden; by IDG Books Australia Publishing Corporation Pty. Ltd. for Australia and New Zealand; by TransQuest Publishers Pte Ltd. for Singapore, Malaysia, Thailand, Indonesia, and Hong Kong; by Gotop Information Inc. for Taiwan; by ICG Muse, Inc. for Japan; by Intersoft for South Africa; by Eyrolles for France; by International Thomson Publishing for Germany, Austria and Switzerland; by Distribuidora Cuspide for Argentina; by LR International for Brazil; by Galileo Libros for Chile; by Ediciones ZETA S.C.R. Ltda. for Peru; by WS Computer Publishing Corporation, Inc., for the Philippines; by Contemporanea de Ediciones for Venezuela; by Express Computer Distributors for the Caribbean and West Indies; by Micronesia Media Distributor, Inc. for Micronesia; by Chips Computadoras S.A. de C.V. for Mexico; by Editorial Norma de Panama S.A. for Panama; by American Bookshops for Finland.

For general information on Hungry Minds' products and services please contact our Customer Care Department within the U.S. at 800-762-2974, outside the U.S. at 317-572-3993 or fax 317-572-4002.

For sales inquiries and reseller information, including discounts, premium and bulk quantity sales, and foreign-language translations, please contact our Customer Care Department at 800-434-3422, fax 317-572-4002, or write to Hungry Minds, Inc., Attn: Customer Care Department, 10475 Crosspoint Boulevard, Indianapolis, IN 46256.

For information on licensing foreign or domestic rights, please contact our Sub-Rights Customer Care Department at 212-884-5000.

For information on using Hungry Minds' products and services in the classroom or for ordering examination copies, please contact our Educational Sales Department at 800-434-2086 or fax 317-572-4005.

Please contact our Public Relations Department at 212-884-5163 for press review copies or 212-884-5000 for author interviews and other publicity information or fax 212-884-5400.

For authorization to photocopy items for corporate, personal, or educational use, please contact Copyright Clearance Center, 222 Rosewood Drive, Danvers, MA 01923, or fax 978-750-4470.

Hungry Minds™ is a trademark of Hungry Minds, Inc.

About the Author

The first thing that comes across clearly when you meet **Sarah Hodgson** is that she's mad about her profession — teaching dogs and training people. For her, it's a life's passion, not a job.

From early childhood, her infatuation with animals and what they were communicating was apparent to everyone. Although she didn't grow up in an animal-centered environment, she soon surrounded herself with all sorts of creatures: from domestic dogs and rodents to wildlife that she rehabilitated. Her first exposure into the dog world was when she began working at a local kennel at age 12. Soon after, she locked into the magic of teaching dogs, and she became a self-proclaimed dog nut. After teaching her own, she went around the neighborhood and offered to train everyone else's dogs.

Sarah entered the pre-veterinarian program at Michigan State University. Although she finished her degree in Biology with an emphasis on Psychology and Animal Behavior, she had already found her life's calling: teaching dogs and training people. At first she trained dogs to earn money through college, but it was clear long before graduation that training dogs was what she loved to do. For her, there was never any other option.

In upstate New York, Sarah has sustained a dog training school for 14 years. During that time, she has built in her love of writing — completing several training books and serving as a corresponding columnist for *The New York Times*. From 1990–1995, she also worked as the press escort under Thelma Boalby, giving her invaluable introductions to those influential and well respected in the dog circles. And the greatest influence on her training methodology came from Job Michael Evans, a former Monk of New Skete.

Sarah continues to teach dogs and people under the business name Simply Sarah, Inc., in Bedford, New York. In addition, she enjoys participating in public events and media appearances to raise canine awareness. But her favorite time of day is when she takes her own dogs, Hope and Shayna May, hiking in the woods. She says that's as essential to her day as drinking water.

Dedication

For Abigail, Martha, and Philippa Biddle, and all the paws to follow

Author's Acknowledgments

So many people to thank — I haven't a clue where to begin.

First, hats off and paw up to my agent, Deborah Schneider. Your steadfast encouragement has been a mystery to me but something I could not do without. Dominique, you're my queen! You've been a good friend, great editor, and — *can you believe it?* — one heck of a publisher. And to the rest of my editing staff . . . Nikki, your upbeat wackiness makes writing for you fun; Sandy Blackthorn, alias "The Saint," I don't know how you do all you do and still remain so cheerful; Dr. Amy Rodriguez (D.V.M.), I love you; and Tracy Barr, initials *tlb*. Thank you all so much.

I can't forget my home team: Laurie Guarino and Louisa Polos, for all your after-school efforts and candid brilliance, Kenny Sohn for your patient explanations, cheery story and long distance advice, and Ridgely Biddle, my final reader and dearest friend. As if you didn't have enough to do!

And, of course, to my foundation of friends and family. Two legged and four. If my arms could reach, I'd hug all of you at once.

Publisher's Acknowledgments

We're proud of this book; please send us your comments through our Online Registration Form located at www.dummies.com.

Some of the people who helped bring this book to market include the following:

Acquisitions, Editorial, and Media Development

Project Editor: Sandra Blackthorn

Acquisitions Editor: Nicole Moustaki

Copy Editor: Tracy Barr

Acquisitions Coordinator: Heather Prince

Technical Editor: Amy Rodriguez, D.V.M.

Editorial Manager: Pam Mourouzis

Editorial Administrator: Michelle L. Hacker

Cover Photo: FPG International LLC,
    © Arthur Tilley

Production

Project Coordinator: Regina Snyder

Layout and Graphics: Amy Adrian, Joe Bucki, Tracy K. Oliver, Jill Piscitelli, Jacque Schneider, Janet Seib, Michael Sullivan

Special Art: Kristin Doney, Illustrator; Mary Bloom, Sarah B. Gilman, Jeannie Harrison, Sarah Hodgson, and Winter/Churchill, photographers.

Proofreaders: Laura Albert, Jennifer Mahern, Susan Moritz, Marianne Santy, Ethel Winslow

Indexer: Sherry Massey

General and Administrative

Hungry Minds, Inc.: John Kilcullen, CEO; Bill Barry, President and COO; John Ball, Executive VP, Operations & Administration; John Harris, Executive VP and CFO

Hungry Minds Consumer Reference Group

Business: Kathleen A. Welton, Vice President and Publisher; Kevin Thornton, Acquisitions Manager

Cooking/Gardening: Jennifer Feldman, Associate Vice President and Publisher

Education/Reference: Diane Graves Steele, Vice President and Publisher

Lifestyles/Pets: Kathleen Nebenhaus, Vice President and Publisher; Tracy Boggier, Managing Editor

Travel: Michael Spring, Vice President and Publisher; Suzanne Jannetta, Editorial Director; Brice Gosnell, Publishing Director

Hungry Minds Consumer Editorial Services: Kathleen Nebenhaus, Vice President and Publisher; Kristin A. Cocks, Editorial Director; Cindy Kitchel, Editorial Director

Hungry Minds Consumer Production: Debbie Stailey, Production Director

◆

The publisher would like to give special thanks to Patrick J. McGovern, without whom this book would not have been possible.

◆

Contents at a Glance

Cartoons at a Glance

By Rich Tennant

"We're hoping he'll grow into it."

page 59

"I don't think teaching the puppy how to help you cheat at cards was the training and bonding experience the Vet. had in mind."

page 313

"WE'VE HAD SOME BEHAVIOR PROBLEMS SINCE GETTING 'SNOWBALL', BUT WITH PATIENCE, REPETITION AND GENTLE DISCIPLINE, I'VE BEEN ABLE TO BREAK ROGER OF MOST OF THEM."

page 119

"When we got him several years ago he was a Golden Retriever. Now, he's more of a Golden Recliner."

page 231

"C'mon boy, don't be scared. Come out and meet your new friend."

page 7

WHY TIMID FAMILIES SHOULDN'T PICK BORDER COLLIES AS HOUSEHOLD PETS.

I have to go to the bathroom, Dad.

page 287

"The first thing I'm going to do is quit my Yoga classes. I'm learning all I need to know about sitting quietly in one position for hours by owning a puppy that falls asleep in my lap."

page 95

Shoot, that ain't nothin', watch this- Roll over, Rusty. C'mon, roll over! Roll over!

page 197

Fax: 978-546-7747
E-mail: richtennant@the5thwave.com
World Wide Web: www.the5thwave.com

Table of Contents

Introduction

W hether you're starting this book with a puppy curled at your feet (or chewing your shoelaces), or you're still in the thinking-about-it stage, welcome. My name is Sarah. Right off the bat — you're not a dummy. You may feel lost and uninformed, but confusion *does not a dummy make.*

All you need is some good information to guide you in your selection, loving hints to help you through those first critical months, and support in training. In these pages, you find straightforward info on what to do and just how to do it — in plain English. Nothing more, nothing less, I promise.

To say that *I love* puppies would be an understatement. Dogs of any age make me giddy. Their paws and silky ears, their little bellies, the infamous puppy breath, and each individual reaction to my "happy voice" awakens the child in me. Though I spend countless hours doing grownup things like driving, cleaning, and cooking, when I've got my arms around a puppy or I'm curled up with my own dogs, my daily responsibilities seem to drift away.

About This Book

The coolest thing about this book? You can jump in anywhere. It's a no-rules reference for everyone who has a puppy or ever thought of getting one. Just look in the table of contents or index for the topic you want to know about. Then flip right to that chapter to get the straight scoop.

Each chapter is divided into sections, and each section contains information about some part of raising a puppy — things like

- ✔ The best age to bring home a puppy
- ✔ Tips for housebreaking success
- ✔ The five stages of development

Conventions Used in This Book

You can read this book straight through from front to back if you want. But you don't have to read it that way. Feel free to use this book as a reference. Just look in the table of contents or the index for the topic you're interested in. Then scoot right to that specific section in the book. You'll see cross-references to other sections or chapters for more or related information about the topic.

To point out new terms or to emphasize something, this book uses italics. And when you're presented with a set of steps to perform, the action you need to take is in bold.

Foolish Assumptions

Here's what I assume about you:

You know that puppies have four paws and a tail — or at least a stump of one.

You either have a puppy right now or are considering getting one, but you don't know the first thing about raising a puppy.

You don't want to become a Ph.D. in training techniques and dog physiology. You just want the basics on things like what supplies to buy, how to train a puppy, the best dog food to use, and how much exercise to give him.

How This Book Is Organized

The book is divided into parts, each one having its own colorful theme. Here's a quick rundown.

Part I: Maximizing Your Chances of Success

Here you find the scoop on choosing a puppy — from the right breed to the perfect personality. Are the breeds all that different? Can their personality be pre-determined? Where's the best place to find a puppy? You'll find all the answers and more in this part.

Part II: I've Picked Out My Pup — What's Next?

Those first few days can be a real challenge. What to do? What to buy? What to expect? You find all the answers in here, plus you find out how to train yourself *and* think like a dog.

Part III: The "What Have I Gotten Myself Into?" Months

By 12 weeks, your puppy's brain is fully developed — and won't you know. He sleeps less and plays more. His true personality emerges, and it may not always jive with yours. Take a deep breath. This part is here to help. It helps you understand your puppy's developmental phases, work with your kids, and get a handle on housetraining.

Part IV: Oh, Behave!

Let training begin. In this section, I cover training stages, tailoring what you teach and how you teach it to the age and personality of your prize pupil. In this part, you discover basic lessons, hints on problem solving, and guidance in finding that help if you need it.

Part V: Behaving in the Big League

Have you mastered the basics? If so, there's plenty more to keep you busy. From off-leash training to canine sporting events to specialized training skills to going out in public — this part examines it all.

Part VI: Ensuring Fitness and Health

If you want a happy dog, you have to take care of more than training. You need to worry about your dog's health, too. This part gives you the information you need to know about good nutrition and exercise, how to take care of your dog when he's feeling fine, and what to do if he gets sick.

Part VII: Dealing with Life in the Real World

This section is a hodge-podge of information that includes topics like good neighborhood manners, handling life changes (babies, roommates, a move, and so on), and traveling with your pet.

Part VIII: The Part of Tens

Last but not least, ten of my favorite games and ten crowd-pleasing tricks. Enjoy. . . .

Icons Used in This Book

The icons in this book point out various things to you:

Useful tidbits and helpful advice — like how to snap the leash *just* right to avoid hurting your pup and still get the response you want.

Friendly reminders to help you never forget — like leaving a full bowl of water for your pup on a hot summer day.

"Warning, Warning!" Need I say more?

Factoids that aren't necessary to know but quite interesting.

Fun information that's good to know.

Where to Go from Here

If you like to start at the beginning of things and work your way from there, go right to Chapter 1 and dig in. Otherwise, feel free to look in the table of contents or index for your topic of choice.

But before you dig in, remember this: Puppies are a lot like babies. They need to be nurtured but not spoiled. They need to be loved but not over-indulged. They need guidelines — not unlimited freedom. They need to play, but they also need limits.

Our ability to reason and understand gives us the responsibility to make the necessary adaptations. Borrowing from one of my poems, you must be your puppy's leader, safe keeper, friend, and voice. Your efforts will forever be your reward.

Our Reward

Treat me with respect, teach me your rules, and train me with patience.

Let me know what pleases you, for if you don't, my unbridled enthusiasm may place unnecessary and stressful demands on you.

There is not an animal on the planet that can offer you the same unconditional devotion that I can, if you show me the path to your heart.

Through my puppyhood I may test you, but only because I am a puppy. Persist, for I will remember your structure as I grow into doghood.

Do not take advantage of me.
Though I have many needs, I cannot speak.

Be my leader, my keeper, my friend, and my voice.
Your efforts will be our reward.

Sarah Hodgson

Part I
Maximizing Your Chances of Success

The 5th Wave   By Rich Tennant

"C'mon boy, don't be scared. Come out and meet your new friend."

In this part . . .

So you've always wanted a puppy. Now you're about to take the big plunge, but you still have lingering questions:

How much consideration should I give to my lifestyle? Are the breeds all that different? Can puppies' personalities be pre-determined? Where's the best place to find a puppy?

You find all the answers and more in this part.

Chapter 1

What's the Big Deal? A Puppy Is Just a Puppy

● ●

In This Chapter

▶ Time commitments and a dog

▶ Lifestyle demands and the dog purchase decision

● ●

"*A puppy is a puppy is a puppy.*" A less true statement was never spoken. Sure, all puppies like biscuits and a belly rub, but the similarities end there. Each puppy, as it grows into doghood, faces — and sees — the world in different and unique ways. Some puppies thrive on human interaction; others prefer an independent lifestyle. Some love the general mayhem created by small children; others find the commotion less than thrilling. Some see all house guests as long-lost friends; others see them as enemies. Some cherish quiet, solitary times; others will tear your house up if you come home too late. What type of puppy sounds good to you?

This chapter considers the many aspects of dog ownership. As you read, consider *your* lifestyle. What breed personality best suits you? (For info on the various types of breeds, head to Chapter 2.) If you abhor the thought of exercise, you probably want to stay away from very active breeds. A great-looking dog loses her appeal when she's climbing your walls. Similarly, if you're the outdoorsy type, bent on strenuous dog/owner hikes through driving snow and scorching sun, don't set your heart on a tiny companion dog. She just won't be up for it, and you'll end up hiking alone. And if your house functions as the local basketball/swimming/video game/bridge club headquarters, a protective breed might develop career stress trying to keep track of all the comings and goings.

You Gotta Consider Your Lifestyle

You can see the importance of thinking about your life and your personality *before* choosing a breed. You have lots to consider — your schedule, your budget, where you live, and more — and you have many breeds to choose from. This section gives you a few things to think about as you begin to decide what kind of dog is right for you.

How crazy are your schedules and commitments?

Puppies need lots of attention, especially when you're breaking them in. Just how much attention depends on the breed and the age, but growing puppies need two to four exercise periods, two to three square meals, and a good block of love and attention every day. Leaving them alone day after day is detrimental to their psychological development, and certain breeds need more interaction than others. Unlike guinea pigs or gerbils, puppies don't accept social isolation very well. You can't expect them to enjoy sitting in a room all day with newspapers and a bowl of water.

Of course, this doesn't mean that if you're a person with a busy social or work calendar, you shouldn't have a puppy. After all, busy people need dog love, too. If you're an always-on-the-go type, choose an independent breed with a medium-to-low energy level *and make time in your schedule for your puppy.* And if you work outside the home, consider a calm breed who won't need a five-mile run twice a day to be happy.

Dogs are social creatures and suffer from extended isolation. Termed *separation anxiety,* this condition is recognized by the medical community. If you're out of the house more than you're in it, you may want to wait until your life eases up before investing your love in a sincerely *needy* dog.

If you're a work-at-home type, you (and your future puppy) are in luck. Although your schedule can be complicated and hectic, you probably have the flexibility to pay lots of attention to the new arrival. But if your schedule is very busy and you don't have the luxury of working at home, you may decide that a puppy isn't the best choice. But don't despair:

- ✔ If you have erratic hours, choose an older puppy or a dog of a breed that's known to tolerate isolation.
- ✔ If your schedule allows it, come home for an hour mid-day or, if your budget allows it, hire a responsible dog walker for the first year.

There are some major developmental differences in young versus adolescent or older dogs. Young puppies' curiosity demands supervision. They are also needy; feedings, walks, and play periods must be carefully woven throughout the day. And keep in mind that some older puppies or dogs act like young ones, so if you do decide to go with an older dog, be sure you find one that's matured a bit.

What do you do for fun and leisure?

What do you do for fun? Can your puppy — who's had all his shots — be included? Dogs don't like to be left out. And they're not choosy. Attending a soccer game, running in the park, or sitting on your lap (small dogs only!) during a Garden Club meeting — it's all a day's fun for your puppy. Being left at home is lonely, and some dogs can be very destructive if they feel deserted.

How are the ol' living quarters?

Do you live in a big house or small apartment? Dogs need room to stretch, and the more energetic the dog, the more room required. Little dogs fit fine in big houses, but the opposite may not be true. In addition to what type of living quarters you have, you also want to consider your neighbors. Some neighbors are less tolerant than others. If your neighbors are the type who complain, you may run into trouble if you get a barker. Yes, complainers are a pain in the neck, but they're within their rights. Table 1-1 lists the living conditions that are ideal for various breeds (see Chapter 2 for detailed information about particular breeds) and how much each type of breed tends to bark.

Table 1-1	Barking Tendency and Recommended Living Conditions by Breed		
Breed	**Big House**	**Small Apt.**	**Bark Proneness**
Pointers	Yes	Not recommended	High
Retrievers	Yes	Not recommended	Medium
Spaniels	Yes	With exercise	Medium
Setters	Yes	Not recommended	Medium
Sighthounds	Yes	With exercise	Low
Scenthounds	Yes	With exercise	High
Large game hunters	Yes	With exercise	Low
Sled/draft	Yes	Not recommended	Medium
Guarding	Yes	With exercise	Medium
Personal protection	Yes	With exercise	Medium
Rescue	Yes	With exercise	Low

(continued)

Table 1-1 *(continued)*			
Breed	*Big House*	*Small Apt.*	*Bark Proneness*
Sheep herders	Yes	With exercise	High
Cattle/sheep driving	Yes	Not recommended	High
Terriers	Yes	With exercise	High
Fighting breeds	Yes	With exercise	Medium
Non-sporting	Yes	With exercise	Varies
Toy	Yes	Yes	Varies

Of course, every rule has an exception or two. Table 1-1 considers the average dog in the group. A particular dog may be better — or worse — than average.

Do you travel? How much?

Are you always flying off somewhere? Some breeds can't handle excessive kenneling. If you're a jet-setter, pick a breed that can.

- ✔ To help you narrow your choices, discuss how much you travel with the breeders you talk to.
- ✔ A few weeks of travel here and there won't hurt.
- ✔ Don't forget that some hotels accept pets (hint, hint).

Can you afford the added expense?

If money's a little tight, avoid high-maintenance dogs, such as those with pushed-in noses or skin flaps, or long-coated breeds. These types of dogs demand more care and can be prone to health problems. Consult a veterinarian about the breeds you're considering before you settle on one.

What Else Is Your Puppy Gonna Be Subjected To?

In addition to your activity level, you need to consider the other people and commitments in your life, too. Are you single? Do you have kids? Are you retired? These things should influence your breed decision. Listed in this section are some *general* lifestyle situations. You might not fit perfectly into any one category — just read them over and keep that thinking cap on.

Single people

Single. Free. No commitments. Few responsibilities. Except one — a new puppy. You need to adjust your schedule around her, and you need to socialize her — take her out to meet your friends if she's had her shots or bring friends in if she hasn't.

A dog isn't a one- or two-year commitment; it's a commitment that lasts the dog's lifetime. So think ahead — a long way ahead. Where will you be in five years? Ten? No pressure here, but do you think you'll have kids? If so, think about getting a kid-friendly breed, even though you may not currently have children. And take the time to familiarize her with kids while she's a puppy — even if that means borrowing your neighbor's kids or corralling your nieces and nephews.

Couples

Do both you and your partner work outside the home? If so, can one be home enough to care for the new four-legged baby? Puppies hate to be alone; the more attention the puppy gets, the better. You also need lots of patience, tolerance, and perseverance. In fact, if you plan to have kids, puppies are great practice. As with raising children, you need to plan and share responsibilities. Someone needs to walk her, feed her, and socialize her.

- ✔ If you're considering a family, avoid protective, guard, and fighting breeds unless you're committed to early training and socialization with children and adults.
- ✔ If you both work all day, consider a more independent breed. You'll still be missed, but it won't be totally traumatic.

Families with children younger than five

Kids this small see puppies as playthings, and I probably don't have to tell you that teaching a three-year-old not to pull and poke the puppy is hard. So get a breed that can tolerate rough handling. You also might want to consider an older puppy — one between four and twelve months old. If properly raised and socialized, an older pup is often calmer and less likely to chew on toys and kids. And unless you're an experienced owner, avoid guard, protection, and fighting breeds. They are less tolerant of visitors and children.

Families with children older than five

Kids over five can participate in a lot of puppy activities. Although you can't expect your children to do all the work, they can learn a lot about responsibility through feeding the puppy, handling its basic health care, and walking it.

- If your kids are pretty rough-and-tumble, you need a breed that tolerates this type of activity.
- If your kids are past the rough-and-tumble stage (leaving for college, perhaps), you can consider many breeds.
- With doors flying open and kids running in and out, you want a kid-tested breed that can take all the commotion in stride.

Again I caution you against protection, guard, and fighting breeds unless you're experienced and can make time in your schedule for extensive training.

Retired people

Retirement is a great time to add a dog to your family. Your schedule is probably more flexible, and you can be very attentive to your new pup. But remember, a puppy can be as demanding as a baby, so if you already did the diaper changing and 4:00 a.m. feeding thing and don't care to repeat these experiences, consider an older pup (between four and twelve months) that has a head start on house training. If your retirement plans call for quiet walks and introspection, investigate the calmer breeds. If you intend to spend your retirement hiking and cross-country skiing, choose a breed that complements your energy level.

Young adults

You're young. You're an adult. College bound or living on your own for the first time, you want a dog. But before you search for your canine soulmate, think carefully:

- Dogs need constant interaction, especially when they're young.
- Dogs cost money. Between upkeep and veterinarian bills, you can expect to spend approximately $150 – 400 per year, not including unexpected diseases or emergency care.
- Most important to consider, owning a dog is a decade-plus commitment. Do you have any idea where you'll be ten years from now? Forget ten years. How about one year or six months or seven days from now?

Impulse ideas can be alluring, but before you involve the loyalty of a dog, consider the commitment. Talk to those closest to you and consider other options if you decide that your lifestyle — now or in the future — should change in such a way that a dog would no longer fit into it.

Households with other pets

Even if you fit into one of the categories previously presented, you may already have other pets. Other animals in the house — especially if your other pet is a dog — change the dynamics between you and your puppy and your puppy and its new environment. Having a well-mannered dog to teach your new addition the ropes can make your life a lot easier. If, on the other hand, your resident dog is a nut case, you may want to consider a little training for him *before* you bring another dog into your home.

Chapter 2

Figuring Out Which Kind of Puppy to Get

*B*efore you find the puppy that's right for you, you need to get a grip on the various breeds that are available. In this chapter, I give you the scoop on the seven standard breed groups assigned by the American Kennel Club, as well as some info about rare breeds and mixed breeds. This chapter also gives you a look at the characteristics of different breeds so that you can begin developing an idea of what kind of canine companion may be right for you.

Understanding What a Breed Is

Long ago, before computers and microwaves, we humans depended on dogs to help us survive. As a result of our tinkering with their reproductive process, dogs have become a species more varied and diverse in abilities and physical characteristics than any other species on Earth today. There are now dogs that weigh two pounds and dogs that weigh two *hundred* pounds, dogs with silky, flowing coats and dogs with no hair at all.

A *breed* is like a cross between a personal ad and a job description. You can find a breed to fit every function — from hunting, herding, and hauling to protection, pest patrol, and companionship. You can even find a hairless breed that was developed in Mexico to serve medicinal purposes as well as be a companion.

With some exceptions, your puppy's innate skills are not necessary to your survival — but don't tell this to your puppy. As he grows, he'll still think his skills are very much in demand. And his breed drive won't let him slack off for lack of work. No sheep to herd? No problem. He'll herd people. No poachers to drive from the grazing lands? Then the mail carrier is a good enough stand in. No ducks to retrieve from the pond? That's okay. A tennis ball will do. Dogs love to work, and you cannot force them to make major career changes.

Although no one really knows for sure when the word "dog" found its way into our vocabulary, some people claim that it was used as much as 15 to 25 centuries ago. The fancy name for dog is *Canis domesticus*. Wolves are called *Canis lupus*. Although dogs and wolves are considered two different species, they can still interbreed because of their common ancestry.

Slugging Through Seven Standard Breed Groups

If you're serious about adding a puppy to your family, you need to consider a suitable breed. Know what you and your family want and know what the breed was bred to do. This section describes the seven breed groups assigned by the American Kennel Club (AKC) and lists the breeds that fall into each breed group. These descriptions, along with Chapter 1, can help you find a breed to go with your personality—the first step in getting a dog that can live up to your expectations.

All about the American Kennel Club

Think of the AKC (American Kennel Club) as a sort of Canine Principals Office. The AKC keeps records of each registered purebred puppy, monitoring all breeding activities in its *Stud Book*. Sound kinky? Don't get your hackles up; the Stud Book is just a handy system for recording lineage. The AKC also sponsors dog shows and other canine sporting events, awarding championship points and titles in conformation, obedience, and other events.

Interestingly, the AKC only recognizes a quarter of the breeds known worldwide. Each breed has its own country of origin, and not all breeds have made it to America's shores. In fact, before a breed is recognized by the AKC, it must have enthusiasts throughout the states and an active parent club that records breeding and births,

has established conformation standards, and sponsors activities for the club. Only after this interest has been established does the AKC have a board meeting to decide whether to consider the breed for inclusion. If everyone gives the thumbs up, the breed is recognized in the *Miscellaneous Class*. Dogs in this class are allowed to compete for obedience titles and in conformation, but they are not awarded points toward a championship. If the interest in these breeds continues, supporters of the breed can then apply for official breed recognition.

For more information about the AKC, go online to www.akc.org or write to the AKC at 5580 Centerview Dr., Raleigh, NC 27606, (919) 233-3600.

Note that although roughly 400 breeds are recognized worldwide, I refer only to the breeds recognized by the AKC. For more information about the AKC and what has to happen before it recognizes a breed, see the sidebar "All about the American Kennel Club."

The 146 breeds registered with the AKC are subdivided into seven groups: Sporting, Hound, Working, Herding, Non-Sporting, Terrier, and Toy. The dogs in each group share common characteristics. But, because these characteristics can be so broad — the Non-Sporting Group, for example, contains both the American Eskimo *and* the Miniature Poodle — I've broken the groups into subgroups and listed which breeds fall under each description. Confused? Feeling dizzy? Read on; it's quite simple.

With all breeds, do your homework first and buy from reputable breeders only.

The Sporting Group

The dogs in the Sporting Group were bred to aid man in hunting fowl (wild birds). Conditioned by nature to retrieve, these dogs can be trained to gather birds from the field or water, or they can simply stay at home and make excellent companions, fetching tennis balls, slippers, and the morning paper.

Four types of dogs comprise the Sporting Group: pointers, retrievers, spaniels, and setters.

The pointers

All pointers belong in the Sporting Group (see Figure 2-1). Tall, leggy dogs, bred to spend entire days running the fields looking for land fowl, these dogs are competitive, attentive, and *very* energetic.

> German Shorthaired Pointer
> German Wirehaired Pointer
> Pointer
> Vizsla
> Weimaraner
> Wirehaired Pointing Griffon

The pointers love an active lifestyle. Without sufficient exercise, the pointing breeds have an abundance of nervous energy, which may result in destructive chewing, digging, jumping, and excessive barking. Given lots of exercise, though, you'll find these dogs friendly, involved, and accepting of children.

Figure 2-1:
The
Wirehaired
Pointing
Griffon.

The retrievers

Also in the Sporting Group, retrievers (see Figure 2-2) were bred to stay close to their masters and retrieve water fowl.

> Chesapeake Bay Retriever
> Curly-Coated Retriever
> Flat-Coated Retriever
> Golden Retriever
> Labrador Retriever

Well-built, large dogs, retrievers are a bright, loyal, and active lot. Happy souls, they love to be involved in all family activities, take to training very well, and generally view all strangers as potential friends. Retrievers are also easy-going, making excellent family pets, but prolonged isolation upsets them. They may develop Hyper Isolation Anxiety, resulting in destructive chewing, digging, barking, and jumping.

Dogs left alone for an excessive number of hours develop *Hyper Isolation Anxiety*. When finally reunited, their tension is so high that they run around grabbing anything that fits into their mouths and jumping on furniture, counters, and people.

The spaniels

The low-riders of the Sporting Group, spaniels were bred to find and flush birds (see Figure 2-3). Trusting and friendly, spaniels fit in well with active families.

American Water Spaniel
American Cocker Spaniel
Clumber Spaniel
English Cocker Spaniel
English Springer Spaniel
Field Spaniel
Irish Water Spaniel
Sussex Spaniel
Welsh Springer Spaniel

Figure 2-2:
The Golden
Retriever.

Figure 2-3:
The English
Springer
Spaniel.

Loyal, spaniels love family excursions and children, but they don't like being left alone. If isolated or untrained, spaniels may become timid, whine a lot, or guard their food and other objects.

The setters

Majestic setters, bred to run the fields and point and flush fowl, also fall under the Sporting Group (see Figure 2-4). Highly intelligent, setters are loyal, non-protective dogs who thrive on family interaction. As an added bonus, you'll look terrifically aristocratic as you stroll through town with a setter at the end of a leash. Exercise is a requirement for these large fellows; without it, they get high-strung and nervous.

> Brittany
> English Setter
> Gordon Setter
> Irish Setter

At first glance, the Brittany might look like a spaniel. In fact, this breed was once called the Brittany Spaniel, but the Spaniel was dropped because this dog hunts more like a setter.

Figure 2-4:
The English
Setter.

The Hound Group

You ain't nothing but a hound dog. (Sorry, I just had to get that in.) These breeds in the Hound Group like following fast-moving game, and this penchant has made them a big hit in the hunting circles. In addition to their keen noses or sharp eyesight, the hounds' easy-going and, at times, stoic personality has endeared them as family pets. The three types of hounds are sighthounds, scent hounds, and large game hounds.

The sighthounds

Relying on their eyesight to hunt fast-moving game, these sighthound breeds have been domesticated to make placid, gentle pets (see Figure 2-5), but the instinct to run after fast-moving targets has never been bred out of the sighthounds. (You'll need to keep them on a lead when outdoors because you can't outrun them.) In addition, you need to socialize sighthounds to common household pets (like cats, birds, and rabbits) at an early age; otherwise, they may confuse them for lunch as they race across your floor. Sighthounds are alert and mild and make wonderful pets in stable households.

Afghan Hound
Basenji
Borzoi
Greyhound
Ibizan Hound

Irish Wolfhound
Pharaoh Hound
Saluki
Scottish Deerhound
Whippet

Figure 2-5:
The Saluki.

The scent hounds

Bred to follow scent, scent hounds are active, lively, and rugged (see Figure 2-6). That sensitive nose, however, makes them somewhat difficult to train; they'd rather trail a rabbit than hang around learning to sit and stay. And, when these dogs are outside, a leash or enclosure is required — that nose again. Although a bit stubborn when it comes to training, scent hounds are happy breeds. Sweet, lively, and tolerant, they thrive on family involvement and accept children and strangers with ease.

> Basset Hound
> Beagle
> Black and Tan Coonhound
> Bloodhound
> Dachshund
> American Foxhound
> English Foxhound
> Harrier
> Otterhound
> Petit Basset Griffon Vendén

Figure 2-6:
The
Dachshund.

The large game hounds

These hounds were originally bred to hunt lions and elk and, as you may guess, are large, powerful, and fearless when challenged (see Figure 2-7). No longer used for their original purpose, the large game hounds now enjoy life as pets and watchdogs.

> Norwegian Elkhound
> Rhodesian Ridgeback

Figure 2-7:
The
Rhodesian
Ridgeback.

Large game hounds are strong-willed and independent and need training to enhance their sociability — and your control. In the right home, they are steady and calm and make devoted pets, but don't expect them to back down from an argument. You need to exercise and socialize these dogs to prevent destructive habits or territorial aggression.

The Working Group

This classification needs little explanation. Though more varied in job description than the other groups, the breeds in the Working Group have one thing in common: Throughout the centuries, they have performed specific jobs that have benefited humans. In the Working Group, you find sled/draft dogs, personal protection dogs, rescue dogs, and estate guarding dogs.

The sled/draft dogs

These working dogs, also referred to as Nordic breeds, love cold weather (see Figure 2-8). Originally bred to pull sleds and live outside, sled dogs have thick, beautiful coats, a fondness for hunting, and a strong instinct to pull. Put one on the end of a leash, and you'll experience this instinct first hand. Rugged and free-spirited, sled dogs thrive outdoors, and they need plenty of exercise.

Don't try to coddle sled dogs — they're not the cushion-by-the-fire type. Although strong-willed and hard to train, Nordic breeds make sweet, friendly pets if you work with them. To prevent destructive behavior, make sure you give them plenty of exercise and attention. And remember that these fearless hunters will wander if given the opportunity.

With their double coat, sledding breeds aren't much for really hot weather. If you live in a hot climate, consider another breed. These dogs would be miserable.

Sled:

Alaskan Malamute
Samoyed
Siberian Husky

Figure 2-8:
The
Samoyed.

Draft dogs were once used to cart heavy loads for their masters. Though they have a fondness for pulling, their similarity with sled dogs ends there. These dogs are true workers whose close and consistent association with their masters also encourages a strong association with their home and territory. Though I've only listed two breeds here, other breeds, such as the Rottweiler and the Newfoundland, were used as draft dogs in addition to their primary role.

Draft:

Bernese Mountain Dog
Greater Swiss Mountain Dog

The guard dogs

Bred to protect territories and livestock without man's direction, the guard breeds are alert, intelligent, courageous, and independent (see Figure 2-9).

Akita
Anatolian Shepherd
Bullmastiff
Great Dane
Great Pyrenees
Komondor
Kuvasz
Mastiff
Rottweiler

Figure 2-9:
The Kuvasz.

These dogs need structured training and a qualified leader. Be sure you are up to the job; otherwise, you'll end up as a sheep instead of the shepherd. Without the proper training and socialization — or with an unqualified owner — guard dogs may attack strangers who enter their territory. But in the right home (with the right owner), these dogs are calm, dignified, and devoted. Train and socialize them early to avoid later difficulties.

Raising children and dogs is challenge enough. Territorial breeds can overstate their job as guardian, protecting your home and children against all intruders — including friends, extended family members, daily workers, and even other children. These dogs quickly suffer career stress in busy houses. If your heart's set on a territorial breed, structured training is a must.

The personal protection dogs

Personal protection dogs were bred to work under the direction of man (see Figure 2-10). As a result, they are intelligent, strong-willed, and intensely loyal to one family unit. These dogs need a structured training program and early socialization to offset potential territorial aggression. For the determined and committed owner, these dogs make extraordinary companions. Without training and exercise, however, they may become aggressive, unruly, and destructive.

> Boxer
> Doberman Pinscher
> Giant Schnauzer
> Standard Schnauzer

What's the difference between *Standard* and *Giant?* About 6 inches and 40 pounds. It's a size thing. The sidebar "So how big is large?" gives more info on size.

Figure 2-10:
The
Standard
Schnauzer.

JUST FOR FUN

So how big is large?

Dogs come in all shapes and sizes. Unfortunately, the sizes aren't as simple as big and little. The following table can help you figure out how big large is and how little small is — just in case you ever need to know.

Category	Height	Weight
Small	Up to 10 inches	2 – 20 pounds
Medium	10 – 20 inches	20 – 50 pounds
Large	20 – 27 inches	50 – 75 pounds
Giant	27+ inches	75+ pounds

The rescue/water dogs

The rescue breeds are large, low-key dogs with dense coats (see Figure 2-11). They prefer cold weather to hot. Steady and intelligent, rescue/water rescue breeds are exceptional around children when raised with them. Untrained and isolated, however, they can develop Hyper Isolation Anxiety.

Newfoundland
Portuguese Water Dog
Saint Bernard

Figure 2-11:
The Saint
Bernard.

The Herding Group

The function of breeds in the Herding Group is to, well, herd livestock. These dogs are a hard-working lot who, in most cases, work under the direction of a shepherd. This group can be broken down into two types: sheep herders and cattle herders.

The sheep herders

These herding dogs were bred not to guard the flock but to move it (see Figure 2-12). They are agile, alert, and very active. Easily trained, the sheep herders are devoted to their family, not prone to roaming, and tolerant of children. They can be protective of their property and suspicious of strangers, but they are not generally prone to serious aggression problems. These dogs love to exercise, work, and play. Always on the lookout for something to herd, they settle happily for children if sheep aren't available.

Australian Shepherd
Bearded Collie
Belgian Malinois
Belgian Sheepdog
Belgian Tervuren
Border Collie
Collie
German Shepherd Dog
Old English Sheepdog
Puli
Shetland Sheepdog

Figure 2-12:
The Border
Collie.

The cattle/sheep driving dogs

These dogs were bred to drive sheep and move cattle long distances, often *without* man's direction. A hardy bunch, cattle/sheep driving dogs are more solidly built and stockier than the sheep herders (see Figure 2-13). Athletic, dominant, and less predictable than their cousins, they need clear and consistent training. Generally reserved with strangers, they need early socialization to prevent aggression.

> Australian Cattle Dog
> Briard
> Bouvier des Flandres
> Canaan Dog
> Cardigan Welsh Corgi
> Pembroke Welsh Corgi

Figure 2-13: The Pembroke Welsh Corgi.

The Terrier Group

Losing is not in a terrier's vocabulary. Own a terrier, and one word springs out at you immediately — determination. Terriers take a bite out of life and don't let go. The two types of terriers are vermin hunters and fighting breeds.

The vermin hunters

These self-assured, spirited breeds are a lively bunch (see Figure 2-14). Originally bred to listen for and hunt vermin on the farm, they are always on the alert and feisty when set to a task. Agile and independent, they don't excel in off-leash training and need to be leashed when outdoors. If you're not a control freak and want a dog with spunk and good humor, take a good look at the dogs on this list. Untrained or over-isolated, however, these dogs can become chronic barkers, chewers, or urination markers, and may develop aggression over objects and food.

Airedale Terrier
Australian Terrier
Bedlington Terrier
Border Terrier
Cairn Terrier
Dandie Dinmont Terrier
Fox Terrier (Smooth and Wirehaired)
Irish Terrier
Jack Russell Terrier
Kerry Blue Terrier
Lakeland Terrier
Manchester Terrier
Miniature Schnauzer
Norfolk Terrier
Norwich Terrier
Scottish Terrier
Sealyham Terrier
Skye Terrier
Soft Coated Wheaten Terrier
Welsh Terrier
West Highland White Terrier

Figure 2-14:
The West Highland White Terrier.

Don't be surprised if your terrier breed lifts his lip as you (or anyone else) reach for his bone or food bowl. It's a natural reaction called *spatial aggression,* and it's similar to what a young child who doesn't want to share a favorite toy does. Other dogs known for this behavior include some working breeds, hounds, and certain toy breeds. For suggestions in overcoming this dilemma, refer to Chapter 15.

The fighters

Originally bred to fight other dogs or to bait bulls, these breeds are cocky and courageous (see Figure 2-15). Thankfully, they are no longer used for fighting, and their combative instincts have been bred down. These dogs can make agreeable and entertaining pets.

> American Staffordshire Terrier
> Bull Terrier
> Miniature Bull Terrier
> Staffordshire Bull Terrier

Figure 2-15:
The Bull
Terrier.

Early socialization and training are important — the pugnacious nature of dogs in this group has been tamed but not eliminated. Without this effort, fighting breeds can be dangerous around other animals, adults, and children.

Some deranged people think that watching dogs rip each other limb from limb is cool. Although illegal, dog fighting as a sport still happens. Consequently, there are breeders who breed for aggression. So be very careful when buying a puppy from one of these breeds; make sure your breeder breeds for mild temperaments only. For information on finding a reputable breeder, head to Chapter 4.

The Non-Sporting Group

Many of the dogs in this group were originally bred for specific work, but because dog work is hard to come by these days, these dogs have become companions (see Figure 2-16). Unlike other breed groups, the personalities of the dogs in this group vary widely because they were all originally bred for different tasks. Before considering any of these breeds, consult breed-specific books and speak to a veterinarian to get a truer sense of what the breed you're looking at is like.

American Eskimo Dog
Bichon Frise
Boston Terrier
Bulldog
Chinese Shar-Pei
Chow Chow
Dalmatian
Finnish Spitz
French Bulldog

Keeshond
Lhasa Apso
Löwchen
Poodle (Standard and Miniature)
Shiba Inu
Schipperke
Tibetan Spaniel
Tibetan Terrier

Figure 2-16:
The
American
Eskimo Dog.

The Toy Group

Many of the breeds in this group are miniaturized versions of working or hunting dogs (see Figure 2-17). Too small to work, these breeds have perfected the art of being adorable. Needing little exercise (though they definitely need exercise), they are perfect for apartment dwellers and older people. Playful and devoted, they demand constant affection and attention.

Affenpinscher
Brussels Griffon
Cavalier King Charles Spaniel
Chihuahua
Chinese Crested
English Toy Spaniel
Havanese
Italian Greyhound
Japanese Chin
Maltese

Miniature Pinscher
Papillon
Pekingese
Pomeranian
Pug
Shih Tzu
Silky Terrier
Toy Manchester Terrier
Toy Poodle
Yorkshire Terrier

Figure 2-17:
The Pug.

Neglecting training for these little guys is easy, but it's a big mistake. Although small, these dogs can become quite tyrannical, ruling the house with constant barking and snapping. To get the most from these precious companions, train them.

Yes, Dahhhling, Maybe a Rare Breed

If you decide that you're drawn to more exotic breeds, you may want to consider a rare breed. Though they're not yet registered by the AKC, rare breeds have their own following and advocate group, the American Rare Breed Association (ARBA).

The following list represents just the tip of the rare breed iceberg.

Although these breeds are more uncommon, they're still dogs with the same needs and demands of all the others.

- ✔ **Cesky Terrier:** From Czechoslovakia, this breed was originally a cross of the Scottish Terrier and the Sealyham Terrier.
- ✔ **Leonberger:** Originally bred in Germany, this dog was meant to resemble a lion.
- ✔ **Louisiana Catahoula Leopard Dog:** The state dog of Louisiana, this breed is known for its incredible work with wild cattle and Brahma bulls.
- ✔ **Norwegian Lundehund:** Meaning "Puffin Dog," this Norwegian breed is known for having six toes and unique abilities traced to puffin hunting during the Ice Age.
- ✔ **Nova Scotia Duck Tolling Retriever:** This breed is proficient at *tolling*, or luring ducks into gun range by running around at the shoreline, causing a disturbance.
- ✔ **Polish Owczarek Nizinny Sheepdog:** This herding breed is the first native Polish breed to be introduced to the United States.
- ✔ **Swedish Vallhund:** This Swedish breed is a cattle herder (Vallhund means "Forest Dog").

Hey, but I've Always Heard That Mixed Breeds Are Better

Many people contend that mixed breed dogs are better than purebred dogs. I've owned both and have loved them equally. Love and loyalty know no pedigree. The biggest difference between a mixed breed and a purebred is predictability. When you throw a ball into the water for a retriever, you can predict what's going to happen next. If you know or can guess something about a mixed breed puppy's background, you may be able to gain some insight into his personality. Like any other dog, a mixed breed needs attention, exercise, and training. Figure 2-18 shows a typical mixed breed dog.

Figure 2-18:
A mixed-
breed dog.

The theory *Hybrid Vigor* contends that due to their larger genetic pools, mixed breed dogs are superior in health and temperament to purebred dogs. What do I think? The theory sounds good. Regarding temperament, though, I've met as many purebred dogs as mixed with good personalities. The choice is up to you.

Chapter 3

Just Do It: Picking Your Breed

So you've looked at your lifestyle and your commitments, and you've factored in the daily-life kinds of things your prospective puppy may be subjected to. You've familiarized yourself with the various breeds that are out there, and now you're, *well*, overwhelmed. How can you siphon this information and make a practical choice?

I wish I could be there to help you in person, but since I can't, this chapter can help. It contains a questionnaire I give to clients who hire me to help them select the right breed. This questionnaire can help you make the right choice when selecting your new best friend.

Oh, and if you haven't yet considered your lifestyle and gotten yourself all up to speed on the various breeds that are available, you may want to put a pencil in the margin right here to save your place and then head over to Chapters 1 and 2 to get the scoop on those things. Then come back here to start working on selecting the puppy of your dreams.

The Puppies For Dummies Choosing a Breed Questionnaire

The questionnaire itself is self-explanatory. When you're filling it out, the main thing to remember is to be really honest with yourself about your wants and needs.

Your name: _____

Number of adults in family: _____

Number and ages of children (under age 18): _____

Your daily schedule (hours at home): _____

Your leisure activities:

_____

_____

_____

Will you include the dog in these activities?

❑ Yes   ❑ No

I have other pets.

❑ Yes   ❑ No

If yes, what kind?

_____ Age _____

_____ Age _____

I've owned a dog before.

❑ Yes   ❑ No

I've had success training a dog.

❑ Yes   ❑ No

I live in a(n)

❑ Large house   ❑ Small house   ❑ Apartment

I have

❑ A large yard   ❑ A small yard   ❑ No yard

Please enter one of the three following responses to the activities listed below.

Very little   Moderate amounts of   Extensive

I have time for a dog that needs _____ grooming.

I have time for a dog that needs _____ training.

I have time for a dog that needs _____ attention.

I have time for a dog that needs _____ exercise.

Please check the appropriate response:

I'm getting a dog to be _____.

❑ A family member   ❑ A watchdog   ❑ Used for work
                                                (type of work: _____)

I'd like a dog who is _____ of children.

❑ Very accepting   ❑ Tolerant but aloof

I'd like a dog who needs _____ affection.

❑ Very little   ❑ Moderate amounts of   ❑ Much

I'd like a dog who _____.

❑ Is naturally active ❑ Enjoys quiet walks ❑ Doesn't need extensive exercise

I'd like a dog who is _____.

❑ Eager to please   ❑ Independent   ❑ Strong willed

I'd like a dog who is _____ with guests.

❑ Enthusiastic   ❑ Calm   ❑ Reserved   ❑ On guard   ❑ Indifferent

I'd like a dog who is _____ strangers.

❑ Naturally protective around   ❑ Accepting of   ❑ Aloof toward

When we go on trips, the dog would be _____.

❑ Taken along   ❑ Kenneled   ❑ Left with friends or family

I'd prefer a dog who sheds _____.

❑ Very little   ❑ A couple of times per year   ❑ Shedding doesn't matter

I'd like a dog whose coat is _____.

❑ Long   ❑ Short   ❑ Thick   ❑ Feathery   ❑ Curly   ❑ Wiry
❑ Any of the above

I envision a(n) _____ size dog.

❑ Extra-large   ❑ Large   ❑ Medium   ❑ Small   ❑ Tiny
❑ Size doesn't matter

I would like a dog who barks _____.

❑ Protectively   ❑ Interactively   ❑ Seldom

So What Do I Need to Do?

After you complete this form, look it over and cross-reference your decisions to other sections of the book. For example, in Chapter 21, you find an exercise chart that can help you determine the energy level of various breeds. Chapter 2 goes over breed size and purpose to help you determine whether your living environment, family situation, and activity levels are suitable for the breed you're considering.

After you complete this masterpiece, you have some choices:

- **Just do it — pick your breed.** After filling out the form and cross-referencing your decisions to other sections of this book, you can make an educated decision on the breed that's right for you.

- **Take the information to a dog professional (trainer or veterinarian) in your area.** This person can give you some advice on which breeds may be best for you and can refer you to a club or reputable breeder specializing in that breed.

- **Mail the questionnaire to me.** I offer a service in which I evaluate your form and suggest breeds that are best suited to your lifestyle. You receive a read-out of two or three breeds and the parent club contact you can use to locate reputable breeders in your area. This service costs $30.00.

Chapter 4

Where Can I Find My Puppy?

Puppies are a major responsibility. If you're reading this chapter, you're off to a good start. Though getting a puppy is definitely one of life's most exciting moments, read these pages carefully before you jump in head first. You need to become familiar with a few things — including a puppy temperament test — ahead of time.

The Ways to Get a Puppy

You can find puppies just about anywhere. You can go to a breeder or visit an animal shelter. You can read about a litter in your hometown newspaper or fall in love with a puppy in a pet store window. And there are pros and cons to every option.

Finding a reputable breeder

If you're getting a purebred puppy, do yourself a *big* favor — find a reputable dog breeder. How? Ask your veterinarian. Call or write the American Kennel Club and ask for the parent club of the breed you're interested in. This club can recommend good breeders in your area.

This information is available from the AKC's North Carolina office:

5580 Centerview Dr.
Raleigh, NC 27606
Phone: (919) 233-3600
Web site: www.akc.org

Of course, just following the advice of these people doesn't mean you're done finding a good breeder. You have to evaluate the breeders you contact. Following are a few things that can help you judge the quality of a breeder:

✔ **Use good sense when you visit a kennel.** Is it clean? How about the smell? What about the dogs? Are they perky and friendly?

✔ **Question the breeder's knowledge of genetic health conditions for your specific breed.** A common example is hip dysplasia, a condition that is found in dogs ranging from 15 to 200 pounds and that affects the proper development of the hip joint. (Dogs prone to hip dysplasia should be OFA certified before they're bred. Insist that your breeder provides you with certification slips before you consider buying a puppy.)

OFA, the Orthopedic Foundation for Animals, rates dogs' hips as excellent, good, fair, borderline, or dysplastic (mild to severe) when the dogs are two years old. Make sure your puppy's parents have been certified and are over two years of age.

✔ **Does the breeder ask you questions?** A good breeder has as many questions for you as you have for him. Don't be offended. Concern is a good sign.

If the breeder is sloppy, the kennels are a mess, and the dogs are listless and poorly kept, you won't be able to trust anything this breeder might tell you — from the pups' pedigree to their immunizations.

Questions to ask the breeder

Here are some questions you can ask a breeder you're considering buying a pup from:

✔ **How long have you been breeding dogs?** Good breeders have been doing it for a while or, if they're just starting out, are involved with other, more experienced breeders.

✔ **Are the puppies socialized to unfamiliar sounds and people?** A well-bred and socialized pup will be more relaxed, less of a chewer, and more acceptable of everyday occurrences.

✔ **Can I meet both parents?** When you visit the breeder, insist on meeting the mother dog and, if possible, the father dog. Their personalities leave their mark.

✔ **Is the purchase of the puppy guaranteed against health or behavioral defects?** Good breeders stand behind their pups.

✔ **Are you willing to take the dog back?** A good breeder loves the puppies as much as you do and will welcome them back if it doesn't work out.

✔ **Have the parents been certified clear of genetic defects inherent to the breed?** You can ask your veterinarian what to look for.

✔ **Do you temperament test the litter?** If the answer is no, perform your own temperament test before you select a puppy. If the breeder objects, chances are, you don't want to do business with this person anyway.

✔ **Do you stress conformation or temperament in your breeding lines?** Temperament is the key word while you're searching for your puppy.

The ideal situation would be to find a breeder who is dedicated to the good temperament of the breed as well as the dog's *conformation* (the dog's physical characteristics compared to the ideals for the breed), who guarantees the puppy's health, and who is willing to let you temperament test the puppies (if he or she hasn't done it) to ensure that you're ending up with a healthy puppy whose personality matches your lifestyle.

Purebred puppies cost money. How much depends on the breed and your location.

Documents to get from the breeder

Be sure to get these important documents from the breeder:

✔ Both an AKC registration application and an AKC registration certificate — make sure they're filled out.

✔ A written bill of sale with the following information:

> The dog's breed, sex, and color
>
> The date when the dog was born
>
> Registration numbers and registered names of the dog's parents
>
> The breeder's name and mailing address

Never accept a promise of later identification unless you do not plan on registering your dog.

Some breeders line-breed, a practice where related dogs are bred to encourage conformation (a look). Although line-breeding is accepted in the breeding community, I don't endorse it. Many line-bred pups are high strung or uncharacteristically difficult. To find out whether the puppy you're considering is line-bred, ask to see the parents' pedigrees *before any money changes hands* and look for names mentioned more than once. Also beware of breeders who breed closely related dogs — for example, father to granddaughter, uncle to niece, and so on.

Considering those pet store puppies

"It's unbelievably cute, it's desperate, it looks so lonely, and it just went on sale — I'll take that doggy in the window!"

Is this happening to you? If you're deliberating over a pet store pup, let me fill you in on the facts and then you can make your own decision. First, you have to know about *puppy mills.* Although not every pet store gets their pups from puppy mills, some do. Puppy mills are farms, found most commonly in mid-western, less populated states, that breed dogs for profit, like chickens. If you haven't seen the pictures, let me tell you, they'd break your heart — cage on top of cage, row upon row, dogs getting little human contact and poor care. Somewhere down the line, someone pays a price for this neglect, and it's usually the puppy buyer.

Early Stress Syndrome (pre-12 weeks of age) can take its toll on these little creatures, leaving many nervous or distrustful. Although I have seen puppies who've tolerated the early stress in stride, developing into mellow dogs, they're the exception, not the rule. If you have a choice — pet store or breeder — I recommend that you choose the breeder.

If you find a pet store you'd like to buy a pup from, insist that the store prove that the puppy came from a breeder. Then call that breeder and get as much information as you can, using the questions for breeders listed in the section "Questions to ask the breeder."

Avoid buying any puppy who looks sickly, acts nervous or afraid, or can't calm down after a half hour of interaction.

Taking a trip to the shelter

Going to the shelter or checking the classifieds for a puppy can be depressing. Prepare yourself. You'll find faces you may see in your soup for a while. You may see some dogs with limp tails and soulful expressions. No matter what, though, resist the temptation to take all the dogs with you. Most dogs coming into a new home suffer from *shelter shock* (stress from feeling totally out of control and abandoned) and need all your love and understanding to pull through.

Don't be scared away from your decision to rescue a dog from a shelter. It's the noblest of acts. I found the sweetest dog I've known at a shelter in Michigan and have never regretted it. But before you go to the shelter, you need to be prepared. Following are some things to keep in mind:

 ✔ **Know what physical and personality traits you are looking for.** Do you want small or big? A young puppy or an older one? Calm or energetic? Make a list before you go and check with the kennel workers, who can be quite helpful and can guide you to puppies that fit your criteria.

✔ **Try to find out each candidate's history.** Most dogs end up at the shelter with an excuse that their owners are "moving" or have "allergies," but there's usually more to it than that. If you're selecting an older puppy, determine whether it has been neglected or abused in any way. This stress can result in behavioral problems that you need to be prepared to cope with.

✔ **If you have children, determine whether a dog likes them before bringing him home.** Take your kids with you to the shelter. If you plan to have children but don't have any now, borrow some to go with you to meet the dog.

✔ **If you have other pets at home, try to determine whether or not the *new dog* will be accepting of them.** Ask the shelter personnel to place the puppy with other animals at the facility to ensure that he's accepting of all creatures.

✔ **Find out what you can about the puppy's health.** Has the puppy's health been checked? Are there any conditions (such as epilepsy, hip dysplasia, or worms or other internal or external parasites) you should know about?

✔ ***Be* with the puppy.** Commune with him. Look into his eyes. Do you feel "something" click? Is it love at first sight? (I do believe in fairy "tails," by the way — at least where dogs are concerned!)

If you adopt an older puppy from a shelter, count on having a behavior problem or two to iron out. Dogs who have spent any time at the shelter may need a refresher course in the house manners department. The staff at the shelter can give you an idea what to expect. But remember: As the dog adjusts to you, more of his personality will emerge.

What is Breed Rescue?

Breed Rescuers are dedicated individuals, generally breeders themselves, who take in dogs of their breed that have been abandoned at a shelter or cannot be kept. Before the dogs are placed, the rescuers neuter, housetrain, and socialize them. The dogs being rescued can range in age from as young as four months to well into their adult years. If you've fallen in love with a breed but can't see yourself going through all the puppy phases, consider adopting one of these dogs. It's is a great way to rescue a dog whose temperament has been pre-determined and whose heart is in desperate need of a permanent home.

If you rescue a puppy who misbehaves, be understanding. Bad habits result from not knowing what was expected from him in his last home. This dog needs a lot of patience and training. Remember, harsh discipline only creates more problems.

If you find a dog, don't just assume it's a stray and in need of a home. Check for tags, notify the police, and call all local shelters to make sure she isn't lost. You'd want someone else to do the same for you.

When your puppy finds you instead

A day may come when a puppy finds you, and if it does, you'll feel like you received a gift from above. The attachment will strike you like lightning. Life, responsibilities, and time commitments are all temporarily non-existent. *Temporarily* is the key word, however. Suddenly, you're faced with a big decision: what to do with the puppy.

First, you must take him to the veterinarian and check his health. If he's sick or has some contagious illness, take care of the problem immediately. Next, sit down and have a heart-to-heart with yourself. Can you really take on the responsibility of caring for this pup? Raising a puppy is the closest thing to having a baby—*without* the benefit of diapers.

If you decide that you can handle the sudden responsibility, great. You have a new member of the family. You can pick a name and begin training. If, on the other hand, you decide — as much as it breaks your heart — that a puppy just wouldn't fit into your life, remember that puppies need more than love to survive. So *don't* feel guilty. Instead, use all your energy and love to find a good home for your new friend. After all, you'd much rather be part of a solution and happy ending than create another problem — an anxiety-ridden dog — and nothing is worse than keeping a puppy cooped up all day.

Most puppies who find you are going to have some baggage (early stress) and probably suffer from isolation anxiety; you need to be aware of that and prepared to deal with it. Also, beware of bugs. Street pups often play host to a whole array of parasites, both internal and external. If you adopt a street pup, do yourself and your new dog a big favor: Get to a veterinarian immediately. (Check out Chapter 23 for all kinds of information about parasites.)

The Art of Picking a Puppy from a Litter

You're on your way to see the puppies. Soon you'll be peering into a box full of wriggling puppies. I'm warning you, they're going to be unbelievably cute. Now, before you actually see them, is the time to take a very firm stand: Say to yourself, "I am only taking one." Then continue to repeat these words until the urge to pile all those cute puppies into the car passes. (For more information on a multi-puppy household, see the section about having two puppies, near the end of this chapter.)

Chances are, one or two pups will capture your fancy right away. Maybe you like the biggest pup, the smallest pup, or the one with the most soulful expression. First impressions can be very persuasive, but you need to look at the puppy behind the pretty face before you make your decision. You can't jump into a long-lasting relationship without asking a few questions.

Each puppy has a character all his own. Each has his own way of approaching other puppies, interacting with you, and exploring his environment. You need to measure these qualities so that you can see how the puppy's personality complements your own.

Studying the littermates' personalities

By seven weeks of age, puppies have begun to develop a world-view. Each has a special way of relating to *littermates* (siblings), mom, and the world beyond.

Litter-land has a pecking order, the beginnings of a *dog pack hierarchy*. Every puppy has a place and behaves accordingly. Bright, energetic, and bossy types are highest in the hierarchy. Puppies with a more laid-back attitude occupy the middle ground, preferring leisure over leading. More timid types rank lowest. For these puppies, who like peace and quiet, sitting on the sidelines is just fine.

Dogs live in a world that's defined by a hierarchy. If you want to impress your dog, think leader, top dog, alpha — whatever. The important thing is that you *both* know who the boss is.

All these puppies have a place in the world, but which puppy is right for you? You need persistence to convince a high-ranking puppy of your authority, patience to train the relaxed middle-grounders, and time to build up a shy puppy's self-esteem. The payback is always worth double the effort, but only *you* know what challenge you're up to.

To get an idea of what puppy personality may be best suited to you, consider a range of personalities in a hypothetical litter of five puppies. You may see litters of more or less than five, but generally, each pup's personality falls into one of these categories.

This litter is composed of three females and two males. For each one, I list its rank, approach to play, exploratory behavior, and greeting behavior. Then I describe what type of person would make the best owner for this dog.

This is a hypothetical litter. In a litter of 9, there may be two #1s, three #2s, three #3s, and one #4. Any mix is possible.

Puppy #1: The top dog

With littermates: "Challenge and win" is this puppy's motto. She loves to play and wrestle, mainly because she always wins. She thinks she's hot stuff, and her behavior shows it. This is the puppy that mock-fights with the squeak toys and relentlessly attempts to break down the barricade.

With you: You'll probably meet her first. She'll charge forward, leap in the air, and wag her tail furiously. Don't get a swelled head — she's like that with everyone. This gal mouths excessively, jumps, and maybe even climbs on top of you to show off her confident flare.

The right owner: Many people fall for this girl's fancy greeting act because it's so flattering. But she's not trying to flatter you — she just wants to be *first*. Very intelligent and funny, she needs an owner with the time and perseverance to train her. Without an owner who has a serious commitment to training, this puppy will become a tyrant and make a difficult family pet.

Puppy #2: The next in line

With littermates: This puppy loves a good wrestle, too, and spends a lot of time fending off the leader of the pack. When he's not under assault, he spends his time mock-fighting with lower-ranking pups and exploring his surroundings.

With you: Confident and happy, he's not as pushy as the leader. He may mouth you and jump just to show you that he's a pretty outgoing puppy, too.

The right owner: Although not as cocky as the Top Dog, this puppy is energetic and boisterous and needs an owner with similar qualities. He'll keep a close eye on you and may take advantage when your back is turned. He's great with older children and a family dedicated to an assertive training regimen.

Puppy #3: The middleman

With littermates: I call this puppy the explorer. She defends herself in a wrestling match, but competition is not really her cup of tea. She'd rather explore her surroundings and pursue more peaceful activities with littermates.

With you: What a relaxing change from the other two. She sits calmly, maybe getting up to follow you as you walk around the room. She may mouth or climb on your chest, but her energy level is moderate compared to you-know-who and her cohort.

The right owner: This dog is often ideal for laid-back families. She'll have a high tolerance for noise and confusion. Although she needs training, occasional lapses won't result in a battle for control.

Puppy #4: The passive pup

With littermates: This puppy is shy with his littermates. He submits passively to the other puppies, who always know a softie when they see one. He interacts with lower-ranking siblings and enjoys quiet exploration and play.

With you: The passive puppy is calm and quiet. He might mouth you tentatively. When you walk around the room, he may be more content to watch.

The right owner: This calm, considerate temperament needs an owner with the same qualities. Older children may enjoy this dog, but everyone must be aware of his sensitivity and use the gentlest handling techniques. This puppy needs training to enhance his self image, but it must be done with much patience, very little discipline, and a lot of positive reinforcement.

Puppy #5: The shy pup

With littermates: Your heart will go out to this little creature. She shows fear when approached by her dominant littermates. She may play with puppy #4, but she usually plays by herself. You find this pup playing with a chew toy in the corner or exploring by herself while the other puppies are wrestling.

With you: You'll feel sorry for this puppy. She'll be happiest curled in your lap and may show fear if you make sudden movements or walk across the room. She doesn't like loud noises at all.

The right owner: The shy puppy is not good with children because loud noises and chaos send her into a state of shock. She needs a very special owner who is patient and supportive. Gentle training methods can help develop her self-esteem.

Selecting the one that's right for you

After you take a look at different puppy personalities, you're ready to select your pup. This section presents seven exercises that you can use to assess each puppy's personality. Perform each exercise with each puppy and then rate each puppy's performance on the Puppy Assessment form. (You can copy the form and take it with you as you visit various puppies.) Afterward, tally your score, and there you go . . . you've found the puppy that's right for you.

Using the Puppy Assessment form

By now, you should know which type of puppy you'd like to bring home with you. Active puppies are a lot of work, but they're also lots of fun. Spirited and intelligent, they are well-appreciated by those who have the time and determination needed to train them. Neutral puppies are relaxed and undemanding — sort of the "regular guys" of the dog world. Passive and shy puppies appreciate love and support but are fearful of change. They do best in a consistent environment.

Using the Puppy Assessment form shown in Figure 4-1, you can perform specific exercises with each puppy and rate each one using the following scale:

A — Active (Top Dog and Next in Line)

N — Neutral (Middleman)

P — Passive (Passive and Shy)

Puppy Assessment Form

Name / Number of Pup	1. Observe	2. Uplift	3. Flip-Flop	4. Gentle Caress	5. Wacky Walk	6. What's That?	7. Crash Test

Figure 4-1: For each exercise, rate each puppy as either A for Active, N for Neutral, or P for Passive.

Be sure to test each puppy while he's awake and active.

Perform each of the following activities with each puppy:

1. **Observe.**

   As they play with each other, observe the puppies and rate each one according to its rank in the litter. (You may want to refer to the preceding "Studying the littermates' personalities" section.)

2. **Uplift.**

   After observing, take each puppy aside one at a time. Cradle him mid-body and suspend him four inches off the ground (see Figure 4-2). If he squirms wildly and reaches out to mouth you, give him an A. If he squirms a bit but then relaxes, give him an N. If he shudders in fear or pins his ears back and tucks his tail, give him a P.

Figure 4-2:
Performing
the Uplift
test.

3. Flip-Flop.

Next, lift the puppy up and cradle her upside-down like a baby (see Figure 4-3). Does she squirm and try to grab at you with her mouth? If so, give her an A. If she wiggles a bit and then settles happily, she gets an N. If she whimpers or pulls her mouth back in tension (a submissive grin), she gets a P.

Figure 4-3:
Performing
the Flip-Flop
test.

4. Gentle Caress.

Okay. Back to Earth. Sit next to the puppy and pet him. Gently stroke him at least 15 times to judge his willingness to be handled. If he immediately jumps toward your face or scampers away toward a more stimulating distraction, give him an A. If he relaxes and sits quietly or climbs into your lap, give him an N. If he cowers, tucks his tail, pins his ears, or pulls his mouth back in tension, give him a P.

5. Wacky Walk.

Stand up, shake your legs, clap your hands, and encourage the pup to follow you. Bend down like a monkey if you must; just do what you have to in order to get her attention. If she attacks your legs or gets distracted by a more interesting stimulant, give her an A. If she follows enthusiastically, looking up to your face for reinforcement, give her an N. If she sits and watches you quietly or withdraws in fear, give her a P.

6. What's That?

You need two spoons for this exercise. When the puppy is distracted, tap the spoons together above his head. If he jumps up and tries to wrestle the spoons, give him an A. If he ignores the sound or sniffs the spoons calmly, give him an N. If he cowers in fear or runs away, give him a P.

7. Crash Test.

Walk at least six paces away from the puppy. Suddenly drop to the floor like you've fallen and hurt your knee. Don't get carried away but make it look fairly realistic. Does the puppy take this as an invitation to play? If so, give her an A. If she walks over and acts curious, give her an N. If she runs away or cowers, give her a P.

Young children can help out on the Gentle Caress and Crash Test exercises. In fact, having them help is a good way to see how your future puppy might get along with your current, less hairy "puppies." Older kids can do all of the tests, but only one test per puppy, please. If everyone in your family starts crashing to the floor, even the bravest puppy will head for the hills.

Tallying the score

To tally the puppy's score, count up your As, Ns, and Ps. Got it? Then take a gander at the following:

- ✔ If you've got all As, you're dealing with a leader type, one who'll want to take control if no one else steps up for the part.

- ✔ All Ns, and you have a middleman on your hands.

- ✔ Ns and Ps mean your dog is likely to be passive and easy going.

- ✔ All Ps means that, without appropriate socialization, your dog may turn out to be shy.

Identifying your pup's personality from the start helps you mold a training program that is good for everyone.

Two Puppies: Double Trouble?

I know, all the puppies are so cute that you'd load them all up if you could. Of course, you probably know you can't (or shouldn't) do that. But what if you're drawn to two in particular? That's even more difficult — it's like picking between day-old chicks. Unfortunately, two puppies can spell more trouble than fun.

- ✔ **They pay more attention to each other than they do to you because they're dogs and you're not (nah, nah!).** Although a single puppy figures out ways to understand you, two puppies don't bother — a situation that impedes training, housebreaking, and efforts to stop chewing and instill overall polite behavior. Your rules are just not as compelling as what the other puppy is doing. If one starts to tear a pillow apart, the other joins in. If one wants to obey but sees the other ignoring you, you're forgotten.

- ✔ **As they grow up, one dog will be more bossy; the other will be a willing follower.** The head honcho will want to take control in all situations, while the follower may show excessive submission and poor coping skills. Both will suffer when separated, often barking, peeing, or chewing until reunited.

- ✔ **At puberty, same-sex pups (especially males) often fight for Top Dog position.** You may notice competition for attention, food, or toys. Without behavioral conditioning, their differences could be irreconcilable.

Still, having two dogs can be a lot of fun for you and for them. So what do you do? I suggest training *one* puppy for the first year and then getting a second. The first puppy has the opportunity to form a bond with you, and then he can teach the newcomer house rules and behavior etiquette.

If your heart is set on two, prepare yourself. (And if you're reading this with two pups on your lap, don't despair; you just have to expend more effort.) Of course, you have to have double the obvious things: two crates, two sets of leashes, two times the toys, and so on, but that's really the least of it. Two puppies demand twice the affection; otherwise, they bond more to each other than to you. If you raise them like inseparable twins, they'll suffer whenever isolated and will pay far more attention to each other than to you. And having two puppies often means four times the cleanup because two puppies together can be twice as destructive.

Raising two dogs is not impossible; it's just more of a challenge. Each needs individual attention, training, and outings to ensure its emotional development. For example, you should walk each one separately in the morning. To effectively housetrain each, you may need to take them out separately, too. Bottom line: It's your life; make sure you have the time and are up to the challenge.

Going for an Older Puppy

Selecting an older puppy of any age can be a lot easier than selecting a younger pup. The cute factor has lost its shine. You're usually testing one at a time, instead of twelve. But if you are tender-hearted, the pup's individual story can suck you in even though the dog may be unsuited for your lifestyle.

A puppy's brain develops until it's 12 weeks old. What unfolds during this critical time period strongly shapes the dog's behavior.

To help you keep your head on straight, following are some guidelines and a few tests you can use to see whether the older pup you're considering is a good match for your lifestyle. You have to be strong enough to let your head lead your heart. Nothing is sadder than rescuing a dog only to have to return it because the dog couldn't cope with your life. Be strong — find out ahead of time whether you and the dog are suited by performing the following tasks:

- ✔ Do you have kids? Make sure you introduce them to the puppy before you bring your dog home.

- ✔ Startle the dog. Toss your keys on the floor. Does the dog fall to pieces or attack them? Neither reaction is a good sign.

- ✔ If you have an animal menagerie at home, make sure the puppy can cope with creature chaos. Are there animals in the current home? Has anyone conditioned this puppy to other creatures?

- ✔ Ask one of the staff (or the previous owner) to lift the dog. What happens? Intense fear or frustration is not a good sign. The ideal puppy may squirm but is still accepting.

- ✔ Bring a soft brush and try to groom the pup while feeding her treats.

Bear in mind, older puppies are less accepting of strangers and strange situations than infant pups, so allow some room for edginess. But if you see anything more extreme, back off, especially if what you see is aggression. Unless you want a major training project, look for a puppy who is accepting in each of the exercises described earlier in the "Selecting the one that's right for you" section and, if they're a factor, shows patience with kids or other animals.

The Best Age to Bring Home a Puppy

You need to decide whether you're going to get a young puppy or a more mature one. If you're getting a baby pup, the best age to bring her home is between 8 and 12 weeks. If you're getting an older pup, 6 months or older, be mindful to select one that has grown out of its young puppy ways (excessive biting and chewing).

Things to consider with a baby pup

Many experts tell you to bring a puppy home when it's between 6 and 8 weeks old. I recommend 8 to 12 weeks. Six-week-old pups nip and play in an early attempt to define a hierarchy. They even use mom as a biting bag; she puts them in their place and teaches them respect. Respect is a must-learn *before* bringing a pup home.

Also, at 6 weeks, puppies are just developing bladder control; waiting for that developmental stage has benefits *far* beyond my ability — or desire — to explain it.

Things to consider with an older pup

Most older puppies are calmer and more tolerant of household chaos — if they've been well socialized and trained in their first home. Nothing is more discouraging than purchasing an older puppy who's been neglected. These dogs can be unpredictable and nervous and aggressive around daily home activities. If you're considering an older pup, *pay attention.* Look before you leap. Handle your candidate plenty. Let everyone in the family meet him or her. And talk to the person at the other end of the leash. Here are some questions you want to ask the owners:

- How old is this dog?
- Why are they looking for another home for the dog?
- Has he had any training?
- How many homes has he had? If more than one, why?
- Do they know of any bad habits — barking, house soiling, aggression, or chewing, for example — that you may encounter?

If the current owners' lifestyle jives with your lifestyle and you get the answers you want to hear, then you're all set. If not, you may have some initial problems. For example, if you work all day and find an older dog who's accustomed to being left alone, you very well may have found your canine match. If, however, you get a dog that has Hyper Isolation Anxiety or one who learned bad manners in his last home, you need to take the time and effort to help your new dog overcome these problems.

Hyper Isolation Anxiety (HIA) is anxiety, canine style, that occurs when you isolate your dog. It usually starts within minutes of separation and may (in severe cases) continue until you come home. HIA may cause destructive behavior like chewing, barking, or house soiling.

If you're getting a puppy older than 10 weeks, make sure the breeder has "socialized" him to everyday situations: people, sounds, and so on. An unsocialized pup may go to pieces around strange new things like vacuums, cars, or new people and grow up to become a nervous dog.

Part II

I've Picked Out My Pup — What's Next?

The 5th Wave   By Rich Tennant

Beware of Dog

THUNDER

"We're hoping he'll grow into it."

In this part . . .

Congratulations. You've selected the perfect puppy for you. Feelings of pride, adoration, and love are emanating all around you.

But out of nowhere, the dreaded "What should I do now?" thought pops into your head. Well, don't hold your breath another minute. In this part, you find everything you need to know about starting out: what to buy, what to do after you bring your puppy home, how to understand your new friend, and how to *think* like a dog.

Chapter 5

Shopping for Initial Supplies

· ·

· ·

You need to do some prep work before the Big Day arrives — the day when you actually bring home your new puppy. You have to get supplies to outfit your home: up-front essentials like a good collar, a few leashes, a realistic containment system, and a few odds and ends. This chapter walks you through the stuff you need.

Soon after you bring home your puppy, you also need to start working on another set of supplies — training supplies. This chapter also fills you in on the essentials for getting your puppy's training started. And since you need to consider outdoor enclosures, too, this chapter gives you a few options to think about.

Outfitting Your Home

The day is arriving — it's time to pull out your plastic and do a little shopping for your new arrival. Although you may be tempted to buy every gimmick — from the latest toy to that designer doggy raincoat — I suggest you bring a list and stick to it. The most important items are discussed in this section.

Gates, crates, and playpens

You need to designate an area for your mischievous puppy to stay while you're not home and cool off when things get out of hand. I like to think of the area as a cubby because it should be small, quiet, and cozy. Don't worry, it reminds them of their wolfish den roots. You can create a cubby by gating your puppy into a small area or buying a crate or playpen for him.

Gates

Gates are a big help in raising a puppy. You can use gates to cubby your puppy in a small area, such as a bathroom. You can also use gates to enclose a play area (kitchens make an ideal play area because they don't isolate your puppy from you).

If you use a gate to create your puppy's cubby, make sure you pick an area that has linoleum or tile floors, in case of accidents. Also ensure that the area's puppy-proofed (see Chapter 24 for tips on puppy-proofing your rooms).

Crates

Crates are comforting for puppies who don't know how to handle open spaces and are useful for toilet training. Crates can be an invaluable training tool, but they can also be emotionally destructive to your puppy if overused. Crates are good in the following situations:

- ✔ When your puppy must be left unattended for less than six hours
- ✔ During sleeping hours for young, unhousebroken, or mischievous puppies
- ✔ As a feeding station if your puppy is easily distracted
- ✔ As a time-out area for over-excitable pups

You can choose from several different types of crates, which come in two varieties. Wire or mesh crates, some of which fold down nicely, are sturdier and allow better ventilation — definitely a must in hot environments. Portable travel kennels are made from polypropylene. Both do the job.

Following are a few things to keep in mind about crates:

- ✔ The size of the crate is also important, especially if you're housebreaking a puppy. If the crate is too large, the puppy may eliminate in one end and sleep in the other.

If you have a growing puppy, buy an adult size crate with a crate divider. Divide it so that your puppy can lie comfortably and turn around only. Do the same if you have a big dog and a bigger crate. If no manufactured dividers are available, create one out of a safe, non-toxic material.

Dogs love to pee on absorbent surfaces. If you're still having housebreaking problems, consider the bedding you're using. Is it thick and plush? If so, maybe it's too plush — change it if needed. (And check out Chapter 11 for more details about housebreaking.)

- ✔ If you can, place the crate in a bedroom because both puppies and dogs hate being alone at night. If having the crate in the bedroom is out of the question, place it in a well-trafficked room, like the kitchen or family room.

✔ Do not use the crate if you're gone for long 8- to 12-hour days. Being confined in a relatively small space for such a long period of time will drive your dog nuts. Isolated all day in a kennel, he'll learn to sleep during the day and keep you up all night. You'll create a nocturnal nightmare with the energy of six stallions, which isn't good for either of you.

Using a crate does have drawbacks. True, your puppy can't get into trouble inside the crate, but being there doesn't teach him how to behave in your home, either. Isolation provides little training and has other drawbacks, too:

✔ It doesn't communicate leadership.

✔ It separates you from your puppy when you're at home.

✔ It can't communicate how to behave in the house.

If the idea of a crate turns your stomach or if you're home all day, you *can* get through the early stages without one. For information, head to Chapter 12, where I discuss the Teaching Lead.

Canine playpens

Do you work all day? In addition to hiring a dog walker, consider purchasing a Canine Playpen (often called X pens). Playpens enclose your puppy, preventing destruction and at the same time giving him plenty of room to stretch and move about. You can open the playpen during work hours and fold it down when you're home.

When you leave your dog, go quietly, dim the lights, close the curtains, and turn on some classical music to encourage peaceful rest while you're out.

Two leashes

I discuss training leashes in the section "More Supplies as Puppy Grows Up." For now, all you need to purchase is a lightweight nylon leash and a long line, which you use for outdoor playtime in open areas (away from streets) and, later, for advanced training.

A drag lead

Drag lead is a fancy term for a short (4 to 6 feet), light-weight nylon lead that stays on your puppy when you're together in the house. A drag lead is useful for quick corrections that distance you from the activity, whether the activity be jumping on the counters, chewing a plant, or nipping at the kids.

A long line

Long lines (30 feet and over) are great to let your puppy romp around the yard and to encourage distance control. Constructed from canvas or nylon mesh, a long line allows freedom to play, and yet it also gives you plenty of leash to grab onto to retrieve your puppy if he should wander off.

For young puppies, long lines are great for wandering in a yard or field — take along some favorite snacks and reward your puppy each time he checks in with you. You can also use long lines to encourage off-lead training (explained in Chapter 17).

A regular tag collar

Have a buckle collar and tag waiting for your new arrival. If you're getting a puppy, purchase a lightweight nylon collar and a small tag. (Don't worry if you haven't picked out a name; a good tag should give your phone number with a short message, such as "Help Me Home 666-555-4444.") When fit properly, you should be able to comfortably slip two fingers under the collar. Check the fit often if you have a puppy — they grow faster than you'd think. If you're getting a dog or puppy over 4 months, invest in a training collar (see the section "More Supplies as Puppy Grows Up").

A tag with your dog's name and your address may endear him to dog-nappers or let thieves know your dog's not home to protect you. No, I'm not paranoid — just cautious. You should be, too.

Call your veterinarian or local animal shelter and ask for information regarding tattooing or ID microchips. These quick and painless procedures are another way to help someone return your dog to you in the event he gets lost or stolen. Both my dogs have chips.

Other up-front necessities

Here's a hodge-podge of other supplies you need to get before your puppy comes home:

- ✔ **Bowls (two for water and one for food):** Stainless steel metal bowls are best for food and water. They're completely hypo-allergenic, wear well, and are easy to clean. I suggest two bowls for water: one as a staple and one to keep by the toilet bowl to discourage bowl sipping. Have the bowls ready and in position before you bring your puppy home. Put water in one dish and some treats in the other dish and in the bedding. What a cool surprise.

- ✔ **Bedding:** Avoid giving your puppy anything plush initially. He'll pee on it. An old sweatshirt or mat is best. Have the bedding ready and in position before you bring your dog home.

- ✔ **Food:** Decide on a nutritional plan ahead of time. Dry food is best in the long run, although it may not be suitable for puppy's first few months with you. Consult your breeder or ask your veterinarian or local pet store clerk about your puppy's nutritional needs. (You can get more information about your dog's nutritional needs in Chapter 20.)

✔ **Toys:** Be sensible. Resist the temptation to buy one of everything. Too many toys can be confusing; your dog may think that everything mouthable is fair game. And avoid designating old shoes, socks, or other household objects as toys. You'll be sorry.

If your plan is to use plastic or gum bones, don't give your dog edible toys. If you do, he won't settle for anything less. Because white, knotted rawhide can expand in the stomach, I don't recommend it. Hard bones are the best. So many new choices are hitting the market; talk with your veterinarian about their safety and then test some out. Puppy pacifiers, compressed rawhide, hooves, or pig ears are usually safe (although some dogs have reactions). Introduce one type at a time. Your puppy will let you know what to stock.

✔ **Soft grooming brush and nail clippers:** Your first brush should be soft bristled — not wire because it can hurt soft puppy skin. Though you won't use nail clippers for a few months, get them now and condition your puppy to their sound. (Check out Chapter 22 for tips on brushing and nail clipping.)

More Supplies As Puppy Grows Up

Later, after your puppy gets settled into his or her new home and starts growing up a bit, you'll need to make another trip to the store — for training leashes and collars. This section covers some of the different kinds of equipment you'll encounter at the store.

Training collars and leashes may make you and your puppy's lifestyle feel restricted, even overly structured. But using them is a temporary thing, and you'll both be a lot happier in the long run.

Training leashes

Leads are a training essential; they also enable you to keep your puppy secured. The car comes to mind quickly. While you're driving, keep your puppy secured for his safety, as well as your own peace of mind. During romps, too. If you're not in a confined area, don't let your dog run free.

The Flexi-Lead

Flexi-Leads are fun, period. The longer, the better. Initially, this leash is great for exercising. Your puppy can run like mad while you stand there reading the morning newspaper. If you feel like exercising, too, all the better. You can quadruple your puppy's workout. When you progress to off-leash work (see Chapter 17), the Flexi is a staple. Its design works like a fishing reel, letting length in and out. Although using it takes some coordination, once you've mastered it, you probably won't be able to live without it.

You do need to take a few precautions, however. Don't use a Flexi-Lead near roads or heavily populated areas. Its high-tech design takes getting used to, and even a seasoned pro can lose hold of the slack. If you're out with other people, watch their legs. Most puppies get a little nutty when you give them some freedom to run. If a person gets sandwiched between you and your prancing puppy, he's in for a wicked rope burn. It's best to keep play times private.

The Teaching Lead

As your puppy matures, he'll want to hang with you when you're home. The same puppy who curled up quietly in the kitchen while you showered will eventually protest the separation. Simply dismantling the gates won't be the answer. A young puppy gets overwhelmed with too much freedom, even inside the house, so you'll want to keep him on a lead. (Don't worry about keeping your puppy on a lead in the house; it's only temporary.)

To keep it simple and structured, you can use a little invention of mine called the Teaching Lead Method. I explain this method in detail in Chapter 12.

The Seat Belt Safety Lead (SBSL)

Letting your puppy ride in your lap or hang his body halfway out the window when you drive may seem like a good idea, but it's really not. Maybe I've witnessed too many accidents, but to me, cars aren't toys, and your puppy is too precious to lose in a fender bender. Here's my safety rule: Confine your puppy while driving. If you're preoccupied with your puppy when you should be paying attention to the road, you're creating a safety hazard for both of you and other motorists.

I devised a system I call the Seat Belt Safety Lead (SBSL) system, which protects puppies in the same way a seat belt protects people. Using it is quick and easy:

1. **Tie or clip a short leash onto a seat belt. (You can leave it in the car permanently.)**

2. **Decorate this area with a blanket and a toy. Make it a special spot.**

3. **Bring your puppy to the car and say "Go to your spot" as you point to the area. Offer a treat for cooperation.**

4. **Hook your puppy up on a buckle collar (not a training collar). Ignore all initial protests. Praise him when he's calm.**

Secure your dog to the SBSL in the back seat of the car so that, in the event of an accident, your dog won't hit the windshield. If you're planning an extended trip on freeways, connect the SBSL to a pre-fitted harness.

Other ways to secure your pup in a car

You don't have to use the SBSL system to secure your puppy for a car trip. You can use car gates, crates, and harness belts. Car gates confine dogs to a back area in a vehicle. You can also use crates to secure your dog in the rear compartment. Another alternative is a harness-type seat belt — a great concept, even though some puppies aren't thrilled about sitting still as you clip them in. To calm your puppy, give him a dab of peanut butter as you're placing on the harness.

The short lead

Short is relative to the size of your puppy. A short lead should not be more than eight inches; for small dogs, one to three inches will do. You can use it for encouraging manners and for off-leash training. Here's the theory behind both:

- ✔ **Encouraging good manners.** A lot of clients complain that their puppies behave like a saint on leash, but when they take the leash off, the old derelict emerges. A short leash can serve as a nice transition from using the Teaching Lead system (see Chapter 12) to full-fledged freedom. Wearing a short lead reminds the puppy that you're still watching him; it also gives you something to grasp for correction purposes if you need to.

- ✔ **Off-lead training.** When you progress into off-leash work (see Chapter 17), the short lead again serves as a reminder of your presence and authority. In addition, it gives you something to grab graciously if your puppy slips up.

Training collars

Adjustable collars made of cotton, nylon, or leather are called *buckle collars*. Buckle collars don't slide or choke. Their purpose is to carry your puppy's I.D. tags. On the flip side, the purpose of a training collar is to encourage your puppy's focus. If you have a dog who would rather chase a leaf than stay with you, you need to invest in a training collar. Spend time learning about the different training collars available. First impressions count.

You can't simply ask for a training collar. You need to be more specific. Many different types of collars are available, and finding the one for your situation is a must. An ineffective training collar can hurt your puppy, as well as hinder the training process.

You have quite a few collars to choose from (see Figure 5-1). If you're confused about which one is most appropriate, ask someone who knows: Other trainers, veterinarians, or groomers may be helpful. Keep in mind, though, that some dog people are one-collar oriented and tell you that only one type works. Stay away from that advice; every situation is different. What may work wonders for you could be someone else's nightmare. Choose a collar that works for you from those described next (try them all out if you have to).

Figure 5-1:
Various
training
collars are
available.

Do not use a training collar on a puppy younger than 16 weeks. Training collars should be used for teaching purposes only. Remove the collar when you leave your dog unattended because it can be deadly if snagged. Put your dog's tags on a buckle collar.

The original correction collar

I call this collar the "original" because it has been around the longest. It has some other names too, like a chain or choke collar, even though when used properly, it should never choke your dog. Choking and restraining only aggravate problems. It is the sound of the collar, *not* the restraint, that teaches. To be effective, you must put on the collar properly and master the zipper snap.

Can a regular tag collar be my training collar?

Some dogs respond to the slightest tug of any collar. If you have a dog in this category, count yourself blessed. If a sharp tug on a regular tag collar convinces your dog to stay at your side, look no further.

Alternatively, a new type of collar, called a *check choke,* is on the market. This collar is like a regular nylon collar, but the top closure is a chain. Because it's the sound of the chain — and not the restraint — that teaches, I find these collars extremely effective for cooperative dogs.

If put on backward, this collar will catch in a vise hold around your puppy's neck and do what the collar is not supposed to do — choke. Take these steps to ensure this doesn't happen (refer to Figure 5-2 as you work through the steps):

1. **Decide which side you want your puppy to walk on.**

   You must be consistent; puppies are easily confused. Because left is traditional, I use *left* as my reference.

2. **Take one loop of the collar and slide the chain slack through it.**

3. **Create the letter** *P* **with the chain.**

4. **Holding the chain out, stand in front of your puppy. Show him the chain.**

5. **Give your puppy a treat as you praise him and slide the loop of the P over his head.**

Figure 5-2: The right way to put on a chain, or choke, collar.

Master the zipper snap. Your puppy should learn by the sound of the collar, not the restraint. Used properly, a quick snap (which sounds like a zipper) corrects your puppy's impulse to disobey or lead. Practice the zipper snap without your puppy:

1. **Stand up straight and relax your shoulders, letting your arms hang loosely at your side.**

2. **Place your hand just behind your thigh and snap your elbow back so that you're swinging at the air behind you.**

   If it helps, pretend that someone else's hand is there and you're trying to hit it.

Once you have the hang of the movement, find your puppy. Place your hand over the leash and snap back as he starts to lead forward.

If you find yourself in a constant pull battle with your puppy that's only broken by occasional hacking, investigate other collar options, especially the self-correcting collar or chin lead.

How many ways do you think you can hold the leash? Just one way when you're training your puppy. If you hold the lead improperly, you pull your puppy off the ground, which chokes him. To hold the lead correctly, wrap your thumb around the bottom of the lead and your fingers over the top. Keep your arm straight as you lead your dog and snap straight back.

The nylon training collar

These collars work best on fine-haired dogs. Like the original choke you slide it over the head in a "p" position. You can use this collar with more cooperative dogs. Count your blessings if your puppy falls into one of these categories.

The self-correcting collar

Yes, I know, it looks torturous, like a choke collar with large prongs. But it is humane for hard-to-manage dogs — especially if you fall into the *I-can't-stop-choking-my-dog* category using an original training collar. Developed by the Germans for many of their bull-necked breeds, this collar works wonders for puppies who are insensitive to pain or too powerful to be persuaded with simpler devices.

Although it's officially termed a *prong collar*, I refer to it as *self-correcting* because it requires little strength to use. By simply locking your arm into place, even the rowdiest of puppies will feel a pinch and slow down.

If you decide to try this collar, let me warn you: Occasionally, these collars pop off. To prevent a possible emergency, purchase an oversized training collar and attach your leash to both when walking in an unconfined area. Use this collar only when you're working with your dog on a leash.

Help at your fingertips

Grabbing at a puppy's collar is like grabbing a person's arms. It often leaves the dog twisting in discomfort and mouthing at you in play or confrontation.

If you can relate, or you find yourself reaching for your puppy and coming up empty-handed,

consider the finger lead. A finger lead is a 3 ½-inch tab that's custom fit for a finger, and you can leave it on your dog's buckle collar or harness to enable a quick correction indoors or outdoors.

The chin lead

Once again, I have given an existing product a more descriptive name. Actually, this product comes in two forms. The pet stores sell a version known as a Halti. The other brand is called a Gentle Leader. What's the difference? Texture (the Gentle Leader is softer), price, fabric, color choice, and a fancy video, which is sometimes made available when you buy the Gentle Leader.

You may think this collar looks like a muzzle when you first see it. Trust me — it's not a muzzle. Puppies can eat, chew, and play happily while sporting their chin lead. In fact, using this lead is probably the most humane way to walk a dog. It eliminates internal or external pressure around the neck. Using it is similar to handling a horse on a halter.

So how does this wonder collar work? It works on the "mommy" principle. When your dog was a pup, his mom would correct him by grasping his muzzle and shaking it. This communicated, "Hey, wild one, settle down!" The chin lead has the same effect. Left on during play, the pressure on the nose discourages rowdiness and mouthing. By placing a short lead on your dog when you're expecting company, you can effectively curb jumping habits. Barking frenzies are drastically reduced and training is made simple as you guide your dog from one exercise to the next.

For those of you who can look beyond its muzzle-like appearance, the chin lead is a safe, effective, humane training tool that gives you a leg up in correcting negative behavior patterns. Another plus is that leading by the chin demands minimal physical strength, so nearly everyone can use it — kids too. Here are a few more notes:

✔ **Wearing time.** How often you should leave the chin lead on is a question best answered by your puppy. If yours is relatively well behaved, you can use it exclusively during training times. If he's the mouthing, jumping, or barking type, leave the lead on whenever you're around. Remove it at night or when you're out.

✔ **Sizing your chin lead.** Chin leads have a sizing scale. The chin lead must fit properly around your dog's neck. If it's too loose, your dog can pull it off and perhaps chew it. You want the lead to fit snugly about his ears, with enough room to fit two fingers under his neck. You may need to tie a knot with the remaining slack after you adjust it to prevent it from loosening.

✔ **Observe how your dog reacts.** Initially, puppies don't love the idea of a head collar. Their reaction reminds me of the first day my mother dressed me in lace — I hated it. But after an hour or so, I hardly noticed it at all. I learned to tolerate it. So will your dog. When you see him flopping about like a flounder, take a breath. Once he realizes he can't get the collar off, he'll forget about it. Some puppies take an hour to adjust to the feel of the collar; some take a day or two. If you give this collar a try, you may have to tolerate some resistance. Be patient.

If a chin lead irritates your dog's nose, buy Dr. Scholl's moleskin at the drug store and wrap it around the nose piece. It's softer and will feel more comfortable. If that treatment is ineffective, remove the chin lead and contact your veterinarian for ointment.

The chin lead is my favorite choice when original training collars fail. Both my dogs have chin leads.

Harnesses and other gadgets

Some people use harnesses. Although you can use a harness, with many dogs, harnesses encourage pulling because they force your puppy in front of you, not beside you. In fact, harnesses may actually encourage *more* pulling when you remove them; for sled dog wanna-be's, when the leg contraption comes off, they feel like they've been released from a shoot — see ya!

Some small dogs need a harness, though, because their tracheas are simply too fragile to bear the resistance of a neck collar. With the exception of tiny breeds, I don't recommend harnesses to anyone who has his heart set on a well-trained dog.

On the market is a No-Pull Harness design that I've found very effective. It prevents pulling by humanely curbing your dog's gait. *Prevent* is the key word.

Outdoor Enclosures

Puppies need to be safely enclosed when you allow them to run free outside. I tell all my clients, "If you can't fence them, leash them." The kind of enclosure you need — pens, tie outs, runs, or electrical fences, for example — differs in every situation. Following are important considerations:

✔ What kind of puppy do you have? What's the puppy's personality?

✔ How do you want to use the fencing system? Are you planning to leave your puppy confined when you're not home or just when you're out with him?

✔ What kind of confinement would his temperament allow? How much property do you own? (If you're lucky enough to have a yard, think seriously about enclosing at least a portion of it.)

Many people ask whether you can just train a dog to stay on your property. *Property training* is not impossible, but it is not a safe idea. To be successful, property training takes a certain canine temperament and consistent training procedures over a long period of time. And even then, you should not allow a dog that is property trained to be outside unsupervised.

Pens and tie outs

Pens and *chain link runner lines (RLs)* designed to leave the puppy out of doors unattended are a good option for older dogs, but they often create what I term *Hyper Isolation Anxiety (HIA)* in puppies. Being social animals, puppies get anxious when left alone, especially when they're very young. This anxiety manifests itself in excessive barking, digging, territorial behavior, destructive chewing, or frenetic activity once they're reunited with the owner.

Runner lines are only beneficial if you remain with the puppy and focus him on exercise games. Left unattended, a puppy can self-inflict a neck injury by chasing an object or animal. Also keep in mind that you need to leash the puppy when you take him to his confinement area; otherwise, he may bolt. Freedom now, confinement later. . . .

What you don't get from outdoor enclosures

The convenience of enclosure can't be argued. Morning rush. Family chaos. Hard days at work. Who has the time to walk, train, and play with the dog? Without supervision, however, puppies become too self-reliant. Alone outside, puppies learn to fend for themselves, which can lead to timidity or territorial behavior — not to mention your loss of control: "Come? Maybe later . . ." Enclosures are useful in keeping your puppy safe, but they can't replace the importance of your interactions.

Full yard fences

Enclosing your entire property is a great option for many puppies. This enclosure enables them to enjoy their freedom and accompany you on your outdoor tasks. You can install a doggy door to let your puppy monitor his own comings and goings between the house and yard.

Unfortunately, full yard fences have their drawbacks, too. If the puppy is left alone for prolonged periods of time, this enclosure also can create HIA. Given close access to the house, some dogs may chew the welcome mat or the base boards around the entrance door. Puppies prone to digging or jumping can also escape quite easily. Hounds, Nordic and Sporting breeds, and Terriers are just a few breeds famed for their acrobatic escapes. It only takes one escape to lose your puppy to a tragic occurrence.

Electrical fences

One option growing in popularity is the *electrical fencing system*. This seemingly magical creation keeps dogs enclosed by an underground wire that creates a shock when a dog wearing a battery-powered collar approaches. This system is ideal for dogs who habitually dig and love to run, as long as the dog is otherwise properly trained. Following are a few things to keep in mind about electrical fences:

- Your puppy must be at least 6 months old to be trained on this system — no matter what any sales person tells you.

- An electrical fence is *not* a substitute for proper training.

- Dogs can get through this fence. The best guarantee is proper and patient training, as well as checking the battery each month and the perimeter to ensure the wired-loop hasn't been short circuited.

- Collars that transmit the stimulus are battery run. You need to check the battery and replace it approximately every six weeks. The wire circuit can also get cut; check it after yard work, an electrical storm, and each month when you replace the battery.

- An electrical fence doesn't keep other dogs or animals from entering your property — a potential hazard.

Chapter 6

Bringing Your Puppy Home

● ●

In This Chapter

▶ Enduring the car ride home

▶ What to do with your puppy when you get there

▶ Surviving those first few days

▶ Making it through the first week

● ●

*T*he day to bring home your new puppy has finally arrived, and your life is never going to be quite the same. If you've planned ahead, rung up some goodies on the plastic (see Chapter 5), and thought through the day's events — from the car ride home to the first 24 hours — you're off to a good start. The day may toss a screwball or two in your direction, but with proper planning, you aren't going to encounter anything you can't handle.

To make this homecoming as smooth as possible, read the suggestions in this chapter and resist the urge to spoil your puppy before you've even brought him home (a pretty tall order, I know).

The Car Ride Home (Or "Ohmydearlord, Will This Trip Never End?")

You've selected your one and only, and the moment's arrived to bring him home. Unless your puppy comes from a neighborhood litter, I'm assuming you came by car. Now, depending on the situation, the car ride can be quite an experience. Worst case scenario: Your new dog gets car sick. It's a sorry sight, but you can take a few precautions:

✔ Have paper towels ready.

✔ Spread a sheet across the seat area prepared for your dog and bring a few clean sheets just in case you need a change.

✔ Bring along a box for the puppy to ride home in. Boxes add a feeling of security. Place a towel on the bottom and bring extras in case your puppy gets sick.

✔ Bring someone along to sit with the puppy (if the pup gets nervous, encourage him/her to talk softly).

✔ Before you leave, secure a light collar with an identification phone number (you can write the number on the collar itself) in case you have an emergency or accident.

✔ Bring along a few chewies in case the puppy gets the urge to chew.

✔ Drive slowly, taking each curve with care.

✔ Play some classical music and speak softly.

You may butt heads with some other nervous behaviors, such as whining, barking at passing objects, or eliminating. Stay calm and don't correct the puppy. Doing so makes for a bad start and only makes him more anxious and homesick. Expect the worst so that, no matter what happens, you'll be prepared.

Home, Home at Last

You made it home, somehow. You've been anxiously awaiting this very moment. The excitement level is probably pretty high, so take a few deep breaths. Too much tension can startle or frighten a young puppy. Even though you want to rush in and give your newest member the full tour, hold your huskies. Remember: Dogs don't see their environment with their eyes; they sniff it with their noses. Sniffing out an entire home might take hours and would be overwhelming.

Pick one room ahead of time, clean it, decorate it with bowls and bedding (see Chapter 5), and take the new pup or dog there initially. Share his curiosity as he checks out the room and speak to him sweetly. If your dog has an accident or grabs something inappropriate, don't correct him. He's too disoriented to retain anything so soon, and you'll just frighten him. So relax. This is just the beginning.

Rub a frozen stick of butter on your palm and encourage your puppy to give "kisses" (see Figure 6-1). This trick makes his first associations of home friendly and positive. You're also conditioning him to come forward when you reach out to him, not back up or jump at your face. (You can repeat this trick with family and friends in the days to come.)

You may be wondering what you should do with the rest of your household. If you have some anticipating eyes waiting for you at home, the next few sections can help.

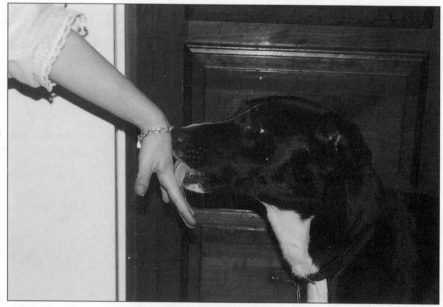

Photo by Sarah Hodgson.

Figure 6-1:
The butter-on-the-hands trick teaches "kisses" and creates a friendly home environment.

Keep the kids calm

Talk about excitement. This day may be on a future "fondest memories of my childhood" list. However, your job is to keep the kids calm. Too much squealing and loving in the first five minutes can be overwhelming for a pup. Explain the situation to your kids ahead of time and ask for their help in making the dog or puppy feel comfortable.

✔ **Set limits.** Make a rule that they can follow quietly and speak gently, but all roughhousing, shouting, and fighting is forbidden. (This may be your last peaceful moment for a while, so enjoy it.)

✔ **Have a pow-wow.** Gather everyone together and create a large circle by spreading your legs so your feet touch. Place the pup in the center of the circle and let him approach each person on his own. Discourage all unfair attention-getting ploys.

Don't over-stimulate your new pal with 300 toys and millions of people. If he is enthusiastic and wants to explore everything, go with him. If he wants to sit in a corner all day, just mill around the room and pet him as a reward for venturing out. Don't pet him if he's cowering in a corner — you'll reinforce that behavior. If you pay attention to a timid dog, you end up with a timid dog.

Really, really forget your friends' advice

Your friends are the hardest creatures to control. They all have ideas on the best way to raise a pup. Don't follow your friends' advice. What works for one person and his dog probably won't work for you, and if you follow everyone's suggestions, you may alienate your puppy. If you need help, seek out a professional.

Now for those guests (your friends *will* want to come over to visit the new puppy) — once your dog has calmed down, encourage guests to get on the floor or sit in a low chair. Bring your new arrival over and cradle him in a sitting position. If he's too excited, offer him a distraction chewy to help him calm down. By ignoring him when he's excited and petting him when he's calm, you're getting a head start on encouraging good manners.

Consider people with special needs

Let your common sense take over. If your dog is going to be around someone who's physically challenged, don't start off introductions by lifting the dog up to the person's face or putting a young puppy in his lap. Oh sure, your puppy may be small now, but what will happen when he grows into a 130-pound Great Dane and *still* wants to sit in Grandma's lap? Better teach that puppy to sit down next to the person and chew a special toy, one he only gets when visiting this person.

Make harmony with your other pets

Don't expect your resident pets to be wearing party hats when you pull into the driveway with the latest addition to the family. In all likelihood, they won't share your enthusiasm for the new family member.

Other dogs

Older dogs don't love sharing their space with puppies. So make the first introductions on neutral ground before you bring them together in your home.

You'll probably see a lot of *bluffing* — showing of the teeth, raised hackles, and shoulder pawing — when the two first meet. It all looks pretty scary but rarely escalates to a fight, so stay calm and don't interfere. (Don't interfere, that is, *unless* you see an unusually aggressive response — glaring eyes, withdrawn lips, and a growl that starts in the throat or belly.) Here are some other harmless behaviors you may see:

✔ Some older dogs will growl or paw at a new puppy — this is a good sign. Big dog is showing little dog who's boss.

✔ Sometimes new dogs shriek if the resident dog even comes near; again, don't interfere. If you comfort the new dog, it may alienate your resident dog and make the relationship between them rocky.

To keep the hierarchy harmonious, pay more attention to your resident dog, greeting and feeding him first. As long as he feels like he's still number one in your heart, he should cope just fine. Although you may find it hard not to meddle and feel protective of your newcomer, remember, you're following dog pack rules.

Cats

Cats have mixed feelings about new dogs. Some cats head for the highest object in the house and stare at you reproachfully. Some wait confidently for the curious dog to get close enough for a good, solid bat on the nose. In either case, keep your response low-key. Overreacting makes both animals nervous.

If your cat can't come to grips with the presence of the new puppy, keep the two in separate areas and bring them together when your dog is experienced with the Teaching Lead (described in Chapter 12).

Other animals

If you have other caged animals in the house, like ferrets or guinea pigs, don't bring them out immediately. Let the puppy get used to you and then show him the cages when he's in a sleepy mood.

How the First 24 Hours Will Go

The first day your new dog is home with you can be a little odd. After all the anticipation and preparation, your dog is home. Some dogs jump right into the swing of things; others prefer a more reserved approach. Don't compare your dog to others you've known and don't worry if he seems too rambunctious, too cautious, or too anything. You, your house, the other people and pets there — all are very new to him; he's trying to figure out what's going on.

If he wants to sleep, let him sleep; put him in his crate (or sleep area) with the door open. At mealtime, put his food and water bowl in or near his crate and leave him alone for 15 minutes. Even if he doesn't touch his food, take it up. (It's probably just his nerves.) After the meal, walk him outside or to the newspapers (see Chapter 11 for more about this kind of training). Water should be made available during meal times and removed with the food. Leave a dish by the door, allowing sips before each outing, and be mindful that if your puppy looks thirsty, he probably is.

Ideally, your dog should sleep near you at night, by your bedside in a large open-topped box or crate that he can't climb out of. He may whine the first few nights, but he'll feel a lot safer beside your bed than alone in another room. If he whines, lay your hand in the box or on the crate to calm him.

I can already feel your temptation to bring your new puppy onto your bed. Don't do it — at least not for now. It will send him mixed messages regarding your direction and may encourage bed-wetting. A true nightmare. When your pup's grown, you can allow him on the bed with your permission, but not now. . . .

If a bedroom is out of the question, crate him or enclose him in a small area, like a bathroom or kitchen. Turn off the lights, turn on some classical music, and be ready to walk him if he cries. Ahhh, the joys of doggy parenthood.

He (and you) may need to get up one to three times during the night to eliminate. If so, quietly take him to his spot and then back to his enclosure. Don't start playing games with the dog at 3:00 in the morning unless you like the habit. For more info about housetraining, head to Chapter 11.

What to Expect the First Week

Having a puppy is a big change, and the first week's a whirlwind. You wake up and remind yourself that you have an extra mouth to feed (unless, of course, that extra mouth is yelping at you for some attention). Even though it's only human to envision every piddle as a lifelong habit, try not to feel overwhelmed. The most important things are taking care of your puppy's needs to eat, play, piddle, and poop. Just like a newborn. Here are a few things you can do this week to help your puppy get off to a good start:

- ✔ Help your puppy learn his name. Place some Cheerios in a cup and shake it as you call out his name. (Avoid using his name if you're disappointed.)

- ✔ Direct your puppy to his bathroom spot using a word like *outside* or *papers* each time you lead him to his spot. (Check out Chapter 11 for more hints on toilet training.)

- ✔ Put butter on your hands and say "Kisses." Encourage your puppy to kiss, not nip.

- ✔ Find a veterinarian. Choosing a doctor for your pet is a very personal and long-term commitment. Asks friends and other pet owners who they recommend. Visit more than one office (with or without your dog), talking to the receptionist and the doctor if their schedule allows it. Are the people friendly? Is the office clean and well organized? Do you feel welcomed and comfortable? Does your dog? The answers to these questions can help you decide which vet is right for your dog.

Chapter 7

How to Be a Good Puppy Trainer

*B*eing able to talk to animals was my lofty aspiration at the age of two. In reality, although they may not actually "talk" to them, lots of people have a way with animals. You can recognize these people in a heartbeat. They can walk into your house and have your puppy behaving in seconds and looking to them as their long-lost leader. When I did this with one particular eight-month-old puppy, it was enough to bring one of my clients (the dog's owner) to tears. "Why doesn't Alice look at me that way?" she asked.

Alice eventually did look at her owner that way, but first I taught the owner what I knew by instinct and experience — a new thought pattern, which began with respect for her pup and an understanding of how she, the owner, had played a role in creating the problem with her dog. In this chapter, I share with you what I shared with her. I help you become a good dog trainer *before* you begin working with your dog. The stuff in this chapter can help you understand and train your dog better.

You Gotta Train Yourself First

A lot goes into being a good dog trainer, and most of it's a mental thing. Puppies have spirits, just like the rest of us, that you must understand and encourage in ways that make sense to your dog. Your puppy has bestowed on you the highest honor, one you'd never receive from a human: a lifetime commitment to respect your judgment and abide by your rules. You need only to show her how.

In order to show your puppy how, you need to remember five *key* things that a good dog trainer does:

- Accepts and modifies his own personality
- Never blames the pup
- Recognizes the pup's unique personality
- Understands his (the trainer's) role in the training process
- Learns from the dog

Recognize and Modify Your Personality

Now's the time to analyze yourself. Take out a pen and paper and write down three adjectives to describe your personality. What kind of person are you? Demanding? Sweet? Forgiving? Compulsive? Be honest. Then compare your personality with your dog's character (see the section "The six common character types," later in this chapter).

Are you demanding, but your dog is a sweetie? If so, someone is going to have to change. Making too many demands on a sweet dog only frightens him; he'll shut down or run away when training begins. If you're compulsive and you have a laid-back dog, you'll be laughed at. Have you ever seen a dog laugh at his owner? It's quite embarrassing. For you to be a good dog trainer, you must modify your personality to suit your dog's.

Never Blame the Pup

Believe it or not, puppies don't react out of spite. Your puppy's behavior is directly related to your reactions. My mantra?

A dog repeats whatever gets attention.

Whatever gets attention. And they don't care whether the attention is negative or positive. So if you're out there saying, "I tell her she's bad, but she just ignores me!" I have something to tell you: Your dog interprets your discipline as interaction and will repeat the unwanted behavior again and again.

So how do you handle unruly situations? The first step to becoming a good dog trainer is to stop blaming the dog.

Never run at your puppy for anything. Racing head long toward a puppy is scary. Visualize someone two to four times your size barreling down on you. Overwhelming. Although your puppy may collapse in fear or run from you, she won't "know" anything. Consider other options like using treat cups, described in Chapter 13.

Recognize the Pup's Unique Personality

Yes, puppies have personalities, too. If you've had more than one, I'm sure you know exactly what I'm talking about. So many of my clients have started their sob stories with "My last dog was so easy!" "But," I respond with a smile, "this isn't your last dog. This dog is unique. And to train him, you must begin by understanding his personality."

No matter what his personality, your dog needs to interact and be understood. Puppies love to share a secret language with you, whatever the commands you use, and are content staying close to you as long as you include them in your daily activities.

The six common character types

Based on my experience over the years working with countless numbers of dogs, I've noticed that most dogs fit into one of six character types. Identify your puppy's character type and remember it as you work through the training chapters later in this book.

- ✔ **Eager Beaver.** These creatures do whatever is required to make you happy, although they can be difficult and manic if you ignore their training. Eager Beavers want to please so much that they stick to whatever gets attention. If you like to toss the ball, puppies with this personality will bring it back 500 times. If you encourage jumping, these dog will jump on you—and everyone else—whenever excitement builds. If you encourage them to sit and settle down on command, that's what they'll do. With this puppy, all you have to do is decide what you want. You don't need to use harsh training techniques.

- ✔ **Joe Cool.** Laid back and relaxed, puppies with this personality have control of every situation and seem to be less focused on you than their image. Give these fellows a command, and they'll look at you as if to say, "in a minute," and then they'll forget. Organize a lesson and they'll fall asleep. Although they're quite funny and easy to live with, training is essential for these dogs. Without it, they may not respond to you off lead. They may also be unmanageable in social situations. Diligent and patient training techniques are necessary.

- **The Jokester.** I've owned a little comedian. A quick-minded perfectionist, Calvin taught me more about dog training than a lot of books I've read. The reason? Dogs with this personality are revved up Wonder Pups who get into a lot of trouble if they're not directed. Dancing on the edge of good behavior, they're biggest accolade is laughter and they must be firmly persuaded to cooperate. Laughter, after all, is attention — trust me, it's hard not to laugh at a dog prancing around with an oversized cantaloupe in his mouth. Given clear, consistent, and stern instruction, comedians take to training well. Their puppyhood will test your patience, but they make wonderful dogs if trained.

- **The Bully.** These dogs take themselves far too seriously. In a pack of puppies, this pup would have been destined to lead, and your home is no different. Unless you're experienced, a pup of this nature can be difficult to train. Aggression, physical leaning, and mounting are common. Training must be consistent and firm and should begin in puppyhood. If your dog fits this profile, you must lay down the law now, and you may need professional training. Do not proceed with training on your own if your puppy threatens you.

- **Sweetie Pie.** Docile and mild, these puppies like to observe situations rather than control them. They adore the people they love and must be trained under a soft hand. If you yell at them—or at anyone else—they crumble. There's little to say against these dear puppies. Although it's easy to skip over training for these pups, training is essential for their safety.

- **Scaredy Cat.** These puppies like to view the world from behind your legs. Soothe this behavior, and you make it worse. Unlike children, who might feel relieved, soothing actually reinforces the dog's fear. You must act confident and relaxed in new and startling situations. Tell your puppy "excuse me," and move her away if she ducks behind you. Only reinforce her if she calms down. Training is essential to help these characters feel more secure. These puppies respond best to a gentle hand.

Psychotic pups are out there

It's very rare that I come across a psychotic puppy, but they do exist. Some puppies have been bred very poorly and suffer brain damage as a result. These dogs can become vicious and are a danger even as very young puppies. This problem is identified by erratic or fearful aggression responses in very atypical situations. There are two categories:

- **Erratic viciousness.** At unpredictable intervals, puppies with erratic viciousness growl fiercely from the belly. It may happen when his owner passes his food bowl, approaches when he's chewing a toy, or even walks by him. At other times, the puppy is perfectly sweet — a "Jekyll and Hyde" personality.

✔ **Fear biters.** These puppies show dramatic fear in or a startled bite response to non-threatening situations, like turning a page of the newspaper or moving an arm. They can act extremely confused or threatened when strangers approach.

Many well-educated dog people use the term *fear biter* incorrectly. There is a big difference in a dog that bites out of fear and a fear biter. Don't automatically assume the worst if someone labels your dog with this term.

Don't panic if your puppy occasionally growls at you in play or barks at the mailman. A lot of puppies growl when protecting a food dish or toy, and the guarding instinct is strong in many breeds. These are behavioral problems that can be cured or controlled with proper training. Even many biters can be rehabilitated. The situations I'm speaking of involve *severe* aggression — bared teeth, hard eyes, a growl that begins in the belly, and a bite response you'd expect from a trained police dog. These personality disturbances are seen very early, usually by four months of age.

Encountering psychotic dogs is both frightening and tragic because nothing can be done to alter their development. Their fate has been sealed by irresponsible, greedy people. If you suspect that your dog might have either of these abnormalities, speak to your breeder and veterinarian immediately and call a specialist to analyze the situation. These puppies must be euthanized. In my career, I've seen only six; five were purchased from unknown or suspect breeders, and the sixth was a mixed breed.

Understand Your Role in the Training Process

One of my clients called me in jubilation one day. After weeks of group training, she had figured it out. "Training is about getting the puppies to *want* to work with you!"

In class, I repeat the same concept many different ways. However, I understand that hearing the words and feeling their meaning rarely happen simultaneously. Although this student had listened to me, she had been training her dog by dictating her commands and muscling through all corrections. Additionally, she carried out my suggestions to the extreme: If I said to enunciate commands, she'd shout them. When I encouraged people to tap their foot lightly to end a heel, she'd stamp it.

She loves her dog tremendously, but when she started training, she was more obsessed with the mechanics than the process itself. "Remember," I would tell her, "Training involves two spirits — yours and your puppy's. One affects the other." To understand your role in the training process, keep these things in mind:

- ✔ Training is about making your puppy want to work with you.
- ✔ Your puppy isn't a machine; he's a spiritual being.
- ✔ You are your puppy's social director and his leader.
- ✔ Every puppy learns at different rates. Frustration is catchy, so stay calm.
- ✔ Your mom's right again — patience is a virtue.

Learn from Your Pup

Isn't dog training about controlling the dog? No. That's not the whole story. Any dog trainer worth his weight in dog biscuits knows that learning is never a one-way street. Raising a puppy teaches you invaluable lessons that you can use with the people in your life as well. From your puppy, you'll learn patience and forgiveness. You'll come to understand behaviors that don't please you. You'll feel a commitment grow inside you and see it in your family. If you listen with your heart, your puppy will teach you many lessons.

Chapter 8

How to Think Like a Dog

In This Chapter

▶ Communicating by using the language of a pup

▶ Establishing who's in charge of the household

▶ Motivating your puppy

There is more to your little fur ball than blinking eyes and four paws. A fascinating creature in his own right, your puppy needs you to understand where he's coming from before he can give you his full cooperation. No matter how many stars you wish on, your pup will never understand what it's like to be human—no matter how much you work together.

Until you can think *with* and *not against* your dog, you can't really train him properly. You need to explore your dog's individual personality and learn his language.

So how do you think like a dog? Read this chapter to find out.

Doglish: Speaking the Language of a Pup

To be the best teacher, you need to be fluent in *Doglish,* the language of your puppy. Give your family or friends a lesson, too, and encourage consistency.

Doglish consist of three elements:

✔ Eye contact

✔ Body language

✔ Tone

In Doglish, words, feelings, and lengthy explanations don't count. Complex reasoning is impossible for your puppy to follow. Puppies are so innocent in their simplicity, it's beautiful.

Eye contact

If you're constantly looking to your puppy in stressful situations (someone's at the door or the dog's stealing the dish rag) and are having trouble encouraging your dog to pay attention to you, guess what? Your puppy thinks you depend on him to be the leader. He thinks you want *him* to make all the judgment calls. Before you can figure out how to handle these situations (which I explain in Chapter 13), you have to understand that to train your puppy, you must encourage *him* to look to *you* for direction.

You reinforce whatever you look at. Look at a well-behaved dog and guess what you have? You got it. A well-behaved dog.

Think of your dog's energy as a scale from 1 to 10, with 1 being sleep and 10 being hyper-excited play. Between 1 and 8 is the happy zone, which includes all the endearing behaviors you love. Between 8 and 10 is the wild zone, which contains all the behaviors that drive you crazy: jumping, stealing, nipping, and running out of control, for example.

Remembering that dogs repeat whatever behavior earns them your attention, you can see that if you pay a lot of attention to a naughty dog, you get Mister or Misses Naughty. By redirecting wild energy (described in Chapter 28) and focusing on the good stuff, you know what you get? A perfect little angel (well, almost). The bottom line is this: Only make eye contact when your dog is calm (in the 1 to 8 zone).

Believe it or not, the 8 to 10 zone is no picnic for your dog. Although he's rowdy, he's unfocused. This manic behavior is a simple reaction to not understanding what you expect—a matter of stress and containment. Discipline does not help because your dog often interprets it as confrontational play. Structure and training help the most.

Body language

Body language is a funny thing. Imagine this: Your puppy becomes excited and hyper when company arrives at the front door. Desperate to save face, you start shouting and pushing your puppy as the company fends the both of you off with their coats. You try every possible command — Sit, Boomer! Down! Off! Bad dog! — but to no avail. The whole arrival scene is one big fiasco.

Body language is an integral part of Doglish. Play, tension, relaxation — they all have different postures. Knowing that your puppy thinks *you're* a dog and doesn't quite grasp the "I'm pushing you frantically because I'm unhappy with your greeting manners" concept, you're not communicating what you think you are. In fact, *you're* copying *his* body language. As you blaze the training trail, remember these three things:

✔ Stand upright and relax when directing your dog. I call this the *Peacock Position*. (Imagine a peacock — beautiful and proud, chest out, confident, and in control.) When giving your puppy direction or a command, throw your shoulders back and stand tall just like a peacock. Tell your family and friends about this position and start strutting your stuff.

✔ Don't face off or chase your puppy when you're mad. To your dog, you'll look like you're playing.

✔ When you're trying to quiet or direct your puppy, stay calm.

✔ And always remember, you set the example.

I hear two questions ringing through the pages already: How on Earth can this be done? Can't I ever get down and play or cuddle with my puppy? Of course you can. Chapter 28 is devoted to appropriate puppy play — one of the biggest perks in having a dog. But don't play with your puppy when he's in a mischievous mood, or you're asking for trouble.

Tone

If your puppy thinks of you as another dog and you start yelling, he hears barking. Barking (yelling) interrupts behavior; it doesn't instruct. And barking increases excitement. Some of you may have a puppy that backs off from a situation when you yell (although he'll probably repeat the same behavior later). The reason he backs off is because your yelling frightens him — he is afraid of you — not because he understands. Yelling is just no good. So what works? Well, Chapter 14 tells you what works. But first, here are three tones you should commit to memory. I call them the three Ds:

✔ **Delighted tone:** Use this tone when you want to praise your puppy. It should soothe him, not excite him. Find a tone that makes your pup feel warm and proud inside.

✔ **Directive tone:** Use this tone for your commands. It should be clear and authoritative, not harsh or sweet. Give your commands once from the Peacock Position.

If you bend over when giving your puppy a command, don't be surprised if your puppy doesn't listen. You're doing the doggy equivalent of a *play bow* (a posture that invites a game). Think of it in human terms: If you ask me to have a seat while you're hunched over and looking at the floor, I'd be less interested in where to sit and more interested in what on Earth you're looking at. When giving your puppy directions, stand tall and proud like a peacock.

Teaching kids how to use the proper tone

Do you have kids? If so, you've probably noticed that sometimes they call out to puppies in a very high-pitched tone, and sometimes they don't pronounce commands properly, either. And you're probably wondering what to do about it.

Well, until kids are 12, you're better off focusing on what they're doing right instead of honing in on their imperfections. So my advice is simply to over-enunciate all your commands so that the kids learn to pronounce them properly and in an appropriate tone. For example, instead of saying *sit,* say *siiit.* If you over enunciate each command, your kids will notice the effects and start mimicking you. And when your kids copy your intonations, the control transfers from you to them.

✔ **Discipline tone:** I'm not much of a disciplinarian. My approach encourages more structure than strictness, but you should have a few tones that tell your dog to back off or move on. I use "No, Sir" and "No, Ma'am" a lot. I go into more detail in Chapter 14, but the word doesn't matter as much as the tone. The tone should be shameful or disapproving, like "How could you?" or "You better not touch that." Discipline has more to do with timing and tone than your puppy's transgressions.

As you can see, Doglish is quite different from English. Many people assume that their puppies understand them when, in fact, they're often picking up the opposite message. If you chase your table snatcher, your English is saying "How dare you!" but your Doglish is saying "PARTY!" Remember, every interaction you have with your puppy gets translated into Doglish. From now on, you're being watched from a canine's eyes, so you had better start acting like a canine.

Don't repeat your commands. Dogs don't understand words; they learn sounds. Saying "Sit, sit, sit, Boomer, sit!" sounds different from "SIT" — and that's what Boomer learns. If you want your dog to listen when you give the first command, make sure you give it only once; then reinforce your expectations by positioning your dog.

Who's In Charge Here, Anyway?
(The Leadership Principle)

Dogs have a lot of team spirit. Many often refer to this as their "pack" instinct, but I like to think of it in "team" terms. Team consciousness and the canine psyche have a lot in common. Teams focus on winning; each player works for it, wants it, thinks about it, and strives for it. Dogs live their entire lives, their every waking moment, by team structure. Instead of winning, however, their mantra is survival. And to your dog, you and your family are his team.

Some other, less obvious factors also determine a team's success. Three come to mind immediately: cooperation, structure, and mutual respect. Without these, even a group of phenomenal players would produce only chaos. A good team is organized so all members know who's in charge and what's expected from them. And should someone get in trouble or get hurt, he can trust that another teammate will help out.

For your dog to feel secure and safe, he *must* know who's in charge, and it's your job to teach him what you expect. In dogland, teams are organized in a hierarchy, so you must teach your four-legged friend that two-legged dogs are the ones in charge. If you have more than one person in your household, teaching this concept requires some cooperation on everyone's part, but it's very do-able.

If *you* don't organize the team hierarchy, your *dog* will, and that can be a real nightmare. If your dog has the personality to lead, you'll find yourself living in a very expensive doghouse under dog rule. If your dog doesn't have the personality to lead but feels he must because no one else is, you'll end up with one big headache because dogs in this state are very hyper and confused.

So how do you organize your team and teach your dog the rules? You have to understand what motivates your dog's behavior (see the following section), and you have to master his communication skills (see the earlier Doglish section).

All this may seem like hard work, but watching the technique in action is quite fascinating. Your dog will respond to you more willingly if you make the effort to understand and learn his language. With an ounce of effort, a little time, and some structure, you can earn your dog's respect, cooperation, and trust. Plus, you'll have a teammate who will be at your side when the cards are down. You can't beat that bargain.

Gimme, Gimme, Gimme (The Attention Factor)

Puppies are motivated by attention. They live for it, love it, and will do anything to keep the spotlight focused on them. Does this remind you of a three year old? Well, add to this similarity the fact that puppies don't care whether the attention is negative or positive.

Why negative attention doesn't work

Picture a very excited jumping puppy. You're trying to read the paper calmly, but he wants your attention. What if you tried to correct the dog by pushing him down and screaming "Off!"? In all likelihood, the puppy will jump again. Do you know why? Because you just gave him attention. Attention in a dog's mind includes anything from dramatic body contact to a simple glance. Yes, even looking at your dog reinforces his behavior.

Though this phenomenon may sound far-fetched at first, it's actually pretty elementary. Puppies think of us as other dogs. If they get excited and then we get excited, we're following their lead. By mimicking their energy level, we communicate that they must interpret new situations. The fact that you might be upset with their behavior just doesn't register. Being upset is a human emotion. Excitement and body contact is a dog thing. Even if you push your puppy so hard that he stops and slinks away, the only thing you've accomplished is scaring him. And who wants to train a dog through fear? Trust me, there's a better way.

Let me give you another example. What happens if a dog grabs a sock and everyone in the household stops to chase him. Dog party? You bet. Because the puppy views everybody as a dog, he's thinking, "What fun!" as he dives behind the couch and under the table. Chasing doesn't come across as discipline; it comes across as *Prize Envy* — "Whatever I have must be really good because everyone wants it!"

Dogs often interpret negative attention as confrontational play: "You're animated, you're loud, you're fierce. Let's play rough!"

Out-of-control negative attention reinforces the very behavior you're trying to change. So how do you resolve these problems? Be patient and read on. (You can find in-depth information on specific problems in Chapter 13.)

The benefits of positive attention

When I ask my clients what they do when they catch their puppy resting or chewing a bone quietly, most say, "Nothing. It's a moment of peace." I appreciate such honesty; however, it's those times when they ought to be showering their puppy with attention. Not wild, twist-and-shout, hoot-and-holler attention. Just calm, soothing, loving attention that makes the puppy smile inside. A soft whispering praise is best mixed with a massage-like pat. My mantra? Your dog will repeat whatever you pay attention to.

So you decide. What would you rather have? A puppy that stays by your side with a chew bone or a frantic sock stealer that races around the house like a maniac? If you like the sock stealer, close the book. But if the bone-chewer image appeals to you, stick with me — we're going places.

Dogs are drawn to positive energy fields. Think of yourself as a Dairy Queen. If you keep up the cheer, your dog won't want to be anywhere else.

Part III

The "What Have I Gotten Myself Into?" Months

The 5th Wave   By Rich Tennant

"The first thing I'm going to do is quit my Yoga classes. I'm learning all I need to know about sitting quietly in one position for hours by owning a puppy that falls asleep in my lap."

In this part . . .

Bringing a puppy into your life isn't all love and happy times. In fact, puppies go through developmental phases just like kids. Sometimes they're cooperative. A lot of times they're not.

If you've already got some children running around, the energy level at your home can be overwhelming. Plus, sibling rivalry can occur between your new puppy and your kids. And there's the housebreaking issue to contend with. A puppy doesn't come with a self-instruction kit.

Not to worry. Part III helps you understand your puppy's developmental phases, work with your kids, and get a handle on housetraining.

Chapter 9

Puppy Phases

• •

In This Chapter

▶ The basic needs of a puppy

▶ What to expect during the five stages of puppy development

• •

Sharing your life with a young puppy is more than just fun and games. Puppies are adorable, and nothing beats the serenity of a sleepy head resting on your leg, but they're also very demanding: They create chaos just when you want to relax. They chew your shoe even though you provide them with dog toys. Come in from a walk, and they pee on the carpet. They're underfoot when you're in a hurry. They bite your pant leg, lick your food, jump on the company, leap on the furniture. . . .

The frustrations puppies introduce can send anyone packing, but you shouldn't overlook this one pearl of wisdom: Naughty puppies are normal puppies. Like infants who pull hair and toddlers who spill milk, active puppies are healthy, curious, and enjoying themselves. Though I share techniques you can use to discourage unacceptable behavior (see Chapter 15), don't expect your puppy to act like a dog. Understanding just how your puppy develops and what's going on behind those adoring eyes is half the battle.

The Needy Pup

Puppies, like babies, have needs. They need to eat, drink, sleep, exercise, and eliminate.

If a human baby needs something, it cries. Crying communicates a need, and the baby's guardian is responsible for figuring out just what that need is. Puppies also attempt to communicate their needs to their caretakers, but they don't cry. They bite. They get hyper. Their signal is oral, fidgety, and persistent interaction. Where a verbal discouragement might refocus wild behavior, a needy pup won't let up. How you respond to your puppy's attempts to communicate affect how that puppy feels when it's with you.

Just like a baby, you build trust with a dog by responding quickly and accurately to its cries. If, time and again, you fail to grasp that Muffy's whining, scratching, and nipping means that she needs to go outside, you're undermining the trust she needs to have in you.

Excessive nipping most often communicates urgency. Pressing poop, fatigue, or heightened energy are often communicated through unrelenting, hard bites. Before you get cross, remember that when your puppy displays these behaviors, she's trying to tell you something. Disciplining her only communicates confrontation and aggravates your relationship.

Are you or is someone in your home forgetful? Make a list of your puppy's needs and post them around the house until everyone's in tune.

The Five Stages of Development

Anyone who has raised a puppy knows that, like kids, puppies develop in stages. How you cope with the ups and downs, your survival tactics, and the solutions you choose all affect your pup's outlook and how comfortable he is with you. Feeling overwhelmed? Take a deep breath. This section gives you an overview of the five stages of development. With this info, you'll know what to expect and how *you* should behave. (Head to Chapter 14 for various training exercises and commands you can use for each of these five stages.)

Infancy (8 to 12 weeks)

At this point in your pup's development, her life centers around satisfying one of four basic needs: sleeping, eating, eliminating, and playing. You should be feeding her three to four times a day, taking her out constantly, and letting her sleep when she wants.

You can also expect to witness the "wild puppy energy spurt." It's something to behold. Several times a day, your pup will get a crazed look in her eye, and then she'll suddenly dash around the house or yard, completely out of control. If she were a cartoon, all four legs would be in the air, and she'd be leaving a trail of smoke. You can't do much to influence her behavior at this time. I've found that the best strategy is to redirect her energy with an empty plastic bottle or soccer ball (see Chapter 28).

Always remove plastic objects after play. Never play with a damaged bottle because the sharp edges can cut or be swallowed. And place it out of reach when you leave your puppy unattended.

Here are a couple of simple, interactive puppy play lessons. These let you get to know your puppy and help her become the well-behaved, well-adjusted dog you've been dreaming about. The first lesson is a simple Name game; use your pup's name before you offer anything positive: food, treats, and love. In the second game, Leash Training, you do the following:

1. **First start with the collar. Put it on your puppy at 20 minute intervals throughout the day until your puppy accepts it.**

2. **Next attach a light 4-foot leash and let your puppy drag it at 20 minute intervals. Once he's used to the feel of the leash, pick it up and follow him. Once this routine is enjoyed, move on to Step 3.**

3. **Call your puppy to you, putting increasingly more pressure on the lead. For the first few real leash walks, carry a cup full of treats to shake and encourage your pup to follow.**

Puppies go through a fear-impression period between 8–10 weeks and again at 4½–5 months. As with people, fear can be a very debilitating emotion for a dog. Puppies can be afraid of anything, including vacuums, hairdryers, food processors, cars, grates, and so on. Unchecked, these fears can last a lifetime. To prevent this, keep these things in mind:

✔ Never race after your puppy or poke him with an unfamiliar object.

✔ If your puppy is experiencing fear, don't bend over to soothe him. Your puppy will think you're afraid, too. Instead, calmly investigate the object and ignore him until he follows your lead.

✔ Set up scenes to introduce your puppy to new appliances, people, and unusual objects. Place treats all around, staying focused on whatever the new thing is until your puppy is confident. Remember, puppies "see" things with their noses; smelling is believing in the canine world.

At this age, your puppy learns best if her new words are part of the fun.

Keep your expectations low; she's got so much new information pouring in she might not remember a new command from one day to the next. That's okay — she's just a baby. Enjoy this stage.

The terrible twos (12 to 16 weeks)

As your puppy matures, his personality develops. At 12–16 weeks, he's a bit bolder, braver, and harder to impress. He marches right up to company and demands attention. He insists on being at the center of all household activities. Your position as all-knowing leader doesn't impress him as much. He's growing up.

Who's in charge here?

Has your puppy begun a training program for you? Here's how to tell:

- He solicits (and gets!) your attention by jumping, nipping, whining, and barking.

- He has taught you how to wrestle and play tug-of-war during walks.

- He grabs your clothing and tries to carry it around the house (while you're still in it).

- When he wants a biscuit or part of your lunch, he expresses this desire by barking in your face. Advanced dogs-as-trainers may simply help themselves.

If any of these scenarios sounds a little too familiar, don't despair. You can turn the training program around so that you're in charge, but in order to do so, you need to understand this stage in your puppy's development.

By 12 weeks, your puppy's brain is fully developed, and he's ready to learn. This age is the best time to begin training because your puppy is old enough to understand and remember your direction but still a little too young to take matters into his own paws. Remember, your puppy is starting to learn things — whether or not you train him — and if you don't train him, he'll train you.

At this age, your pup's starting to learn what behaviors get attention and what games last the longest, and he's keeping score on who wins. Your puppy may be acting bold, but he's still unsure about his world and needs direction from you now more than ever. Keep these points in mind while you're working with him during this important developmental stage:

- **Attention is key.** He wants it, he needs it, and he'll do anything to get it. Remember the canine credo: All attention is good; positive or negative doesn't matter.

- **Eye contact — who's watching who?** If you watch him more than he watches you, he thinks you're looking for direction.

- **Is your house a dog house or people house?** You need to tighten up the rules on housebreaking, chewing, nipping, and jumping. If your puppy is making the decisions on these things, you're living in his house. That's one expensive dog house.

Sometimes I think puppies are made so cute because they can be so annoying. And sometimes I think they know it. I've seen looks that as much as say, "How can you possibly get mad at me when I'm so completely precious?" Just remember: This darling little bundle is keeping score.

The budding adolescent (16 to 24 weeks)

It's going to happen — be prepared. That sweet little compliant puppy you held in your arms days before is going to do a 180-degree turnaround. He'll become defiant, strong-willed, and fussy. He's entering the bratty zone. But don't panic. This stage is normal. It's even survivable. And it won't last forever if you train him through it.

Here are some surefire signs that let you know this stage has begun:

- Leash walks become confrontational battles over who holds the leash and who is walking whom, and corrections only result in jumping.

- You call him. He looks, he pauses, he bolts — in the other direction.

- He insists on being the center of attention every moment of every day.

- Corrections make the behavior worse.

- He's driving you crazy.

Remember, this stage (like the others) is normal. As much as you want to hide under the couch for the next three months, don't. This stage is the best time to start the training outlined in Chapter 14. Keep your lessons short and use each new command during lesson time only for the first week. This process allows your puppy to feel successful mastering each word before you apply it to his day-to-day world; the concept is similar to letting children master their addition skills in school before asking them to balance your checkbook.

I call this stage the "rude awakening." When confronted with the sometimes aggravating adolescent, all dog owners think wistfully of the endearing infant stage. But try to look at the situation from your puppy's point of view: He's getting bigger, the world is less scary, and he's aching to find out just how much he can get away with. Teach him your expectations patiently, be persistent with your training, and take a deep breath because the adventure isn't over yet.

Puppy puberty (6 to 9 months)

Your puppy is about to go through a major transformation. He's growing up. Remember growing up? Hormones, rebellion, confusion, curiosity . . . in another word, *puberty.* An exciting time but not always pretty. Well, puberty's no different for your puppy.

At about six months, those hormones start coursing through his veins, and he begins to experience a jumbled mix of internal signals: Dominate! Submit! Explore! Hide! Approach! Retreat! If he were a child, he'd get an unusual haircut and laugh at your clothes but still be a little nervous when you're not home. On top of these typical growing pains, add the awakening of breed-specific instincts that tell herders to herd, hunters to hunt, guarders to guard, pullers to pull, and so on. You end up in utter canine chaos, and he's still cutting his baby teeth.

So here you have this puppy/dog, pumped full of hormones, high spirits, and anxiety. No wonder he may give you the puppy equivalent of a teenage eye roll when you give him a command.

You may wonder whether you can tell when your puppy is shifting into this stage. You can. Trust me. The most telling sign is unpredictability. You may feel like you have two different dogs: The precious angel who gazes up at you with adoring eyes and the wide-eyed demon dancing just out of reach with your shoe in his mouth. The one you show off during walks through the park and the one you say belongs to your brother. The one who makes you smile and the one who makes you cringe. The ease and speed with which your puppy can transform herself is truly amazing. Here are some other signs that your pup has hit puberty:

- ✔ He knows all his commands but is selective in his response.
- ✔ You see a recurrence of jumping, nipping, and leash pulling.
- ✔ If you leave him alone, he begins destructive chewing or house soiling.
- ✔ You see excessive whining and bossiness.

As if the bratty stage wasn't fun enough.

The toughest thing to control during puberty isn't your dog; it's your temper. Having the right attitude is extremely important. We humans are a control-oriented bunch, and we want our dogs to come when called, stay calm in exciting situations, and control their gamy impulses. But these young dogs want to play! Have fun! Chase a butterfly! They are often unimpressed by your frustration. Some may show fear, but most think a shouting, foot-stomping Top Dog is inviting play, and the game accelerates — as does your blood pressure.

The trying teen (9 to 12 months)

By now your puppy is starting to calm down. He manages better on his own. He chews his bone. He responds immediately to your command. He doesn't assault your visitors. Why, he's almost perfect.

Okay, sometimes he ignores you. Every now and then, he runs right by you when you call him to come. Occasionally, he fidgets himself out of a Sit-Stay or faces you when he ought to be at your side. What you have to understand is that he *wants* to behave, but his teenage genes are relentlessly telling him to make one more glorious attempt for Top Dog status. To that end, he begins a subtle campaign of defiance. You may not think a sloppy sideways sit is a very big deal, but your dog makes a little mental check mark every time you let him get away with it. Here are some other signs he's trying to make his ascent to Top Dog position:

✔ He shifts positions before responding to a Sit or Down command.

✔ He faces away or pivots in front of you during a Heel command.

✔ He slams into your leg on the Come command.

These are all little acts of defiance. Nothing earth-shattering but not acceptable. During this stage, some dogs become more aware of your weaknesses and continue to highlight them in a last attempt to lead the pack. They will continue this until they have exhausted all options and are content to follow your lead. If your dog remains skeptical of your leadership, hang tough. Persist in making your point clear. Consider an investment in group or personal dog training. Don't quit.

Think for a moment. If you asked your puppy to describe you, what would he bark out? "Fun to be around, confident, and in control!" Or would he wag his tail nervously and say, "Impatient, easily fooled, and unsure." Don't think for a minute that your dog doesn't have an option. During your time together, he's learned to read you well. Make a good impression. Stand tall, be patient and firm, and don't be afraid to have fun.

Chapter 10

Kids and Puppies (Reality Bites)

· ·

In This Chapter

▶ Catching the signs that your child is jealous of the new puppy

▶ Overcoming Sibling Rivalry Syndrome

▶ Helping the kids and puppy bond

▶ Recognizing when you need professional help

· ·

*O*ne of the hallmarks of my childhood was my dog, Shawbee, who was a Husky-Shepherd mix. She was my constant companion, waiting for me at the bus stop, hanging outside the church while I took ballet lessons, sharing my ice cream cone on a hot summer day. Nowadays, dogs and kids rarely have the freedom to bond this way. The world is different from when I was a child. There are computers. Most communities have leash laws. Dogs left outside are stolen. People are more dog phobic. Unfortunately, times have changed, and new problems are cropping up.

Today, kids are often over-stimulated at a young age, and they have less time to hang out with dogs. Riding bikes and running around is often limited to parks where dogs aren't allowed. Both parents usually work, which limits the amount of quality time a child spends with his parents, and quality time is something some kids don't like to share. To boot, young puppies and young kids don't always hit it off. More often than not, the puppy views the child as another puppy to bite and bully. I've dealt with many situations where the kids don't like playing with the puppy anymore because "she bites too hard." At other times, a child becomes jealous of the attention the new addition is getting, which leads to an all-out war between the child and the puppy.

All this may sound depressing, but these are things you must think about. Though a good child–puppy relationship may develop, it takes time, patience, and understanding. Don't worry. This chapter can help.

The Classic Signs of Sibling Rivalry

Sibling Rivalry Syndrome happens when a child becomes jealous of the attention your new puppy is getting. In a sibling rivalry situation, the child takes his anger out on the dog, which increases rough puppy play and turns what was supposed to be a beautiful relationship into a hostile one.

Here are some classic scenarios typical of sibling rivalry:

- ✔ "My puppy, Tucker, is a four-month-old Labrador-Doberman Pincher mix. I got him for the kids, but I haven't had a moment's peace since the day we brought him home. Tucker bites the children and tugs at their clothes. The other day, when my son Alex went to take a toy, Tucker snapped at him."

- ✔ "Sasha is a great dog when the kids aren't around. But when the kids get home from school, she jumps at them, knocks them down, and tries to make away with their backpacks."

- ✔ "My puppy, Darby, is always stealing the kids' food from their hands. She also snatches their toys from them. The other day when my daughter lifted her doll above her head, Darby jumped up and scratched her in the eye."

- ✔ "My eight-month-old Pug has taken to mounting my son whenever he comes through the door. It's totally embarrassing."

So the cards are dealt. Suddenly you find yourself in a situation that's less than ideal, full of mayhem and chaos. You love the kids. You love the puppy. You want them to love each other. What can you do?

You can develop a game plan, nip the situation in the bud, and watch a beautiful, lasting relationship develop between the loves of your life.

Overcoming Sibling Rivalry

Kids love *positive* involvement. If they always hear "don't do that and stop doing this," interacting with the puppy is a real downer. To offset this predicament, I've developed a five-step plan to help clients overcome sibling rivalry between their kids and puppies.

Step 1: Get the kids involved

Kids like to help and be involved, but training exercises can bore them to death. Let's face it. Mud wrestling to a five-year-old is more exciting than a two-minute heel. Training exercises are just no fun, and the phrase "it's your responsibility to feed Rex" has a negative spin. The good news is that you *can* get the kids happily involved, but you must be very upbeat and creative. Staying positive is a plus. Here are some ideas:

✔ **Butter Magic:** This trick is fabulous. Rub a frozen stick of butter or peanut butter on the back of the kids' hands, have them extend their hands, and together instruct "Kisses." The trick not only teaches your puppy to kiss a hand that reaches toward him, but it also discourages nipping.

✔ **The Treat Cup Name Game:** Fill plastic party cups half-way with Cheerios. Encourage the kids to shake the cup and call the puppy (see Figure 10-1). Help them enforce the four paw rule (see the section "Step 3: Teach catch phrases," later in this chapter) by leaving a leash on your dog, enabling you to control any jumping. You can also use commands like Sit, Paw, and Down (see Chapter 14 for details on commands).

✔ **Fun Charts:** Make a responsibility chart (except think of a better name for it, like "the sticker chart"). Every time one of the kids completes a task (feeding, walking, or brushing your puppy), he can add a sticker to his column. Be clever. If you have more than one kid, you'll need plenty of column space.

✔ **Super Schedule:** Kids love to be creative. Ask them to help you write "the SUPER schedule for REX." Include times for everything: feeding, brushing, playing, and napping. Let the kids decorate around the edges and place the finished schedule somewhere where all your friends can see what cool kids you have.

Figure 10-1: Playing the Treat Cup Name Game.

Photo by Sarah Hodgson.

Step 2: Transfer the control

Let go of the idea that the kids can communicate leadership. Though some can, they don't have all the time in the world, and the responsibility to teach your dog will fall (like everything else) in your lap. Young kids can't "train" dogs until they grow tall enough to stare *you* eye-to-eye — when they're 12–14 years old. Before then, they're just too close to the puppy to be taken seriously. Kids also bend and bark too much. So it's up to you to teach the puppy to respect the children.

Teach your puppy some basic commands, like Sit, Wait, Excuse Me, and Let's Go (see Chapter 14 for details on teaching commands) and then walk through the commands with the children, issuing lead corrections if your puppy disobeys. Encourage the kids to say the commands clearly. Teach the puppy a negative sound for unacceptable behavior, such as nipping, and then use it regularly when you see your puppy wind up with the kids.

If your puppy is nippy and wild when the kids are around, place him on a drag lead. He can wear this light leash around the house, and it's great for giving indiscrete corrections. Avoid yelling at your puppy when energy escalates; he views your interaction as confrontational, not corrective.

Monkey see, monkey do. You are your children's best example. If you remain calm and structured with your puppy, your child copies you. If you're frantically confused or encourage rough play, your child copies that, too.

Step 3: Teach catch phrases

Kids don't respond well to nagging. "Don't do this, don't do that" has a tendency to go in one ear and out the other. Like dogs and puppies, kids respond better to a more positive approach. Catch phrases can be very helpful:

- **"Four paw rule":** This catch phrase helps the kids remember not to pet Rex until all four paws are planted on the floor, and it sounds a lot better than "Stop calling the dog on the couch." (At which point, I would defiantly do exactly what you said not to do, if I were the kid.)

- **"Look for rain":** When the kids come in from school, have them look for rain until Rex calms down — that is, tell them to cross their arms in front of their body and look to the sky (see Figure 10-2). Also have them look for rain when he jumps into their laps for attention.

If looking for rain sounds scary or your puppy is just too big for it to be effective, use a spray bottle filled with water or a water-vinegar mix to discourage your pup. Rather than aiming at his face, spray the mist in between your bodies.

Figure 10-2:
Kids should "look for rain" until the puppy calms down.

Photo by Sarah Hodgson.

✔ **"Peacock position":** This catch phrase helps the kids remember to stand straight when they give Rex commands — and it's a lot less wordy than "If you bend over, Rex thinks you want to play."

✔ **"Stand like a statue":** Ask your kids if they've ever seen a dog chasing a statue. Answer, no. Why? Because statues don't move. When the puppy gets out of hand, encourage the kids to stand like a statue.

Those catch phrases are just some of my all-time favorites. Think hard, add to the list, and keep me informed. I'm always on the lookout for clever ways to help kids and dogs get along together.

Step 4: Set up everyday situations

Set up situations your pup can expect to encounter — like the kids' running frenzies or building/doll sets — to teach your puppy how to handle himself. Use your Teaching Lead as described in Chapter 12. With the right training techniques, you can remedy many everyday occurrences between kids and puppies — things like mouthing and nipping, food grabbing, and chasing. Take a look at Chapter 13 for details on overcoming these and other daily hassles.

Step 5: Provide games for the kids

You've got to eliminate tug of war. You must take away the shared stuffed animals and socks. Absolutely no more wrestling, teasing, or chasing the puppy. Jeez, what's a kid supposed to do for fun?

Glad you asked. Check out Chapter 28. It's loaded with great games that keep the puppy's attention off the kids. Soda Bottle Soccer, Hide and Seek, Fishing for Fido, the Treat Cup Name Game — they're all great games that the kids can play with the puppy.

Knowing When to Ask for Help

The sad truth is, sometimes the game plan for conquering Sibling Rivalry Syndrome doesn't work. You go through all the steps, you try all the suggestions, and, well, nothing.

If your puppy is becoming less tolerant of your child, showing signs of aggression, or creating so much havoc that your normal daily tasks and parental responsibilities are stressed, call an animal trainer or behaviorist immediately. They really can help. Ask your veterinarian for a referral.

Uh, mom? Can you make him stop doing that to my leg?

Some puppies mount kids (and even adults) when they get too excited. Don't be too embarrassed. Mounting is more a sign of dominance than sexual preference. Knowing this makes it no less acceptable, however. Mounting dogs are bossy dogs who get over-stimulated in exciting situations. To rehabilitate yours, do the following:

1. Leave a 4-foot lead on your dog inside or out.

2. When the mounting starts, calmly grasp the short lead and snap down firmly.

Do not face off to a mounting dog. Also, don't make eye contact and don't push him away.

3. Once your dog is grounded, stand very tall, glare at your dog, and say "Shame on you!" in your most indignant tone.

4. Station your dog for 15 minutes with no attention.

Do not storm into the situation.

5. If your dog acts aggressively, terminate the corrections and seek help.

Chapter 11

Not on the Rug!

I wish I had a nickel for every time I hear "She knows it's wrong! Just look at her eyes — guilt's written all over her face." Interesting enough, although they know you're mad, puppies cannot connect a reaction now to a bathroom thought they had minutes before.

Dogs shouldn't soil the house, but some do, especially young pups. I know — a puddle or poop on the carpet is a wrenching sight, but think about it from the canine perspective. They're puppies, genetically predisposed to cave life, a free-ranging toilet, nature's toys, and an interactive community. They're not human home-proud. Sure, you want your puppy to be respectful of your carpets, but be patient. To be effective, you need to set aside your feelings of frustration and condition habits that jive with your puppy's instinctive tidiness.

So if toilet training has got you down, cheer up. Although teaching your puppy how to behave in your house is no small trick, it's very do-able — as long as you have the right mind-set. After-the-fact corrections don't help your long-term goal. You need a new approach, outlined start to finish. A program that you can apply whether your target is grass, papers, city cement, or gravel. Pull up a chair. Read this chapter start to finish; then read it again to everyone in the house. When the effort's concentrated, house-training your puppy is just a matter of time.

Getting into a Housebreaking Routine

Believe it or not, your puppy's elimination habits have a pattern. Puppies go after they sleep, after they play, after they eat, and after long bouts of confinement. As you prepare to house-train your puppy, be aware of these habits.

And be patient. You can train some in days; with others, training may take months. The best way to house-train your puppy is to establish a strategy and follow a consistent routine, like this:

✔ Don't greet or praise your puppy until after he has pottied.

✔ Use one specific word as you walk your pup to her toilet spot. I use "Outside!" You can say anything as long as it sounds punchy and everyone uses it consistently. I've heard "Papers!" "Elevator!" and "Potty time!"

   The outside toilet area you pick should be in a discrete place relatively close to the house.

✔ Blaze a trail and be consistent. Always follow the same path to the toilet spot.

✔ When you arrive, ignore your puppy.

   Do not let your dog roam until he's relieved himself.

✔ As your puppy is eliminating, use a second command like "Get busy!" After a month of saying this phrase while she's in the process of toileting, your puppy learns to go on cue. How cool is that?

✔ When your puppy's done, greet, praise, and walk her as usual.

Think of yourself as the social planner — the person who can walk into a crowd and manage to grab everyone's attention and direct them smoothly through just about any activity. When you train your dog, talk like a planner, walk like a planner, and remember that attitude is everything. If your voice directs, your puppy will follow.

If you have a small dog or young puppy, don't carry her to her toilet area. Let her walk so she can learn how to navigate on her own.

Getting on a Potty-Time Schedule

So just how many potty breaks does your puppy need per day? Well, that depends. Really young puppies — younger than 12 weeks — may need to go outside every hour or two. Older puppies can hold out quite a bit longer. Use the following general guidelines for your puppy:

Puppy's Age	*Number of Potty Breaks a Day*
6 to 14 weeks	8 to 10
14 to 20 weeks	6 to 8
20 to 30 weeks	4 to 6
30 weeks to adulthood	3 to 4

Based on the preceding guidelines, you need to set up a daily housebreaking schedule. If you're able to be home during the day, follow the schedule shown in Table 11-1. If you work outside the home during the day, follow the schedule shown in Table 11-2. *Note:* In both tables, italicized events may no longer be necessary as your puppy grows up.

Dogs of all ages need interaction between the times listed in the tables, so remember that playtimes are extremely important throughout the day.

If you work outside the home, try to come home for lunch or hire a dog walker to split up your dog's day. If given a good run midday, your dog should be able to tolerate confinement while you're out.

Table 11-1   Housebreaking Schedule for Work-At-Home Owners

Time of Day	Potty Time
Early morning wake up	Go outside
Breakfast	Go outside after breakfast
Midmorning	*Go outside*
Afternoon feeding	*Go outside after eating*
Midafternoon	Go outside
Dinnertime (4 to 6 P.M.)	Go outside after dinner
7:30	Remove water
Midevening	*Go outside*
Before bed	Go outside
Middle of the night	*Go outside if necessary*

Table 11-2   Housebreaking Schedule for Owners Who Work Outside the Home

Time of Day	Potty Time
Early morning wake up	Go outside
Breakfast	Go outside after breakfast
Lunch break feeding & walk	Go outside
Midafternoon	*Young Puppies must go out*
Arrival home	Go outside

Table 11-2 *(continued)*	
Time of Day	*Potty Time*
Dinnertime (4 to 6 P.M.)	Go outside after dinner
7:30	Remove water
Before bed	Go outside
Middle of the night	*Go outside if necessary*

If you work outside the home, take heed: If you expect your puppy to hold his bladder while you're gone during the day, you'll be disappointed. Puppies lack the bladder muscles necessary to accomplish such a feat. If you have to leave your puppy all day, create a space that allows for a good stretch as well as a place to potty. Although your puppy will be confused if you expect him to go outside when you're home, you have little choice.

Select a be-alone space — a small room, for example — or invest in a puppy playpen, which you can find at most pet stores (make sure the flooring is non-absorbent). Place your dog's bedding, bowls, and toys in one side of the space; cover the other side of the space with papers or wee-wee pads. (Cover more area than necessary, taping it down if your puppy insists on shredding it.) In most cases, a puppy will choose to eliminate in the absorbent area. That's great. Take your puppy outside when you get home and follow the scheduled routine outlined in Table 11-2. To discourage accidents inside, do not allow access to the be-alone space when you're home.

Changing the Routine

Once you have the routine down pat (give it about a week), interrupt it. Instead of chanting "Outside!" lead your puppy to the door. Wait until she gives you a signal to continue. If her signal is subtly staring at the door, call her back to you and pump her up: "What is it? *Outside?* Good dog!" Then let her out. Repeat the process in rooms farther and farther from the door or her papers.

Are you having trouble getting your dog to give you a signal? Is your dog just too polite to rock the boat? If you can't get your dog to articulate a signal, try hanging bells from the door. Hang them to the side of the door at your dog's nose level (see Figure 11-1). Each time you pass through the door, slap the bells with your "paw" and say "Outside." Soon your dog will join in the fun.

Photo by Sarah Hodgson.

Figure 11-1:
Hang bells
and encour-
age your
puppy to
signal you
when he
has to go
potty.

Using Papers versus Going Outside

You may decide that you're going to paper-train your puppy to a spot inside your home instead of teaching your puppy to go outside. That's fine, but you have to get in the mindset of using either one or the other. Doing both or paper training in one season only to switch your priorities to outside confuses your dog.

Paper-training is a good option if you have a small puppy, you live in an apartment, you're physically challenged, or you're just not the outdoor sort. It also has several similarities to outdoor training (see "Getting into a Housebreaking Routine," earlier in this chapter):

- ✔ Consistently use the same bathroom spot (inside or out).
- ✔ Use a word or phrase — like "Papers" or "Outside" — when you lead your puppy to the area.
- ✔ After you bring your dog to the area, ignore him until he eliminates.
- ✔ As your puppy's eliminating, use a word or phrase like "Get Busy."
- ✔ Do *not* use the place as a play or interaction area.

Paper-training does have some differences from outdoor training, however, namely that the papers are within the home. If you're paper-training, keep the papers away from your dog's food and water bowls and sleeping areas. Place the papers in a discrete location, like a corner of the kitchen or bathroom, and make sure they're easily accessible to your puppy, even when you're not home.

Tips for Housebreaking Success

Though house-training a puppy can be a real challenge, there are steps you can take to make it easier on both of you. Consistency is key. Dramatization of the routine helps make learning this lesson fun. This section covers a few of my quick tips.

Start with a small confinement area

Puppies are den animals, but the classic den wasn't more than about 90 square feet. Most young or untrained dogs won't soil the area right around them, but if they can race upstairs or into an adjacent room, they're more than happy to relieve themselves there.

So keep your puppy confined. Crate your puppy when you're out and at night, if she's not stationed. After she learns the rules, you can grant her more freedom, but not now. And before you give your puppy freedom in new areas, use the Teaching Lead methods described in Chapter 12 for each location.

Special confinement issues for pet store pups

Pet store pups often have a rough go of the *don't-soil-your-area* concept. After all, they had no choice in that early impressionable time away from Mom. If they were from a puppy mill, not only do those dogs have to go in their kennel space, but they're often stacked on top of other dogs who are forced to do the same thing. Mind boggling. If any Mom-dog had her way, she'd teach her pups to move far away from their sleeping area to go potty.

If your pet-store puppy is having a problem not soiling in his sleeping area, the crate may not be the best option for house-training beause it symbolizes a potty area. At night, a young puppy can sleep at your bedside in a large open-topped box. During the day, keep your puppy with you or confine him in a small room, taking him outside or to the papers every half hour. Take him to the same area, over and over, following the routine described in the house-training sections ("Getting into a Housebreaking Routine" and "Using Papers Versus Going Outside"). If you can get another dog to eliminate in this area all the better because the scent will give your puppy the right idea.

Know when corrections count

If you catch your puppy in the process of eliminating in the house, startle her: Clap your hands as you say "Ep, Ep, Ep!" Jump up and down like an excited chimp. Do whatever you have to to get her to stop. Then direct her to the elimination area as if nothing happened. When she's done, praise her for finishing.

Know when corrections don't count

You're getting mad at a puppy. As much as you'd like to think she's human, she isn't, and your frustration just makes you look foolish. Even though I've heard the idea a thousand times, I'm still not convinced that a "puppy understands the meaning of a correction." Sure, you can frighten a puppy into a fearful posture, but scaring her isn't the point you're trying to make.

If you catch her soiling someplace other than her designated area, you can interrupt the process but lay off all other corrections.

Maintain a stable diet

Avoid changing dog food brands unless your veterinarian directs you to do so. Puppies don't digest the way humans do. Their stomachs can get upset if you change their diet. Also lay off treats for a while until they're housebroken (see Chapter 20 for nutritional hints).

Watch the water intake

Puppies, especially young ones, drink water excessively if they're bored or nervous. If your dog is having peeing problems, monitor his water intake by giving him access to his water bowl during meal times and as you take him to his area.

Be careful not to dehydrate your pup. If she looks thirsty, let her lap. Remove water after 7:30 P.M. If she needs a drink, give her ice cubes, which absorb faster into the bloodstream.

City Pups versus Country Pups

House-training a puppy is challenging regardless of the environment, but there are some key differences between living in a metropolis versus the countryside.

Here are the similarities:

- ✔ Dogs must learn to go in one area.
- ✔ Until the process is understood, you must use the outside for elimination only.
- ✔ No matter the location, you must coach your dog until he's got the process down pat. Words help direct behavior.

And here are the differences:

- ✔ City dogs must be *curbed* (taught to eliminate at the curb). Curbing is tough for leg-lifting males who prefer to mark upright objects. Unfortunately, they don't have a choice. When you train your dog, use the curb close to your home.
- ✔ City dogs have to navigate hallways and escalators before reaching their target. Holding a young puppy until you're outside often helps.
- ✔ Many country or suburban dogs have a large property to choose from, which can be both a blessing and a curse. The blessings are obvious; however, as you house-train your dog, you must stay with him. Just plopping a puppy outside by himself often creates more anxiety than cooperation. You puppy will perform best when you're there to influence his actions.

Regardless of where you live, picking up after your dogs is a good idea. Stools attract bugs and worms. In the city and many suburbs, cleaning up after your dog is the law. Retail scoopers are available at pet stores, or you can do what I do:

1. **Place your hand in a plastic bag.**

2. **Clasp the mess with your bagged hand.**

3. **Turn the bag inside out.**

Bags are easy to carry on walks as well.

Part IV
Oh, Behave!

The 5th Wave — By Rich Tennant

"WE'VE HAD SOME BEHAVIOR PROBLEMS SINCE GETTING 'SNOWBALL', BUT WITH PATIENCE, REPETITION AND GENTLE DISCIPLINE, I'VE BEEN ABLE TO BREAK ROGER OF MOST OF THEM."

In this part . . .

Are you beginning to think that your puppy is as much work as a child? You're right. Both need training and structure. Both need help containing naughty impulses. Both must be socialized properly. And, well, you may need some help to make it all come together.

In this part, you get the scoop on basic training lessons — from teaching your puppy some control and manners to teaching your puppy basic commands. You also get hints on problem solving and guidance in finding additional help if you need it.

Yorkshire Terriers, though tiny in size, retain the hunting instincts true to their "terrier" nature. This puppy is happy to explore the wood pile for possible intruders. *Photo by Jeannie Harrison.*

Puppies, like this mixed breed, explore with their mouths, and you can expect that everything within their reach will be fair game for chewing. Rather than scold your pup for doing the wrong thing, encourage him to do the right thing by providing safe and acceptable chew toys.
Photo by Mary Bloom.

These West Highland White Terrier puppies are ready for action. Playful puppies grow into well-adjusted dogs when they're kindly and safely exposed to different people and environments.
Photo by Jeannie Harrison.

A lot of exploring leads to a lot of napping. This Beagle puppy has found a nest between two boots.
Photo by Jeannie Harrison.

Remember when you bring home your puppy that, like these Bulldogs, he is used to sleeping with his mother and littermates. He'll be lonely at first, but soon he'll learn that you are his source of companionship. *Photo by Mary Bloom.*

You may want to get two puppies so they can grow up together as pals, like these Pembroke Welsh Corgis. But if you do, be sure to spend individual time with each so that they bond with you as well as each other. *Photo by Mary Bloom.*

Housetraining is one of the first things you'll want to help your puppy with. The golden rule? Set your puppy up to succeed: Encourage *her* to look at *you* for direction. This cutey is a Cavalier King Charles Spaniel.
Photo by Mary Bloom.

The Miniature Schnauzer puppy is enjoying his time in the great outdoors. *Photo by Jeannie Harrison.*

Consult with your vet about proper nutrition for large breeds, like this Great Dane. *Photo by Mary Bloom.*

Raising a puppy, like this Jack Russell Terrier, is a big responsibility for kids. Time, patience, and understanding are key. *Photo by Mary Bloom.*

Labrador Retrievers are America's #1 breed, and it's no wonder: They're good-natured, athletic, easy to care for, and great family dogs. *Photo by Mary Bloom.*

When you own a pointing breed, like this German Shorthaired Pointer, expect to spend a lot of time outdoors burning off his desire to run, run, run. To encourage some peaceful rest time for him (*and* you), buy some chew toys. *Photo by Mary Bloom.*

These Pug puppies won't have to look long for loving homes. Pugs are becoming increasingly popular – who can resist their faces? *Photo by Mary Bloom.*

Play classical music to soothe your puppy. It works wonders when she's left at home alone, as well as when she's taking a ride in the car. This heavenly duo is a pair of Cocker Spaniels. *Photo by Winter/Churchill.*

Regular grooming makes your puppy look *and* feel good. And dressing her up in a costume is a great way for the two of you to play. Just make sure that clothes, hats, and such are safe and comfortable for your puppy – and supervise your pet while playing this way. This mixed-breed puppy is a charmer in her flowery bonnet. *Photo by Mary Bloom.*

Puppies are all individuals and should be treated as such. They have their own thoughts, feelings, and behaviors, and it's up to us, their owners, to provide the best possible compassionate care for them. This Boxer likes what he sees in the mirror! *Photo by Winter/Churchill.*

Have bedding ready and in position before bringing a puppy home. These ready-for-bed sweeties are Chihuahua puppies. *Photo by Mary Bloom.*

Their curiosity and *joie de vivre* can get puppies into trouble – even when you think you've successfully puppy-proofed your home with things like baby gates. There's no holding back this boisterous Golden Retriever! *Photo by Winter/Churchill.*

This French Bulldog is almost too cute. But before falling for a breed that may not fit your lifestyle, be sure you know what the dog will look and act like as an adult. *Photo by Mary Bloom.*

The word *bassett* in French means low to the ground, and these short-legged, long-eared dogs are indeed that. The reason for these features is so Basset Hounds can more closely follow the scent trail of the rabbit. Their ears help pick up and retain scent, their noses process the information, and their legs keep them moving on the trail.
Photo by Mary Bloom.

The watchful eye of an Australian Cattle Dog is intense even in puppyhood. This breed takes its work very seriously, and owners will soon find their super-motivated ACDs herding the people and objects in their life with zeal. *Photo by Winter/Churchill.*

A well-behaved puppy is a welcomed social guest anywhere, like at a picnic or parade. These bundle-of-fluff Maltese puppies are fun-loving beauties.
Photo by Jeannie Harrison.

Chapter 12

Teaching Your Pup Some Control and Manners

*W*hen you begin training, the first thing you must accept is that your puppy really doesn't know too much. The complexity of the human household — the furnishings, the walls, the counters, the garbage pail — doesn't mean a lot to him either. Although he's willing to learn, until you structure his environment, he probably won't respect your rules. Don't worry, though. He'll understand soon enough.

Teaching involves communication. You must convey your expectations in a way that gets through to your puppy. Remember, dogs aren't human. Lengthy explanations don't impress them. You have to be a little more inventive. This chapter can help you out. In it, I share a little invention of mine called the Teaching Lead Method.

What the Teaching Lead Is

I invented the Teaching Lead Method when training one of my own dogs, Kyia. Coming from the shelter, Kyia was nervous, peed frequently in the house, and chewed things. Because the crate terrified her, I tied her to me and clipped her to things around the house. Soon she caught on, and the Teaching Lead Method was born. Since then, I've shared my theory with many of my two- and four-legged clients.

Years later, I read about similar ideas in books by the monks of New Skete, Job Evans, and Carol Lea Benjamin. I was encouraged to know others used this technique and set out to design a leash that would make the methods available to everyone.

Although you can find the Teaching Lead in stores, you can make your own from a sturdy leash and extra clip. Just buy a sturdy leather lead and tie it around your waist. (Leather leashes provide better leverage as you train your dog.) Although a homemade lead is more cumbersome, it is equally effective.

If you have a chewer, protect your leash with Bitter Apple (available from pet stores) or Tabasco sauce.

What the Teaching Lead Method Can Do

The Teaching Lead Method is designed to communicate control and condition appropriate household manners without using discipline or force. Following are a few other things that using the Teaching Lead Method can do:

- Take the place of the crate when you're home
- Help you house-train your puppy
- Eliminate excessive jumping and counter sniffing
- Encourage appropriate chewing habits
- Discourage nipping
- Calm your puppy around company

And this list is just the tip of the iceberg. Using the Teaching Lead Method has many hidden benefits. For example, another added perk is the freedom it gives to parents of very young children. With the Teaching Lead Method, you can keep your dog with you and hang onto your sanity.

You can use the Teaching Lead in three different ways: to lead, to station, and to anchor — all of which you use interchangeably to train your dog and communicate leadership in a friendly fashion.

- *Leading* communicates leadership calmly.
- *Anchoring* teaches your puppy that when you're calm, he must be, too.
- *Stationing* provides a special place in each room for your dog and gives you a place to direct him to during meals or when things are hectic.

Although the Teaching Lead is no magic wand, it's pretty handy. But most important, it's humane. When you use the Teaching Lead, you can see your relationship with your puppy go from confusion and chaos to peace and harmony, which is, I feel, as it should be.

Please visit my online site (`www.dogperfect.com`) for monthly tips on the Teaching Lead Method.

Use it for leading

Letting your puppy run free in your house before he's trained can be a big mistake. He runs wild, you chase him, and he remembers the whole thing as one big game. He will even learn to think dogs lead and people follow. Instead, leading gives *you* the upper hand. Your puppy learns to follow your lead, and you can quickly discourage all inappropriate behavior and reinforce the good stuff.

The Teaching Lead Method is the most humane training technique out there, and mastering it is not as hard as you may think. *Leading* involves securing your puppy to your side and leading her around the house using specific commands. (Once she understands the commands *inside,* you can extend your control outside.) Eventually, your puppy will respond to you off-lead. Until then, however, she needs some direction.

Here's how to lead with the Teaching Lead Method:

1. **Make sure you are using the right training collar.**

   If you don't know what collar is the right one, consider your options by asking your veterinarian, checking out Chapter 5, or visiting me online (`www.dogperfect.com`). Until your puppy is 16 weeks, use a regular buckle collar/harness.

2. **Slide the leash around your waist like a belt and connect the end clip to the appropriate waist hole.**

   Put the clip to your left side if you want your puppy on the left; put it on your right side if you want him on the right. You're ready to begin.

   Everyone who walks your puppy must keep him on the same side (do not have one person walk him on the left and another on the right).

3. **To teach your puppy proper leash manners and prevent pulling, take him to a hallway. Walk straight ahead but be mindful of his whereabouts.**

4. **The second he walks ahead of you, call out his name as you pivot and dart in the opposite direction.**

   Praise him, even though you may feel a tug.

5. **Continue to turn away from him until he pays attention to his name and stops trying to race ahead.**

   Gauge your darting style for the dog's size. Do you have a monster? Dart big. A little guy? A strong step will do.

   Now you're walking in style. Where you lead your puppy must follow. This is your big chance. All household decisions are up to you. It may seem awkward at first, but soon you won't even know he's there. You might even call it fun. Remember, you're teaching your puppy to follow *you*, so if there's a conflict of interest (he wants to go left when you're going right), go *your* way and encourage him to follow.

   Some dogs love to walk their owners. It's enormously fun and reminds them of all those tug-of-war games you play together. The first step in correcting this problem is eliminating those tug-of-war games. When your dog takes the leash in his mouth, snap it back *into* the roof of his mouth (not out of his mouth) sharply and give a firm "No!"

6. **As you lead your puppy around, start using commands conversationally. Encourage everyone around your puppy to use them, too.**

   Speak clearly, give your commands once, and enunciate your syllables; puppies understand sounds, not words.

Using basic commands

Here are six foundation commands to get you started:

✔ **"*Name*, let's go!"** Give this command whenever you start walking or change direction. As you turn, hold your head high and don't look at your puppy until he turns with you.

   If your dog or puppy isn't leash trained, put some biscuits in a cup, place your dog on lead, and shake the cup as you walk around, encouraging him to follow by saying "Let's go!" Then pick up the lead and walk around with the cup. Stop every ten feet or so and give the dog a treat.

✔ **"Sit."** Use this command whenever you offer your dog something positive like food, praise, a toy, or a pat. Say the command once, helping him into position if he doesn't respond. The most important rule is to say "Sit" once only. Puppies understand sounds; "Sit-Sit-Sit" sounds much different from "Sit."

   Is your puppy just learning to sit? To position your dog properly, avoid pushing on his spine. With your right hand, gently lift the chin or pull upward on the collar, as you squeeze his waist gently with your left thumb and forefinger (see Figure 12-1). This pressure point tucks him neatly into place without pressuring the skeletal system.

Figure 12-1:
Teach a puppy to sit by squeezing his waist gently with your thumb and forefinger.

Photo by Sarah Hodgson.

✔ **"Name."** A few times each day, stand in front of your puppy (proud and tall as a peacock!) and call out his name. If he doesn't look up immediately, direct his eyes toward you with a finger and a fun clucking sound.

✔ **"Wait" and "OK."** This duo is a real prize. Imagine getting your puppy to stop before he races downstairs or across thresholds. Each time you cross a threshold or heavily trafficked area, command "Wait" and bring your dog behind you with his lead. He may get excited, but wait until he settles down before you command "OK." Make sure *your* feet cross the threshold first (see Figure 12-2). Leaders must lead.

✔ **"Excuse me."** Use this command whenever your puppy crosses in front of or behind you. Also use it if your dog presses against you or blocks your path. As you say "Excuse me," gently knock your puppy out of your way with your foot or knee (hands are perceived as interactive). Remember, puppies respond to hierarchies, so you need to establish yourself as the leader.

✔ **"Settle."** Teaching your dog to lie quietly in a new environment is no easy task. Read the next sections on anchoring and stationing, and soon your dog will quiet down on command.

Figure 12-2:
Teach the
Wait and OK
commands
so that you
cross
thresholds
first.

Photo by Mary Bloom.

If you feel like taking a break, you can do two things: have interactive play time in an outdoor enclosure or using a Flexi-Lead, or station your puppy as described later in this chapter (make sure his bladder is empty). Some days you will station much more than lead — that's okay. Use both methods interchangeably, but keep that puppy with you when you're home.

Everyone who can lead the puppy around should. You don't want your hierarchy to become a dictatorship. The only unacceptable combination is small children and big puppies. Other than that, everyone should take part. If the lead is too long for a child, he/she can use a short leash or wear it like a banner across the chest.

Dealing with resistance

Some dogs like to imitate *mules.* It's a passive form of resistance. Your dog is hoping that you will rush back and give him lots of attention, but don't. Following are two approaches you can use to discourage this habit. Which approach you use depends on the puppy and the situation:

✔ **Keep trucking.** Don't turn around. Praise the air in front of you and walk a little faster. When your puppy catches up, praise him happily and continue. This method works well with large breeds that have a reputation of being stubborn.

> ✔ **Kneel forward.** If you have a more delicate breed or a puppy with a timid temperament, kneel down in front of your puppy (facing forward) when he puts on the brakes. Tap the floor and encourage him to come to you. When he does, praise him warmly; then go to the end of the leash again and repeat yourself. He'll catch on soon. Remember, no attention for stubborn stopping and absolutely no pickups.

Use it for anchoring

As you lead your puppy around, you may need to sit down to talk on the phone, work on the computer, or entertain guests. If you let your puppy free, he might create havoc in his constant vigil to get your attention. Jumping on the counter or chewing the drapes are real eye catchers. To discourage these habits, I advise using a more civilized routine called anchoring:

1. **With your puppy secured to your side, slide the end clip around to your tailbone and sit on the remaining slack of the leash.**

2. **Leave enough room for your dog to lie comfortably behind your feet and offer him a favorite chew toy.**

3. **Instruct "Settle down"; pet and praise your puppy when he does so.**

Use it for stationing

Your dog wants to be with you or another family member whenever you're around. *Stationing* gives you the freedom to take your puppy into each room of the house and show him how to behave there.

To station your puppy, you first need to select your areas. Go into each room you'd like your dog to behave in and pick a good area for him to settle in — perhaps a place near the couch in the TV room but away from the table in the dining room. Decorate the area with a comfy cushion or blanket and a favorite chew toy. Doing so helps your puppy identify his special space, his *station.* Puppies like to have a special place. Think of it on human terms: When you go into your living room, don't you have a favorite couch or chair?

The point of stationing is to teach your puppy how to behave in social situations, so make sure you station him in a room with people. And make sure the station is away from stairs, electrical cords and outlets, or entanglements.

✔ Select bedding that is easy to wash and transport. When you're riding in the car, going to the veterinarian or visiting, bring the bedding along. A bonafide canine security blanket.

✔ As for chew toys, ask your veterinarian for suggestions. Avoid rawhide bones with big knots — they can cause indigestion and other problems. Remove end fragments of hoofs or rawhide to discourage gulping.

Eventually, your puppy will go to his station automatically. Initially, though, you must secure your dog at his station until he learns his place. When stationing, attach your puppy to his buckle or tag collar, never a training collar. If using the Teaching Lead, hook the lead around an immovable object by attaching the top clip to the opposite end of the leash (see Figure 12-3).

Figure 12-3:
Hook the
Teaching
Lead around
an immov-
able object
to secure a
puppy to his
station.

Photo by Mary Bloom.

Be sure the object is immovable, sturdy, and unable to tip. If you have nothing to secure the lead to, screw an eye hook into the wall and clip the leash through it. When stationed, your puppy should have no more than three feet of freedom. Given too much room, he may piddle or pace.

Does your puppy insist on chewing the leash? Using Bitter Apple can stop this activity. (Bitter Apple also discourages test-chewing of the surrounding furniture or rugs, too.) You can find the product at your local pet store. It's vile tasting but harmless. If Bitter Apple isn't effective, try a home-cooked mixture: some red pepper juice with a little garlic or Tabasco sauce. If all else fails, get a chain lead and temporarily station him on that.

As you lead your dog to his station, give him the command "Settle down" and point to his spot.

When first practicing the stationing procedure, stay with your dog. Make him feel comfortable in the area and encourage him to chew his bone. Leave him only when he's busy with a chew toy or resting.

Some dogs panic when initially stationed. If you're concerned, determine whether your dog's reaction is really a panic attack or simply a persuasive protest. Panicked dogs don't focus on you. Dogs that protest are very focused on you and usually bark. Ignore the protest. If he is truly panicked, initially station him only when you can sit with him. Encourage bone chewing and begin to leave his side only when he's sleeping. Pretty soon, he'll get the hang of it.

If you must leave your puppy, give the command "Wait." Short departures are good because they get your puppy used to being left alone and show him that you won't desert him. Go calmly. If he's excited when you return, ignore him because you don't want to reinforce that behavior. When he's calm, give him attention.

Bravely ignore whining or barking, unless your puppy's communicating a need. If he barks and you soothe him, you're teaching a lesson with headache written all over it. You can try distracting your puppy by using a fancy long-distance squirt gun. (I found the Super Soaker to be very effective — long range and accurate, too.) But you must be very discrete; he can't know where the water is coming from. Only release a dog from a station when he's calm and quiet.

Your puppy must be at least 12 weeks old before you begin stationing him. Young puppies (under 12 weeks) can't handle being stationed too long. How long you can station your puppy depends on his age and mental state. A sleepyhead of any age can handle an hour or more. An older pup can handle more extended periods. The best gauge is your puppy; keep him stationed near you and be aware of his signals. If your pup has been napping at his station for an hour and suddenly gets up and starts acting restless, he probably needs to go to his bathroom spot. If your puppy chews on a bone for 15 minutes and then starts acting like a jumping bean, it's probably an energy spurt, and he needs time for a little play.

Use it for other stuff, too

The Teaching Lead Method also helps you with many problem situations, like the following:

✔ **Housebreaking.** The leash follows the same logic as the crate; puppies don't like to mess in a confined area. By keeping your puppy connected or stationed, you're aware of his needs and know when he needs to go out. You'll quickly learn his "I've gotta go bad!" signal. See Chapter 11 for more on housebreaking your puppy.

✔ **Jumping.** Using the Teaching Lead Method, you can handle your puppy's behavior without touching him. If he jumps up, grasp the leash and snap him down saying "Off!" in a very firm tone. Don't look at him or touch him until he calms down. When he does, command "Sit" and give him attention. To find out more about curbing a jumper, head to Chapter 13.

✔ **Discouraging nipping.** Any time your dog is mouthing you or anyone else, remove his head from your hand and say "No." Do this by pulling his collar/lead back sharply or by spritzing in front of his nose with Binaca Mouth Spray (found at your local pharmacy). If you pull your hand away or push your puppy, you could inadvertently encourage rougher play. Chapter 13 has more tips on handling nipping and mouthing.

When using Binaca Mouth Spray to discourage your puppy, do not stare at your dog simultaneously; otherwise, you just encourage confrontation. Avoid spraying your dog in the face (eyes don't tolerate the mouth spray well); just mist it in front of his nose.

✔ **Crunching habits.** Find a bone or similar chew toy that your puppy likes. Buy the same one for every station, plus a few extras to keep handy when you're sitting on the leash. Too many different toys confuse him.

Each time you give your puppy his bone, say "Where's your bone?"

✔ **Outside control.** Connect your puppy to your side. Every time he gets distracted, call out his name and scurry in the opposite direction. Praise him immediately, whether he turned with you or was tugged by the leash. Repeat this move until he is attentive to you when you call out his name.

Chapter 13

Daily Hassles

In This Chapter

▶ Handling a chewer

▶ Nipping and mouthing — nip them in the bud

▶ Dealing with a jumper

▶ Breaking the barking habit

*W*hat you consider bad behavior can be extremely frustrating. After all, no one likes having chewed carpets, scratched doors, or company that hides from a jumping puppy when you open the door. The first step in resolving actions you don't approve of is to understand that you and your puppy are not sharing the same worldview. When your puppy jumps on company, he's enjoying every minute of the chaos that follows. A chewed carpet is usually a sign of boredom, anxiety, or teething. To resolve the behaviors that you don't like, you have to look at them from your puppy's perspective and then modify *your* behavior to change his reactions.

The process isn't too difficult, but you need a few guidelines to get on the right track. In this chapter, I cover chewing, the infamous grab-'n'-go, jumping, barking, and nipping. (The more serious infractions are covered in Chapter 15.) By following my advice in this chapter, you'll soon have the reward of seeing a change in your puppy's reaction and behavior.

Stopping the Chewing Frenzy

Chewing is a puppy thing. It's nothing personal. They don't know a stick from a table leg or a doll's head from a chestnut. Fortunately, they can be rehabilitated. If you have a chewer on your hands, be patient and use some of the tried-and-true techniques described next.

Just like kids, pups are curious about the world around them, and they love to explore. Kids use their hands; puppies use their mouths. Additionally, pups between 3½–8 months are teething. During this time, your puppy may chew on the furniture or your favorite shoes to alleviate discomfort. To ward off possible destruction, supply and encourage the use of appropriate chew toys.

Get Bitter Apple — and lots of it

Bitter Apple is nasty-tasting stuff that you can buy at most pet stores. You spray it on things you want to prevent your dog from chewing. If you notice your puppy chewing on the furniture surrounding her station, spray everything but her bed and bone.

Believe it or not, some dogs like Bitter Apple. If your pup is one of these, try some red pepper juice with a little garlic or Tabasco sauce.

Offer one main toy plus a surplus of surprises

Having too many objects to choose from can confuse your dog. Pick a bone or toy that satisfies your puppy's penchant for chewing, buy multiples of that item, and spread them around the house for quick access. Here are some other suggestions:

✔ Keep your supply of play toys in a special place (designating a box or drawer), bringing them out for special interaction times.

✔ Designate one toy that's only offered during greetings. I use a hollow bone stuffed with peanut butter.

Be aware of Prize Envy

If you yell at your dog *after* she's begun to grab an object she shouldn't or after she's finished chewing, you only damage your relationship with her. Yelling afterwards communicates *Prize Envy* — what's being grabbed is valuable because of the challenge to get it back. If you give the correction too late, your dog thinks, "Wow, what a great prize. Everybody wants to take it from me!" Instead of disciplining after the fact, set up situations so that you can correct your puppy's thought process. Also learn to use treat cups after the dog has already gotten ahold of something you don't want her to have.

Correct the thought process

Correcting a puppy after the fact is ineffective and damaging to your relationship. On the flip side, correcting the thought process — and then shaming the object of interest — puts the negative focus outside your relationship.

Set up a situation with something your dog's obsessed with — tissues, shoes, a Barbie doll, whatever strikes her fancy.

1. **While your puppy's resting in another room, set the object in the middle of the floor.**

2. **Bring your dog to the object on her Teaching Lead.**

   See Chapter 12 on how to use the Teaching Lead.

3. **The second your dog notices the object, say "No, Ma'am" and snap back on the leash.**

4. **Pick up the object and shout at it — without looking at your dog (see Figure 13-1).**

   You read right. Get angry at the object, not your dog. You're doing the dog version of telling a child the stove is hot.

5. **Walk by the object again.**

   Your dog should avoid it like the plague (see Figure 13-2).

Use this technique to catch your dog in the thought process; if your dog already has an object in her mouth, you're too late.

Figure 13-1: "Bad sock!" Shout at the object, not your puppy.

Photo by Mary Bloom.

Figure 13-2:
"What sock?" Your puppy then avoids the object.

You're correcting the object, not your dog. Don't even look at your dog as you mouth off to the naughty thing. Your neighbors may commit you, but your dog will love you for it.

Do not practice this exercise off lead. Your dog will think the object's a mouse and join in the kill.

Use treat cups

Making a *treat cup* is easy. Break up your dog's favorite treats or cereal and put the tidbits in a cup. Shake the cup and offer your dog a treat. Continue this until your dog associates the sound of the cup with getting a treat. Now spread treat cups all over your home and be consistent. Use the same kind of cups. Party cups or deli containers work best.

First you need to communicate to your puppy that your approach with the treat cup is a good thing. So anytime your puppy is chewing on an *acceptable* object, go over with the treat cup, say "Give," offer her a treat, and leave. When your puppy's eating a meal, shake the cup, say "Give," offer her a treat, and leave.

After she understands that your approach is not threatening, the next time your dog grabs something you don't want her to have, find a treat cup and say "Out," as you offer a treat. Praise her when she releases the object and help her find a chew toy. "Where's your bone?"

I can hear some of you already: "Isn't treating encouraging the behavior?" Although this technique doesn't discourage your puppy's mischief, it does encourage him to share his treasures, which can save you a lot in replacement fees. A delivery system is better than a destruction dog.

Consider all objects your puppy grabs, good or bad, as treasures, and she'll be much more cooperative.

Kiss it goodbye

If your puppy has destroyed something, let it go. Yelling or hitting your puppy only makes him nervous and frightened, which leads to more chewing. Any puppy owner can commiserate, and I know first hand how angry you feel, but don't take your anger out on your pup. He doesn't know any better. Remember, your puppy's mouth is equivalent to your hands; if your dog is nervous or fidgety, he chews. I'm sure if your dog could surf the Net, scan the soaps, or pull his hair out, he would, but since he can't, chewing has to do.

Dogs do things that are natural to them: eat food, pick up objects (with their teeth, of course), investigate trash bins. Instead of losing your cool, which only frightens your dog, try the options mentioned in this book. Both you and your dog will be glad you did.

Controlling Nipping and Mouthing

Mouthing and nipping are two different issues. *Mouthing* is a lesser infraction; it's more of a communication skill to get you to do a particular thing. Less pressure, less annoying, but still not particularly charming. *Nipping* is a puppy thing; it's interactive and playful. If you have an older puppy who still nips, read Chapter 15's section on aggression. Nipping puppies are bossy and manipulative and need a firmer regimen.

Mouthing is often an attention-getting behavior. If your dog uses it to communicate a need to go out, respond. If, on the other hand, your dog mouths you for a pat, ignore it. Pretend she isn't there. If she becomes too annoying, get Binaca Mouth Spray and spritz her discreetly in front of her nose, hiding the Binaca in your hand and spritzing as you avoid all eye contact, comments, or pushing. When you use the Binaca spritz this way, you're performing a *cause-and-effect correction* rather than interactive discipline. Interaction involves eye contact and physical manipulation — not good. Cause-and-effect corrections result in unpleasant reactions that your puppy will try to avoid.

Dogs interpret discipline as confrontational play. Excessive physical corrections result in aggression, so be wise: Stay cool.

Nipping is different from mouthing (nipping with sharp little needle teeth can hurt!), and it's another one of those puppy things that you need to refocus. Consider this: When your puppy still hung out with her littermates, she nipped during play and to determine her rank. She also soft-mouthed her mother affectionately. When you bring your puppy home, this behavior continues.

What your puppy wants to know is who's a puppy and who's not. The answer determines the type of mouthing or nipping: soft or playful. Usually, everyone gets categorized as a puppy. Why? Well, for starters, most people pull their hands away when nipped. To a human, drawing back is self-defense; to a pup, however, it's an invitation to play. Even if you were to correct your young puppy, she wouldn't understand (it's like correcting a one-year-old baby for pulling your hair). So what should you do? Good question. Your approach depends on your puppy's age.

Pups younger than 16 weeks

Young puppies mouth a lot. They mouth when playing; they also mouth to communicate their needs. If your puppy starts mouthing, ask yourself these questions: Is she hungry or thirsty? Does she need to eliminate? Is she sleepy? Does she need to play? Remember, puppies nip when they feel needy (just like a baby cries). If your puppy won't let up, ask yourself if she wants something, like an outing, exercise, or a drink.

The following things can help you control mouthing and nipping:

- ✔ If your puppy *doesn't* need anything and she still won't quit, crate or isolate her with a favorite bone. Do not scold your puppy as you isolate her. Calmly place the puppy in her area.

- ✔ Whenever your puppy licks you, say "Kisses" and praise her warmly. Encourage licking by slathering your hands with a frozen stick of butter. Yummm.

- ✔ Withhold your attention when your puppy nips softly. Keep your hand still; withdrawing your hand is an invitation to play and nip harder.

- ✔ If your puppy starts biting down hard, turn quickly, say "Ep, Ep!" and glare into her eyes for two seconds; then go back to your normal routine. If she persists, try spritzing yourself with Bitter Apple or affix a leash onto your puppy so that you can tug the lead sharply to the side. If necessary, place her in a quiet area to cool off.

Pups over 16 weeks

If you have a Peter Pan pup, one who still nips when she's older than 16 weeks, you need to start curbing it now. Although nipping will continue (for a few weeks yet), you need to make clear that it's unacceptable. Following are a few tips to help you:

✔ Stop all challenge games. These games include wrestling, tug-of-war, chasing your dog around, and teasing. When you engage in these types of activities, you're sending the wrong message. These games teach dogs to clamp down hard on *any* object — a leash, the laundry, your shirt, or even your skin — and challenge. For game alternatives, see Chapter 28.

✔ Discourage all nipping, whether it's a bite on your arm or a nibble on your finger. Teeth do not belong on human skin, period.

✔ Put the Teaching Lead applications in Chapter 12 into action. It's time for you to start structuring your interaction.

✔ Purchase a few weapons to use in defense, such as Binaca Mouth Spray, Bitter Apple spray, or a long-distance squirt gun.

Never stare at your pup while you spritz or spray her; doing so turns an unpleasant result into a confrontational interaction.

✔ Leave a leash on your puppy so you have something to direct her with and can avoid physical confrontation. If your dog's not wearing the Teaching Lead, place a short lead onto her buckle collar.

✔ If your puppy begins to mouth, turn to her, use a lead or collar to snap her head from your body, or spritz the region she's nipping with a spray. Do not glare at her; otherwise, she'll perceive your actions as confrontational play.

✔ If she continues to nip, ask yourself these questions: Do I look convincing? Am I snapping or pulling? (Pulling encourages play.) Is my dog taking me seriously? You may need more training before you earn her respect.

Pups with the kids

Kids act a lot like puppies. They're always on the floor and into everything. If you have children, teach your puppy not to mouth them from the start. Here's how.

✔ Leave your puppy on a four-foot long nylon leash whenever she's with your children. If she starts playing too rough, pick up the leash, snap back, and say "Ep, Ep."

✔ If you're still having trouble, buy a long-distance squirt gun or plant mister and fill it with water and vinegar, and spray your dog discreetly when she starts getting riled up.

✔ If all else fails, give the puppy a time-out attached to you, stationed, or crated. Help the kids see that their restlessness leads to your withdrawing the puppy.

If things get out of hand, avoid yelling at the kids. Yelling sounds like barking to your dog and ups the fun ante. Calmly station, crate, or isolate your puppy until she mellows.

When grabbing and chasing are involved

Puppies, being puppies, are bound to chase and grab at things. If the thing is a ball or squeak toy, there's no problem. But if it's the children or your clothing, well, that's a problem. Your next goal is to teach the puppy what's acceptable to grab and pull at and what's off limits.

The bathrobe assault

If your puppy's a clothing grabber, dilute some Bitter Apple spray in a plant mister and carry it with you when you suspect the assault. Do not turn and face your dog when she jumps (she will interpret your actions as confrontational). Without looking or responding, spray your dog discreetly and continue walking.

If this problem persists, get help now. It can develop into post-puberty aggression. No joke.

The child chaser

Kids running around the yard, apartment, or house are a big temptation. If you were a puppy, you'd be jumping and nipping, too. Because you can't teach kids to stop being kids, you need to help your puppy control her impulses.

1. **Put your pup on the Teaching Lead and ask the kids to race around in front of you.**

2. **Anytime your puppy looks tempted to lunge, snap back and say "Shhh."**

3. **Repeat as often as necessary to gain control.**

Once you've tamed your dog inside, repeat the routine outside: first on the Teaching Lead and then on a long line.

Grounding the Joyous Jumper

Everybody knows a jumper — a knock-you-over-when-you-come-in jumper, a muddy-paws-on-the-couch jumper, and a counter cruiser (the puppy who likes to sniff along counter tops). Jumping is a sure-fire attention getter. So what gives? The first step in solving your problem is to understand how it became a problem in the first place. Once again, your puppy's not to blame.

Puppies see us as other dogs, and eye contact is a big method of canine communication. Our eyes are above theirs, so to be gracious and greet us properly, puppies must jump. The first time this happens, a hug follows. "Isn't that cute?" After about the tenth jump, it's not so cute. So the puppy usually gets a shove. But what's a shove to a dog? Confrontational play. The puppy jumps higher and harder the next time. So you try a little toe stepping, paw grabbing, and yelling — all with the same effect. Your dog thinks jumping is very interactive and very fun.

Counter jumping is another favorite pastime. After all, we're looking at the counter constantly, so why shouldn't the puppy as well? When a dog jumps up, you react by shouting and shoving. The puppy interpretation? Prize Envy. The dog thinks, "Whatever I was reaching for must be excellent because everybody raced over for it." So the puppy reconsiders. He jumps when your back is turned or you're out of the room. This behavior isn't spiteful; it's just plain smart. The following helps you dissect and correct the jumping problem one situation at a time.

Dogs that jump need to learn the Four Paw Rule. No attention until all four paws are on the floor.

You're home! You're home!

The best way to remedy jumping when you arrive home is to ignore your pup. Try it for a week.

- ✔ Come home and ignore your dog until he's given up the jumping vigil.
- ✔ Keep a basket of balls or squeaky toys by the door. When you come in, toss one on the ground to refocus your dog's energy.
- ✔ If your dog's crated, don't let him out immediately; wait until he's calm.

If you have a big puppy or a super persistent jumper, you have two options: Fill a plant mister with 50 percent vinegar and water to spray a boundary in between your bodies, or put on an overcoat to protect yourself, and calmly look away. Whether it takes 2 minutes or 20, go about your business until your dog calms down.

If you have kids, tell them to "look for rain" (see Chapter 10), and you do the same. Cross your arms in front of your chest and look to the sky. Don't look down until the coast is clear. Consistency is key. If one family member follows the program but the others encourage jumping, your dog will jump-test all visitors.

Puppies mimic their leaders' energy levels. If you come home to an excited dog and you get excited, you're sending the message that his excitement is acceptable. Instead, come in calm and wait to greet your puppy until he's settled down, too.

Oh goody — company!

The doorbell rings, and here's what happens: Your dog runs to the door, paws flying everywhere, jumps all over the arriving guests, and, because all eyes are on him, gets even more wound up — until, that is, you drag him to the basement. Then you apologize to your guests, who are no doubt wondering why you don't train your crazy dog. Bummer.

It's a common routine. Nobody's in control. Nobody's comfortable, except maybe the puppy. But even that passes if you have to isolate him. Fortunately, there's a better way. Remember the idiom "Good manners start at home"? Well, the same rule applies for puppies.

First, be stern with your regimen and train your company how to act around your dog — and you thought training your dog was tough.

- ✔ **Practice doorbell setups.** Put your dog on her Teaching Lead. Position someone at the door and ask him to ring the bell 10 times at 20-second intervals. Tell the visitor to come through another door when he's done. Each time the bell rings, call your dog's name and walk away from the door. Practice these setups twice a day until your dog tones down her reaction.

  If your dog is a real maniac, try the chin lead (described in Chapter 5) and discreetly spray Binaca Mouth Spray in front of her nose as you say "Shhh."

- ✔ **Do the reverse yo-yo.** Secure a four-foot lead to your puppy's nylon collar. Tie a knot in the lead 4 inches past where the lead passes your dog's toe. Before you open the door, step on the knot. Your puppy will still jump, but this rig forces him down. Encourage attention only when your puppy is calm.

- ✔ **Create a greeting station.** Designate an area by the door to send your pup to when company arrives. Secure a leash to the area and place a favorite ball or toy there. When the bell rings, station/secure your puppy as you instruct "Go to your place." Then answer the door. Instruct your visitors to ignore the puppy while greeting you. Wait until your puppy is calm to introduce her, even if it takes an hour.

> ✔ **Designate a greeting toy.** If your dog's a real tennis ball fanatic (or any other toy), withhold that toy until you have company arriving. Each time you enter your home or company arrives, say "Get your toy" as you toss the favorite toy on the floor. Spritz your dog if she jumps and continue to ignore her until she's settled down.

If you're sitting down, anchor your dog until she's calm enough to greet your guests. (Chapter 12 gives details on anchoring.)

Yoo hoo! Some attention, please

If you can ignore your puppy, the silent treatment is your most effective response. If I kept bugging you for a game of Parcheesi and you didn't look up once, I'd go elsewhere for fun. Once your dog stops jumping, encourage her by saying "Get your toy!" and let her pay attention to that.

If your dog's a real nudge, keep a lead (short or long) attached to her collar. When she jumps, grasp the lead and snap your puppy sideways quickly (this move is called a *fly flick*) as you continue to ignore her (give no eye contact, body language, or verbal corrections).

The fly flick says "How dare you" in the most passive manner; it's not tough or abusive. You just grasp the collar or leash with your thumb and forefinger and flick your puppy off to one side. You might need to perform the fly flick several times before your pup gets the message. When he finally sits down perplexed, give him a great big hug.

Also effective is using Binaca Mouth Spray to create a boundary between your bodies.

I wanna see what's on the counter, too!

Counter cruising is a bad habit that's hard to break. Blatant corrections actually encourage sneaky behavior. Though I've heard it a thousand times, your dog's not grabbing out of spite. The reason your dog grabs when your back is turned or you leave the room is so that she can avoid a challenge: Your puppy sees your eyes and mouth (hands equals mouths in the dog world) interacting with objects on the countertops all day. When she copies you, you bark (shouting is the same as barking to a dog) and challenge her for whatever the prize is. Canine message? Whatever is on the counter must be great, but I better grab it when all backs are turned or I'll have to give it up.

Try to solve this problem with dignity:

1. **With your puppy on the Teaching Lead, place something tempting on the counter.**

2. **The instant your puppy looks up to sniff the counter, snap the lead back, say "Ep, Ep," and shout at the counter "Bad turkey!"**

3. **Continue to work in the kitchen, correcting your puppy whenever she even thinks about approaching what's on the counter.**

If your dog's already on the counter, you're too late to correct her; instead, flick her off by curling a finger under her collar or grabbing her lead. Do not yell at your dog once she's on the counter. Do not lurch, shove, snatch, or hit. Touching reinforces behavior. After all, a touch is attention. If you push your dog, you're just reinforcing her behavior.

If mealtimes are too distracting to your dog, station her while you cook (see Chapter 12).

That couch sure do look comfy

Most people invite puppies on the furniture only to regret it later. If you have a puppy and you don't want him on your furniture permanently, do yourself a favor and discourage it from the start. If you have a delinquent furniture lover, however, the problem's not too hard to break; you just need to be consistent.

1. **Place your puppy on the Teaching Lead and walk up to your couch or bed.**

2. **The second she prepares for the jump, snap back and say "No!"**

3. **Encourage her to sit and, when she does, pet her.**

4. **Walk back and forth until she sits automatically.**

Try the same setup with a family member on the couch. Next, lead your puppy up and sit down yourself. If she goes to jump, snap sideways and ignore her until she sits quietly. Reward her cooperation with a chew toy.

Quieting That Bark-Bark-Barker

A barking dog's a real headache — a complete nightmare. How you handle the situation depends on what's prompting the barking in the first place. In the meantime, you need to watch your reaction. The cardinal sin when rehabilitating your barker is for you to yell. When you yell, your dog thinks you're barking, which leads to — you guessed it — more barking. A bark-along. To solve your problem, stay cool.

Barking at the door

Almost everyone appreciates a dog-alarm at the door — a few woofs to announce new arrivals. It gets annoying, however, when the alarm can't be shut off. The optimal situation would be to have an alarm bark with an off switch. Here's how:

1. **Place a penny can or spray bottle (filled with a 50/50 mix of vinegar and water) at the door.**

   To make a *penny can,* fill an empty soda can with ten pennies and tape the top. The shaking sound startles many dogs.

2. **Position someone outside the door and ask him to ring the bell 10 times in 20-second intervals.**

3. **When your dog starts barking, approach the door calmly. Spray her or shake the penny can discreetly as you say "Shhh!!!" and instruct "Back" to clear the greeting area.**

4. **Keep your dog behind you as you open the door, even if you need to station her there (see Chapter 12).**

   Never hold your dog while you open the door. Doing so just makes her more wild.

5. **Repeat these steps as often as necessary to condition respect.**

If your dog is aggressive, consult Chapter 15 and call a professional. Aggression is a serious problem.

Barking at e-v-e-r-y-thing

Does your dog bark at everything he sees and hears? Nothing goes unnoticed — a biker, the neighborhood kids, or little lively creatures passing through your yard. For some people, after a while, the dog's barking can seem as much a part of their daily routine as the wind passing through the trees. For those of us who don't fall into that category, however, perpetual barking is a big pain.

Barking has an added lure. Whenever your dog barks at something, whether from the window or the yard, that thing goes away. Sure, you and I know that the postman's going to keep moving, but don't tell your dog. She thinks her strength and prowess drove the postman away — quite an ego boost.

> ✔ Start training immediately. Dogs who bark at everything perceive themselves (not you) as the leader, and one of the leader's duties is to guard her territory and her group from intruders. Your dog needs to understand that you're the boss.

✔ Avoid leaving your puppy alone outdoors for long stretches of time. Unsupervised confinement often breeds boredom and territorial behavior. Put those two together, and you're likely to end up with a barkaholic.

✔ Block off areas that your puppy uses as lookout posts such as a living room couch or windowsill. If she's a night guard, secure her on lead in your room at night. Give her 3 feet of freedom — just enough to lie comfortably on her bed.

Screaming at your puppy is translated into barking. Your puppy feels supported, and her role as leader (she barked first) is reinforced. Anytime you see (or hear) your dog start to perk up, say "Shhh" and call her to your side. If she ignores you, place her on the Teaching Lead or let her drag a leash so you can quickly gain control. Use spray misters or penny cans to reinforce your verbal "Shhh!"

Many collars are on the market to help discourage the barking habit. Although I've never tried the electrical stimulation collars (my dog would freak out), I have used the citronella collars. These spray citronella toward the muzzle if the barking is continuous.

Barking in the car

Being locked in a car with a barking dog is my version of purgatory. The car creates an effect similar to the territorial situation described in the preceding section. Your dog barks, and the passing object disappears — only faster in the case of a moving car.

Yelling at your dog isn't the thing to do. Pleading doesn't win you any brownie points. This problem tends to disappear slowly as you progress through training; however, you can do a few things in the interim to discourage this behavior:

✔ Enforce stillness while you drive. Station your puppy in the car with a Seat Belt Safety Lead (SBSL), described in Chapter 5.

✔ Have your puppy pause before you let her enter or exit the car. Instruct "Wait" and give her permission to enter with "OK." After all, the car is yours, not hers.

✔ Play classical music and stay cool. Your dog perceives any frustration on your part as backup and ups the ferocity.

✔ If your situation is unbearable, secure your dog on a chin lead (see Chapter 5).

✔ Ignore the barking if your car's moving. Driving is a job in itself.

✔ If you're stationary, try to spritz your dog with a plant mister (without turning and glaring — quite a feat) or shake a penny can as you say "Shhh."

✔ If your dog barks at gas-station or toll-booth attendants, ask them to toss a piece of cheese into the car window from afar. Hopefully, your dog will make a more positive association.

If you think your dog is bordering on territorial aggression, refer to Chapter 15 and call for professional help.

Barking for attention or protest

All puppies go through a phase when they can't bear to be left alone. If you soothe a protest or attention barker, you end up with a real spoiled dog on your hands. If you ignore the situation, your partner may threaten to leave you. Is there a happy medium? Well, not really, but I'll give it my best shot:

✔ Ignore the barking if you can. Never yell.

✔ Avoid grandiose departures and arrivals. They're too exciting.

✔ Dogs like to be with you. Avoid problems in your home by using the Teaching Lead.

✔ Place peanut butter in a hollow bone and give it to your dog as you leave.

✔ Use a water pistol or toss a penny can toward (not at) your dog when she starts up. Be careful, though; she can't know where the can or water is coming from.

✔ Return to your puppy only after she's calmed down. If you must interfere with her barking tantrum, go to her quietly without eye contact or comments, place her on the Teaching Lead, and ignore her for half an hour while you lead her around.

Chapter 14

Training Through the Phases

*W*elcome to boot camp. This chapter covers the basic, bare-bones commands to teach your puppy at various stages of its development.

I suggest that you practice each command five to ten minutes a day. As you practice, you'll notice that your puppy picks up certain commands quickly but that other commands take weeks. Don't fret. That's how training usually goes. After all, think of what you're accomplishing. You're teaching another *species* your language. My best advice? Be patient. Puppies learn best from an understanding teacher.

Infant Lessons: 8 to 12 Weeks

Don't expect too much from this age group. Although a puppy at this age is capable of learning, her brain won't finish developing until she's 12 weeks old. Your puppy learns best when you incorporate training into her playtime. Hang around with her, use her name as you offer her good things (like toys and treats), introduce her to the leash — pretty basic stuff. Begin housebreaking, but don't expect a totally housebroken puppy in four weeks. Forget discipline right now because she's just too young to understand it. You succeed only in frightening her and eroding your relationship — and that's not good.

Use your puppy's name

Pick a short name or nickname and use it each time you offer your puppy something positive like food or praise. Speak in a warm, happy tone. Watch that squealing.

Start leash training

Put a collar on your puppy immediately. It's okay if she fusses at first; she'll get used to it. Next, attach a light leash and let her drag it around. After a day, pick up the leash and follow her around. As she gets used to having you follow her, start to call out her name and encourage her to follow you.

Do any number of foolish things to pique her interest. When she starts following you, praise her generously. Say "Let's go!" and kneel often to hug her. If she resists strongly, don't run over to her; you'd be reinforcing the resistance. Instead, tug the leash gently and lower yourself to the floor while you praise her.

Puppies grow fast, so keep an eye on the collar size and loosen it when necessary.

Work on Sit and Okay

Say "Sit" as you position your puppy: Put your right hand under her chin and use your left hand to squeeze the waist muscles below the ribs.

Use the happy word Okay to give your puppy permission. Say "Okay" as you give your puppy good things: a meal, pat, toy, and so on.

Walk the stairs

Stairs can be a very formidable obstacle. Some small breeds are just too little to negotiate the stairs and must be carried. That's okay; in time, they'll be scampering up and down like big dogs. Some large-breed puppies are big enough, but they're afraid because their depth perception isn't completely developed.

If you've got a puppy with stair phobia, help her walk the stairs by cradling her belly and guiding her paws. If possible, have someone crouch a few stairs away to cheer her on.

Work on handling and socialization

When you handle your puppy, you're teaching her that human contact is good. Without frequent and gentle handling, your dog will grow up to be wary of people. In addition, puppies who are not socialized often develop a fear of unfamiliar situations and people. By handling and socializing your puppy, you're helping her grow into a well-adjusted, gentle dog who's comfortable around people and new situations.

Handling

When you're calmly petting your puppy, occasionally play veterinarian. Peek into your puppy's ears; check out what's going on in her mouth and eyes. Press her belly gently and handle the base of the tail. Handle the paws like you're trimming her nails. Praise your puppy gently as you do this or give her a treat so she won't get scared. You'll be helping yourself and your veterinarian, who always appreciates a good patient. Every other day go to your puppy during one of her meals. Offer her a biscuit and a pat and say "Good girl!" Once she anticipates your offering, remove her bowl while she eats the treat; then return the bowl and leave. At this point, if you have children in the house, bring them with you and start the process from the beginning. Early food bowl conditioning prevents food guarding later in her development.

Socialization

Puppies at this age are too young to be taken out on the town, but between 8 and 12 weeks is the best age to socialize your puppy with new people and other dogs. Invite your neighbors and friends over, borrow a group of active kids, have a puppy playdate with another healthy canine and socialize that puppy.

Correct that mischievous behavior

If your puppy is rough or jumpy during playtime, attach a short leash onto his collar. If he starts misbehaving, take the leash and snap him away or off. If you use your hands, the behavior may escalate because hands are interactive, and in your puppy's mind, interactive is good, good, good.

When your puppy is attached to the leash, you can correct any mischief without physical interaction. If Mini the Mastiff puts her front paw in my lap and I push her away with my hands, I'm actually encouraging her to put her paw up on my lap again because, in her mind, pushing is interactive. If, instead of pushing, I grab the leash, tug her off, and ignore her until she's calm, she learns that calm puppies get petted.

Clicker-happy training

Clickers are a fun and fast way to speed up your puppy's learning process. Although it may seem magical, clicker training relies on behavior shaping principles that mark desired behavior.

To start, get ten treats. Click and treat; before you're finished, your puppy will be happily alert to the sound.

Now use the clicker for training and to encourage good habits.

✔ **House-training:** When your puppy eliminates in the right area, say "*get busy.*" Click the instant he finishes; then treat and praise warmly.

✔ **Jumping:** When your puppy jumps, look away. Click, treat, and pet him after all four paws are on the ground. Four on the floor — that's a good dog.

✔ **Chewing:** Anytime your dog is chewing an appropriate object, click, treat, and praise warmly.

You can iron out even everyday frustrations with the clicker. Use it to encourage silence, to train him to ask to be let out, to create a positive association to kids, and more. You can also use a clicker to teach basic commands:

✔ **Sit:** Command "Sit," luring your dog into position with a toy or treat if necessary. Click, reward, and praise. Good dog!

✔ **Down:** Command "Down," luring your dog into position with a toy or treat. Click, reward, and praise. Hurray!

✔ **Come:** Throughout the day, command "Come" when your dog's near you. Encourage him to look up by sweeping your hands to your eyes. Click and reward. Gradually extend the distance and increase the distractions, working within a safe environment.

You can also use the same clicker principles to teach tricks. See Chapter 29 for more information on trick training.

Don't forget to follow each click with a treat and praise and avoid over-clicking. It's too confusing; soon your dog will be conditioned to the sound and not respond as well. Be cheerful and have fun.

Terrible Twos Lessons: 12 to 16 Weeks

During this age, your puppy is beginning to recognize what behaviors get your attention, what games seem to last the longest (and these aren't necessarily the games *you* want to be playing), and who the boss is (and in his eyes, it may not be you). Although he may act pretty confident, your pup still needs direction from you. The suggestions in this section can help you guide your puppy successfully through his Terrible Twos. (For a complete rundown of what you can expect from a puppy at this stage, head to Chapter 9.)

Keep control

When you're home, always know where your puppy is. If you give him complete freedom, he'll misbehave and you'll end up paying for it — in more ways than one. Unsupervised, a puppy will rearrange your closets, eat garbage, and chew on the chairs. Remember: You're still dealing with a puppy. Keep yours near you in one of four ways:

- ✔ Using the Teaching Lead concepts (Chapter 12 has details on how to use this method)
- ✔ Under observation in an enclosed area, such as a gated kitchen
- ✔ In a crate
- ✔ With you around the home, attached to a short lead that's attached to the buckle collar

When he's confined, give him attention for good behavior. Continue to organize free time around the home, using the Teaching Lead, unless you're able to devote your complete attention in an enclosed area.

If your puppy begins to respond on his own, you can attach a short lead and give him some supervised free time around your home (but don't rush giving him freedom). If he does well for the most part but falls apart when company comes, put him on the Teaching Lead when you have visitors.

Work on ten commands

Your puppy is still very young. Although he can learn a lot, he's still very sensitive and vulnerable to your impressions. So stay cool. Getting frustrated or impatient only frightens him and makes him less responsive to you.

- ✔ Keep your lessons short and snappy, no more than a couple of minutes.
- ✔ Speak your commands clearly and enunciate your syllables. Repeated commands sound different from commands given once (the indecipherable "sitsitsitcomeonpleasesitdown").
- ✔ Continue to use your commands during playtime.

I encourage hand signals even at this age because they help you get visual attention. I also use treats with some of the commands, but once the command is understood, food rewards can be eliminated. Believe it or not, your puppy can have a ten-word vocabulary by the time he's four months old.

Your dog's name

You need to teach your puppy the importance of alerting to his name. Follow this sequence twice a day:

1. **Place your puppy in a sit position.**

2. **Pivot six inches in front of him (standing or kneeling) so that your feet are facing his paws.**

3. **Keeping your back straight, snap your finger above his nose.**

4. **Call his name as you rapidly draw your finger to your eyes.**

5. **When he looks up, freeze. Look away *after* your puppy breaks the stare.**

Try to get at least three seconds of eye contact.

Let's Go

Continue to use this command whenever you're walking your puppy on his leash. Remember that Let's Go is not optional. If your puppy doesn't want to go and you stop to cajole him, you reinforce his resistance. Say the command happily; then skip, bounce, or dart ahead — whatever you can do to encourage his quick and willing participation.

Sit

Twice a day for four days do the following:

1. **Take your puppy aside with a handful of small treats.**

2. **Place a treat between your index finger and thumb and say "Sit" as you bring the treat slightly above your puppy's nose (see Figure 14-1).**

3. **When he sits, give him the treat, say "Okay," and praise him (see Figure 14-2).**

Repeat these steps no more than five times per session. The hand signals will become lifting your index finger above his nose. As the days progress and your puppy seems to catch on, try giving the command and signal outside of a lesson time and without a treat. After four days, fade off the treat and stop using this command in lessons. Continue to use the command and signal throughout the day.

Figure 14-1:
To position
your puppy
to sit, bring
the treat
slightly
above his
nose.

Photo by Sarah Hodgson.

Down

Once your puppy has mastered Sit, you can work on this command. Twice a day for four days do the following:

1. **Take your puppy aside with some treats.**

2. **Placing the treats between your fingers, instruct "Sit," but before you let go of the treat, drop your hand between the puppy's paws and say "Down."**

3. **Your puppy may not know what to do, so as he looks down, cradle his shoulders with your left hand and press him gently into position (see Figure 14-3).**

4. **Let go of the treat when his elbows hit the floor, praise him, and say "Okay" to release.**

5. **Repeat Steps 2 through 4 five times.**

Figure 14-2:
When your
puppy sits,
give a treat,
say "Okay,"
and give
praise.

Photo by Sarah Hodgson.

Figure 14-3:
Teaching
the Down
command
by cradling
a puppy's
shoulders
and press-
ing him
gently into
position.

Photo by Sarah Hodgson.

The eventual hand signal is pointing to the ground. As the days progress, try this command out of lesson time without a treat. After four days, fade off the treat and stop using this command in lessons. Continue to use the command and signal throughout the day.

Stand

This command is handy when you want to clean muddy paws and during general grooming sessions. Twice a day for four days, take your puppy aside with some treats and do the following:

1. **Place one between your fingers and give the command as you pull an imaginary string from your puppy's nose forward.**

2. **When your puppy stands, stop your fingers and cradle his belly as you repeat "Stand."**

3. **Pause and then release with "Okay" as you allow your puppy to have the treat.**

   Your pup may try to snatch the treat, but hold it firmly and don't release it until he's standing.

4. **Repeat these steps five times.**

The eventual hand signal is a short point forward from his nose. As the days progress, try this command out of lesson time without a treat. After four days fade off the treat and stop using this command in lessons. Continue to use the command and signal throughout the day.

Bring and Out

Most puppies enjoy this game. Try it first with your puppy on a leash and some treats in your pocket. Take your puppy into a small, quiet room with a favorite ball or squeak toy and then follow these steps:

1. **Kneel on the floor and praise your puppy happily for nearly a minute before you bring out the toy.**

2. **When you bring the toy out, toss it in the air to encourage his interest; then give it a short toss.**

3. **If he takes the toy, go to him and say "Good Boy-Out" as you offer him a treat.**

4. **Continue this until you notice that he looks to you as soon as he picks the toy up.**

5. **Gradually encourage him to walk toward you with the toy as you command "Bring."**

He should release the toy quickly, but if he doesn't, you can encourage him by squeezing his upper muzzle just behind the canines. Praise him for releasing.

6. **Repeat these steps five times and praise him profusely when the game is over.**

Practice these commands in the confines of a small room for five days; then bring the command into normally populated areas, fading off the treats gradually.

Settle Down

In each room, your puppy should have a special corner or area equipped with a bed and a chew bone. Eventually, you want to be able to send your puppy to this area on command — a tactic that is especially useful during mealtime or when you have company. To teach him this principle, select areas in each room and then, with your puppy on leash, command "Settle Down" and point to the area with a free hand. He will probably need an escort, so take him there and then hook him to his area with the lead. Soon you'll notice that your puppy leads you over and lies down quickly. He may start to take himself to the area when he's tired. What a good puppy.

Before you begin teaching this command, make sure you read and understand the stationing concept. See Chapter 12 for details.

Wait and Okay

When approaching doors or stairs, command "Wait" and bring your puppy behind your feet. This maneuver is best accomplished by bringing the leash behind your back. Pause a couple of seconds and then command "Okay" as you step out first. The leader must always lead.

Excuse Me

Puppies like to get in the way. It gets them attention. But it makes you look subservient, and it can be dangerous as they get older. Whenever your puppy trips you up, gets on the wrong side of the leash, or just basically gets in your way, command "Excuse Me" and move him out of your way with the leash or by shuffling your feet under his body. Don't yell or kick your puppy and don't use your hands (he'll just interpret this as an invitation to play). Thank him for respecting you; soon he'll move with his tail wagging.

No Sir or No Ma'am

The No Sir/No Ma'am command is a discipline command. Eventually, you will be able to use it to curb your dog from chasing small animals or from approaching food or strangers. But first you must teach him what you mean.

1. **Place your puppy on a leash.**

2. **With your puppy stationed in the next room, prepare a plate of crackers and place it on the floor.**

3. **Go get your puppy and take him toward the setup.**

4. **When your puppy starts to sniff and approach the food, pull back sharply on his leash and command "No Sir" in a stern, disciplining tone.**

5. **Release the pressure immediately and continue walking.**

   If he lunges again, repeat the corrections but continue walking.

6. **Praise your puppy when he refocuses his attention on you.**

7. **Walk by as often as necessary until he avoids the setup altogether.**

   Don't forget to praise him when he does.

Work on handling and socialization

Early handling benefits both you and your veterinarian. Continue to manipulate his paws, ears, eyes, belly, and tail as you would if you were grooming or medicating him. If your puppy will be around children, be sure he can handle it. Act like a kid. Pull his coat gently, squeal, make sudden movements. Praise your puppy and give him treats during your performance. Your puppy loves to party. He loves friends with four legs and friends with two legs. If he's too young to be taken out (ask your veterinarian), invite people in — kids included. If you don't have kids, borrow some. Once your veterinarian has completed your puppy's shots, start taking him out on the town and introduce him to everyone you meet. Take him to three new areas a week.

Ask your veterinarian if he can recommend a well-managed puppy kindergarten class in your town. Joining a class is a fun way to meet other puppies and people.

Lots of socialization doesn't create a dog who won't protect his home or his people. Socialization simply encourages your dog to trust your judgement where people are concerned. Lack of socialization creates a dog who is over-bonded to his family and intolerant of visitors. Depending on his breed and temperament, this dog will become fearful or defensive of other people on or off your property. Such dogs are difficult to manage and are a constant concern around people. Spare yourself the agony and socialize that puppy.

Budding Adolescent Lessons: 16 to 24 Weeks

When you and your puppy reach this stage, you may feel like hiding in the closet. Some days are livable. Other days you feel like moving. Your puppy won't listen or respond to known commands. She bolts, chases, and nips at everything that moves. She demands your attention and barks or mounts you if she doesn't get it. She insists on being the center of attention, every moment of every day.

Remember, this stage is normal. I lived through it, and you will too. This is the stage to start a regimented training schedule. Keep your sessions short and lively and use each new command during lesson time only for the first week. This process allows your puppy to be successful, mastering each command before you start applying it to her day-to-day world — similar to letting children master their addition skills in school before asking them to balance your checkbook.

Keep control

When you're home, you should always know where your puppy is. If you give your puppy complete freedom, she *will* misbehave, and you'll end up paying a lot of attention to naughty behavior. Unsupervised, she'll rearrange your closets, eat garbage, and chew the couch. Remember, you're dealing with a puppy. Keep her nearby you in one of three ways:

- On a lead by your side
- Under complete observation in an enclosed area
- On a short lead (attached to the buckle collar)

Restrained, she'll get attention for *good* behavior. Continue to organize her free time in the house with the Teaching Lead unless you're able to give her your complete attention in an enclosed area. If she begins to respond well on her own, attach a short lead and give her some freedom in the house. Don't rush it, though. If she does well for the most part but falls apart when company arrives, put her on the Teaching Lead when you have visitors.

Continue politeness training

Continue to use the command "Sit" throughout the day. Use it before you pet her, put her food down, or offer a treat. Use it when you let her out of the car or house and before her admirers approach. Remember: Give the command *once*, correcting her with "No" and a leash tug (position her if it's a new distraction).

Know the difference between praise and petting

When your puppy learns something new, it's very exciting for everyone. But try to control yourself. If you get fired up, your puppy does, too. Learning takes a lot of concentration, and an excited pup can't learn much. As you practice your exercises, remember that there's a difference between praise and petting. Petting comes from your hand; it excites your puppy and communicates play intentions. Praise comes from your voice and eyes and is given from an upright position; it calms your puppy and communicates your leadership. Remember this handy phrase: *Praise between exercises; pet to end them.*

Work on five commands

As your puppy is developing, both physically and mentally, you need to start teaching these useful commands: Heel, No, Stay, Come, and Stand-Stay. Together, they help your puppy be more mindful of your presence.

Heel

A puppy standing calmly at his owner's side, walking when he moves and sitting when he stops, is a beautiful thing to watch. Yes, such control can be yours, too, if you're patient. Though it takes a while to synchronize, eventually you'll be maneuvering through crowded streets and calling your puppy to heel from a distance. Sound miraculous? It all starts with one small step. Use these exercises to train your puppy to stay at your heel.

How many ways were you taught to sit at the dinner table? One. Guess how many ways there are to heel? You're right — one. Picture this: your puppy at your heel, toes aligned, heads facing in the same direction. Such a pretty picture.

Do the simple circle

Practice this heeling exercise in an open, quiet place (inside or out). Clear an area to walk in a circle. Position your puppy next to you at your left side, all heads facing in the same direction, and your puppy's paws lined up with your heel (see Figure 14-4). You're ready to start.

1. **Relax your arms straight, keeping your left thumb behind your thigh. Snap the leash back whenever your puppy pulls from your side.**

2. **Command "*Name*, Heel" as you begin to walk in a counterclockwise (dog on the inside) circle.**

   Walk in a cheerful manner, head held high and shoulders back to communicate the right attitude.

Figure 14-4:
Setting up to
do the
simple
circle
heeling
exercise.

Photo by Sarah Hodgson.

3. **Praise your puppy for walking with you and snap the leash if your puppy's attention starts to stray.**

4. **Stop after each circle by slowing your pace and reminding "Heel."**

5. **Place your puppy into a sitting position.**

   To position the sit when you stop, grasp the *base* of the leash (where the leash attaches to your puppy's collar) with your right hand and use your left hand to squeeze the waist.

6. **Practice five circles twice a day.**

If your dog turns to face you when you stop, guess what? He's facing off. Another attempt for control. To discourage this habit, grab the base of the leash with your left hand. Step back on your left foot and swiftly swing your dog into the proper position. Now you can praise.

A good leash snap doesn't involve knuckles, shoulder, or chest muscles. Think of your elbow as a hinge. Without the leash, rock your elbow back and forth. Now imagine that I was holding my hand behind your back. Slap my hand without bending your elbow. Now pick up the leash. Holding the lead behind your back, snap your elbow. Pretend my hand's there and you're trying to hit it.

Float the finish

When you're preparing to stop, slow your pace slightly, lift your left foot high in the air (like you're marching), and then drop it lightly to the floor. This action gives your puppy an added clue that he's supposed to stop and sit.

Change your pace

As you change your pace, keep your leash hand steady. Move faster by trotting. Slow your pace by lengthening your stride. Make sure you change gears smoothly and indicate the change by saying "Clk, Clk" or "Shh." Remember, your puppy's a dog, not a Porsche.

Do an about face

Walking at a normal speed, command "Heel" and pivot to the right. To help your puppy keep up, slow down as you turn; cluck, bend your knees, or slap your leg to keep him with you. Walk on six paces, position the sit and stop, and hug your puppy for a job well done. (Remember: Avoid choking him through the turn; that's no fun.)

Heeling practice tips

You know you're ready to practice the Heel command in everyday situations when your puppy responds without pressure on his collar. Use it everywhere:

- ✔ Keep a short lead on your puppy around the home. Pick the lead up occasionally and command "Heel" as you walk from room to room.

- ✔ Use the Heel command on your walks. If your puppy's young or just beginning to learn, heel him for one-fourth of your walk. Increase the distance over the next month until your puppy is always walking at your side.

- ✔ Finally, you can practice in a parking lot and more crowded situations (make sure it's not too crowded). No sniffing or lunging at neighborhood pals. Be mindful of your puppy, no matter what the distractions.

- ✔ If things get out of hand when you're in public, stay calm. If you yell "Heel, Heel, Heel!" and jerk your poor puppy back and forth, he'll just get excited. If this is a problem for you, determine whether you're asking too much too soon. Maybe your puppy simply needs to exercise more before you practice in public.

Be sure to keep your hand behind you — left arm straight and behind your back (see Figure 14-5). If your left hand is in front of your thigh, your puppy is the leader, not you.

Figure 14-5:
The right
way to hold
the leash for
heeling.

Photo by Mary Bloom.

No

There are a few inconsistencies with the way people use this little word that leaves dogs baffled as to its meaning.

- ✔ **People usually shout it.** Shouting to a dog sounds like barking. Would barking excite a situation or calm it down?

- ✔ **People use it with their dogs' names.** (In fact, many dogs think No is the second half of their name: "Buddy No!" "Tristan No!" "Molly No!") You should only use your puppy's name when you're happy, not mad.

- ✔ **People say it after the action has occurred.** If I yelled at you after you ate a bowl of soup, would you understand that I was upset at you for opening the can? Said at the wrong time, No communicates nothing.

- ✔ **People say it repetitively.** "No, No, No, No" sounds different from "No."

What's an owner to do to teach a dog not to get into trouble? Fortunately, I have the answer. First, you need to teach your puppy the concept of No by setting up situations to catch your puppy in the thought process. As you train your pup to understand No, work indoors first; then out.

Indoors, put your puppy on his Teaching Lead and have someone secretly place a piece of cheese on the floor in a neighboring room (this is your prop). Follow these steps and pay attention to timing.

1. **Bring your puppy into the heel position and casually walk toward the cheese.**

2. **The second your puppy notices the cheese, snap back on the lead and say "No!"**

   Your puppy has a built-in antenna system: his ears. If his ears perk up, your puppy is alert. When teaching No, watch your puppy's ears. Correct your puppy the second he becomes alert to something inappropriate.

3. **Continue to walk like nothing has happened.**

   Remember: You're the boss. No means No.

4. **Walk by the cheese several times to ensure that your puppy got the message.**

If you don't like to say "No," use another word or sound. Just be consistent. Personally, I like "Ep, Ep." It sounds softer, but the dog gets the message — "Don't even think about it!" — loud and clear.

After your indoor training, practice No when you're out for a walk. When your puppy notices a passing jogger, car, kid, another dog, or two tidbits climbing a tree, say "No" just like you did with the cheese. Sidestep away from the temptation to emphasize your snap. Continue to snap each time the antennas flicker. Praise your puppy for focusing on you and relaxing his radar system.

Stay

If this is your dream command, you're not alone. I'm not sure why people have so much trouble teaching this one, but it's probably because they rush it. They teach the command one day and expect their dog to stay while they welcome company or walk into the kitchen for a sandwich. Promise this: You won't rush. Taught progressively, this command's a real winner.

To prepare for your first lesson:

1. **Take your puppy into a quiet room.**

   No TV. No kids. No cats. Just you two.

2. **Slide your puppy's training collar high near his head and center it between his ears.**

3. **Fold the leash in your left hand to hip level.**

4. **Position your puppy behind your heels.**

Now you're ready to teach your puppy his first lesson. You do six sequences. No more, no less. Here are a couple of rules for your puppy's sake:

- Look over your puppy's head when you practice; never look directly into his eyes. It's too daunting.

- Stand tall. When you bend, you look like you want to play.

- Stay close to your puppy when you start out, about six inches from toe to paw. Creating too much distance too soon can be really scary.

- While doing each exercise, hold the lead directly above your puppy's head. That way, if he confuses Stay with Go, you're ready for a quick correction.

- Vary the length of each pause at the end of the exercise. If you don't, your puppy will break ahead of time. He's just trying to please.

- Resist petting your puppy until you finish the following steps. Too much petting ruins his concentration.

To teach Stay, get in the proper position (see the preceding steps) and then follow these steps:

1. **Command "Sit" and align your puppy with your ankles.**

2. **Command "Stay" as you flash your hand in front of your puppy's nose; remove the signal and pause for five seconds.**

3. **Command "OK" as you swing your arm forward and step out of position.**

4. **Again. Command "Sit, Stay." This time, pivot to face away from your puppy and pause ten seconds. Return to the starting point and release with "OK!"**

5. **Back again. Command "Stay." Pivot in front of your puppy. Pause. Now march.**

   Yes, march, slowly at first, like you're sleepwalking. Once your puppy holds still for that, start marching like a proud soldier.

6. **Command "Stay" and pivot and pause. Now try jumping and waving your arms.**

   Go slowly at first; ease into it. Now for some noise.

7. **Pivot, pause, and then bark at your puppy; then return, pause, and release.**

   Remember, no staring; keep looking over his head. Add a meow or two when he can handle it.

8. **From your starting position, command "Stay," pivot in front, and pause for 30 seconds.**

Stand up tall, relax your shoulders, and keep the leash above your puppy's head just in case he's tempted to break.

9. **When the time is up, return to his side, pause, and release with "OK!"**

10. **Now it's time to hug that puppy.**

Practice this simplified sequence twice a day until your puppy's feeling mighty fine about his accomplishments.

Now you're ready to increase the three Ds: duration, distractions, and distance.

- ✔ **Distraction:** Step up your march, add a new aerobics twist, walk around your puppy full circle, and chant like a chimp. Can you do all this without tempting your puppy to move?

  Are you wondering why you're jumping around and making noise while your puppy's expected to stay? Eventually, your puppy will have to concentrate around motion and sound distractions; you're helping him get accustomed to temptations.

- ✔ **Duration:** Stretch your 30-second stand-still to two minutes.

- ✔ **Distance:** Move out one foot at a time. When you're successful, reintroduce distractions gradually and increase the duration.

Now the two of you should feel like pros.

Come

Now for everybody's most desired command. First you need to ask yourself a couple of things. Have you said "Come" more than once and yelled it repeatedly? Have you chased your puppy and bribed him with his favorite delicacy? If so, trouble is brewing. Your puppy thinks Come means disobedience or game time. Fortunately, you can straighten him out, but doing so will take time, concentration, structure, patience, and a lot of praise. Read on.

Hand signals can help your puppy to focus

Your puppy can start learning hand signals, which helps him focus on you. Use hand signals in front of your puppy's nose to direct his attention to you. Here are three hand signals to start with:

- ✔ **Sit.** Swing your right hand from your puppy's nose to your face, like you're scooping his attention toward you, and say "Sit."

- ✔ **Stay.** Flatten your palm like a paddle. Flash it quickly in front of your puppy's nose and say "Stay."

- ✔ **OK.** Swing your right hand out from your puppy's nose as you step forward. Use OK to say "Job well done!"

Going for up-close control first

You first need to teach Come as a position near to you. Then later, when you introduce it as a distance command, your puppy will want to close the gap.

When you say "Come Front," you want your dog to face you and look up. To teach your puppy how to do this, follow these steps:

1. **Walk in front of your puppy while he's standing calmly.**

2. **Standing tall, say "*Name*, Come" as you zip your finger up your belly from his nose level to your eyes.**

   Make a funny sound to encourage focus.

3. **If he looks up but doesn't sit, guide him into the proper position.**

   Lift up on his buckle collar and tuck his hind quarters into position, squeezing his waist muscles below his ribs as you press down. Avoid jerky motions, don't press his backbone, and don't command as you position.

4. **Once your puppy sits and makes eye contact, give him a big hug.**

Repeat this exercise throughout the day, whenever you have something positive to share — a pat, treat, dinner, or toy. Make sure your puppy's first associations to this command are warm and welcoming.

Going for distance control

Before you can teach this command, your puppy must understand that Come means a specific spot near you, looking up. Once he does, you're ready to go for distance control. (No, you're not off-lead yet. Be patient.)

Practice this exercise in a quiet room. No TV. No kids. No cats. Keep your lesson short and upbeat.

To teach distance control, make sure your dog is wearing a leash and then follow these steps:

1. **Practice three regular Sit-Stays; then return to your puppy's side and release him with "OK!"**

2. **Leave your puppy in a stay position and walk to the end of the leash.**

3. **Pause. (Vary the duration each time.)**

4. **Call "*Name*, Come!" in a directional tone. Signal it by sweeping your right arm across your body.**

5. **As soon as you issue the command, scurry backward and reel in the leash.**

6. **When your pup gets near your feet, signal up your belly and tap your heel to the floor (as described in the preceding steps) to encourage the finish.**

7. **Encourage eye contact by standing tall and making kissing sounds.**

8. **Release him with an "OK." Good puppy.**

Practice Come three times per session. That's all. More than that is stressful.

Remember to blend each Come call with a few regular Sit-Stays. If you don't, your puppy will break his Stay early to please you. Sweet thing.

Building focus by throwing in distractions

If your puppy gets excited when she hears Come, you're doing a good job. Now you can start encouraging focus around low-level distractions and increasing the distance from which you call her. Here are some ideas (see if you can add to the list): Try this exercise in front of the TV, in the backyard, in front of the kids, and during mealtime. In a quiet hallway or garage, attach the Flexi-Lead (see Chapter 5) and increase your distance slowly.

Using the Come command around distractions is harder than using the command in a quiet living room. Most dogs try to pay attention to the distraction and you at the same time, which is impossible. If your puppy's torn, say "No" and snap the lead when he turns toward the distraction. Then praise him when he focuses on you: "Good Dog!"

If you're having trouble getting your puppy's attention around distractions, you're not alone. My advice: Stick with it. Don't give up. You must communicate that there's only one way to Come and that is to sit directly in front of you. Practice in a quiet room for a day, enthusiastically praising your puppy's focus. Then try it with your TV on:

1. **Leave him, using the Stay command.**

2. **Pause at least a minute (building up anticipation).**

3. **With a straight back, deep voice, and gigantic hand signal, call "*Name*, Come!"**

4. **Flag him in.**

5. **If he sits straight, praise him happily. If not, side-step from the distraction, snap the chain firmly, and say "No."**

6. **Encourage and praise any focus immediately.**

Work up the distraction chain slowly. If your puppy's too stimulated, practice around simpler distractions for a while. Remember: You're not in a rush. Training your puppy isn't a race. And whatever you do, don't get frustrated. Frustration kills enthusiasm.

Use Come in two of the following situations daily. You can add to the list (only two Comes a day, though): when your puppy's distracted on a walk; during regular teaching or with the Flexi-Lead; indoors, as your puppy's waking up from a nap; as your puppy's getting out of the car; or when the neighbor's jogging by.

Fall back. Even if you've successfully weaned your puppy from the Teaching Lead, you'll probably need it again during this stage. When your puppy is over-stimulated and unable to focus, connect him to your side or station him for a while with a bone.

Have three plans. During behavior emergencies — for example, out-of-control door greetings, article stealing, running away, and so forth — use your commands, if they work. Most dogs, however, become temporarily deaf during these situations, so have alternative plans. See the section "Handling common problems" for alternatives.

Handling common problems

Some problems may surface — or resurface — when your puppy hits puberty. A dog who used to calmly greet guests now goes into a frenzy when people arrive. Or maybe an open door is just too much temptation, and he darts out. Following are some suggestions to help you deal with situations you may find yourself and your pup in.

Door greeting

Always ask guests to ignore your puppy until he has settled down. Your three options might include stationing him to a far corner of the greeting room; connecting him around your waist to maintain leash control; or if all else fails, crating or confining him with a favorite toy. Bring him out when he has calmed down.

Article stealing

When your puppy steals an article of clothing, leave the area and shut the door behind you. At this age, most puppies are more concerned with playing than with chewing. If you ignore him, he'll lose interest in the game.

Another option would be leaving the house: Put on your coat, grab your keys. . . that should be enough to distract him. Take your pup out for a minute or two if you try this trick; otherwise, he'll start to see through it.

As a last recourse, follow him around without eye contact or corrections, slowly cornering him in a small area. Calmly remove the object by squeezing his muzzle and commanding "Out." Never correct a puppy while you're doing this, or he'll quickly distrust you.

Runaway puppy

Running away is not just frustrating; it's also dangerous. You should never let your puppy off leash unless you're in a confined area. If you want to give him freedom in an unconfined area, put him on a 25–50-foot long line so that you can grab the leash for quick control if needed. If your puppy does sneak off, have your plans well thought out.

✔ Try a command or two. If they don't work, stop. Don't panic.

✔ Try running around like a lunatic (without eye contact), screaming and waving your arms. Drop to the ground in a heap and see whether this strange and interesting behavior brings him running.

✔ Try getting in the car. Many dogs can't bear the thought of missing out on a trip.

✔ If nothing works, follow him quietly to make sure he stays out of danger. Yelling only makes matters worse.

Avoid getting angry at your puppy after the fact. Otherwise, he'll learn to be more wary of your ploys. Never use treats as bribery. Used in this way, treats actually reinforce the naughty behavior.

The top five commands

When training during this age, you extend your control on all the commands your pup has learned so far (see the preceding sections). Following are the top five commands that I encourage you to use most often.

Heel

Continue using this command to encourage good walking control. In addition, use this command to call your puppy to your side. To teach your puppy this concept:

1. **Place her on a leash and let her walk ahead of you.**

2. **Suddenly call her name and command "Heel" as you slap your left thigh.**

3. **Lead her to your side by reeling in the leash.**

   Lead her around your left side in a U or to your right around your back. When she reaches your side, make sure she sits before you release her.

Once she gets the hang of this Heel (thigh-slap), begin to encourage her to come to your side around distractions (on-leash at first) and when you're sitting down. Always give the command positively, enforce a proper sit, and praise her warmly before you release her with "Okay."

Sit

Continue to ask your puppy to Sit in all situations. Give the command once; if she doesn't respond, give her collar or leash a tug that says "No" and ask her again. Position her sharply if she doesn't listen.

Down

Continue to work on this command even if your puppy doesn't want to coop-erate. Slide your left foot under the leash, point to the ground, and command "Down" as you pull the leash upward under your foot; press on her back if necessary (see Figure 14-6). Ignore her if she rolls around wildly on the floor or nips your shoelaces. Release her only after she's calmed down.

When your dog begins cooperating, use Down for everything: before treating (hold the treat to the ground and command "Down"), dinner (cover the bowl with your hand and, as you put it down, say "Down"), or with a Toy Toss (hide it in your hand, hold it to the ground, and command "Down").

Wait

Continue to use this command to catch your puppy's attention at doorways, cars, stairs, or before entering an area of high stimulation (for example, the veterinarian's, a room full of children, or dog-training class). This command means your puppy should stop dead in her tracks and wait to follow you. If you're successful using this command in the situations described in the sec-tion "Wait and Okay" (earlier in this chapter) begin to practice it when walk-ing your puppy on her regular lead or Flexi-Lead:

Figure 14-6:
Using the Down command with an uncoopera-tive puppy in puberty.

Photo by Sarah Hodgson.

1. **Stop in your tracks as you command "Wait."**

2. **Pull back on the leash if your pup doesn't stop with you.**

3. **Release with "Okay."**

No Sir or Ma'am

You worked on this correction in previous sections. When your puppy understands that when you say "No Sir" you mean it, begin to practice this command outside with dogs, bikers, and other temptations passing by. Tug the leash sharply as you say "No Sir" in your sternest correction tone.

Trying Teen Lessons: 9 to 12 Months

During the preceding last stage (puppy puberty), I discourage all but the mildest corrective techniques during training. Now that your dog has become a teen, however, he's emotionally ready to learn that not everything he does pleases you. Your dog is only acting naturally when he tests your flexibility on the commands he's learned. He wonders if perhaps the Sit in front of company means something *juuuuust* a little different from the Sit in front of you.

In the previous stages you labored over the teaching process. You showed your dog exactly what each command meant. Now he knows. Every time he doesn't respond or responds in *his* fashion, he's questioning you. If you repeat yourself or position him, he'll never learn to respond on his own. Like teaching a child to tie shoelaces, eventually it must be done independently.

To develop the all-important canine consciousness, you must do two things:

✔ Decide what you want when you give a command.

✔ Follow through. If your expectations are unclear, your puppy's reaction will be, too.

When practicing your commands, avoid repeating yourself or positioning your dog. If he doesn't respond, snap the leash as firmly as required and say "No" in a corrective tone. If he still doesn't respond, review your tone (stern enough?) and make adjustments as needed. If your dog still ignores you, position him without praise.

If your dog pivots out of position when you stop in Heel, inches forward on the Stay commands, or moves in front of you during stationary commands, he's testing you. If you position him sweetly, you're actually giving him attention for his defiance. In these situations, snap the leash firmly as you say "No" and position him by maneuvering him into place with the leash. This may take several tries and a temper tantrum from your beloved pet, but if you let the structure slide, you'll never have a reliable off-leash dog. (Refer to Chapter 17 for info on training off the leash.)

Chapter 15

Dealing with Socially Unacceptable Behavior

*W*hat's socially unacceptable canine behavior? Aggression for one. Although it's a normal form of canine communication, similar to our anger, it's not cool. Other socially unacceptable behaviors include eating stool, ingesting socks, digging to China, and excited/submissive sprinkling. These transgressions have a common theme: Puppies do these things when they're anxious. Some puppies have anxiety due to lack of structure, and some are just a bit more obsessive-compulsive. This chapter identifies these problems and tells you how to help.

Coping with Aggression

The word *aggression* strikes fear into the heart of dog owners. Yes, the occasional growl is a frightening sight but not as uncommon as most people think. Even dogs get frustrated and defensive.

Remember, a puppy is not a member of the human species, able to articulate angry feelings through words. Puppies are dogs and dogs communicate through vocal tones, eye contact, and body language. What we communicate in words, some dogs communicate through aggression. How you cope and re-direct this behavior determines how your puppy copes with these feelings as he grows into doghood.

Aggression is a serious topic. If you're having a problem, get help. Seek a well-known and respected animal behaviorist or trainer in your area. Your veterinarian may be able to help you find one. My recommendations are just that, recommendations. Do not follow them if you are unsure. Aggression, if approached incorrectly or with caution or fear, can result in a serious bite.

If your puppy has bitten, no one can guarantee you that he won't do it again. Your effort to remedy the problem can only help, however, and remedying the problem is your only option other than euthanasia. Passing an aggressive puppy onto another home or into a shelter is irresponsible. You'd be responsible if he bit someone or maimed a child. So get help if you need it.

Determining how serious the problem is

To determine how serious the aggressive behavior is, you need to list these factors:

Breed: Is your puppy a spatial or protective breed (for example, a Terrier, Nordic, or Guarding dog)? These breeds have a greater propensity towards aggression. Seeing a 17-week-old Golden Retriever, known for its passive nature, growling over its dish is more alarming than seeing a protective dog growl over its possessions. Neither should growl, but a growling Golden indicates that you may have a deeper problem that just a breed-inherent trait. Know your breed, understand its natural inclinations, and work through them at the earliest age possible.

Research your breed. Understand your puppy's personality. An ounce of foresight can give you a pound of prevention.

Age: A puppy under 20 weeks should not show any sign of serious aggression. An occasional play growl is common, but if you witness any hard stares and belly growling, you may have a serious problem on your hands. Seek out a professional. Beyond 20 weeks, aggression usually coincides with the release of adult hormones. If this is the case, try not to be too alarmed. This chapter can help you understand the problem, although if you witness any hard stares and belly growling, you may have a serious problem on your hands. Seek out a professional and call the breeder, if applicable, immediately.

Temperament: Aggression is most commonly seen in puppies that are head strong and bold. These guys determine early whether you're giving direction or taking it. If you're not considered "leadership worthy," then your puppy takes charge. As he grows, he becomes more mindful of sounds and stimulation and may often show aggression in order to keep "his" group under tight surveillance. Of course, passive dogs can show a similar type of aggression. If you pamper a passive, fearful dog, she too will assume the leadership role (by default) and be cautious with any slight changes in her environment.

Early play patterns: If you bring your puppy up on a play diet of rough wrestling and tug-of-war, he often becomes aggressive during adolescence. These challenge games set the stage for larger confrontations, which the puppy may not back off from just because you issue the word "No."

Corrective techniques: If a young puppy is subject to heavy-handed corrections early in its life, it learns self-control through fear, not through understanding. For example, if you slap your puppy for grabbing a sock, it may grab the sock less when it's with you, but it will be more protective of the sock once it's obtained (Prize Envy). Read the section "Preventing aggression" to avoid some of these pitfalls.

If you have a dog that shows aggression, keep him off your bed. This *is* a big deal. An aggressive dog thinks it's his duty to protect or keep you in line. The first step in resolving this issue is to take over the high sleeping grounds. Station (leash) your dog to your dresser if you must, but no bed for now.

Preventing aggression

There a different types of aggression. Understanding what may be developing enables you to react appropriately. This section identifies the various types of aggression and gives prevention advice.

If you meet up with an aggressive dog, do not run away. (Think about it: Have you ever seen a dog attack a post?) If you must approach the dog, move in sideways. Approaching from the front equals a challenge. You can extend a stick to distract the dog from your body.

The following descriptions and suggestions do not take the place of professional attention.

Dominant aggression

Do you have a dominant pup under your roof — who steals clothing for fun, barks for attention, leans against you in new environments or around strangers, or successfully solicits attention whenever the mood strikes? Constant attention and dedication to his every need puts you at servant status. When you assert yourself, he has no other choice than to remind you to get back in line. To regain control, for starters:

✔ Use the Excuse Me command when your puppy gets in your way. This is the most passive way to communicate your leadership. (Chapter 14 covers Excuse Me and other training commands.)

✔ Ignore all his attempts to get your attention, including but not limited to barking, pawing, head butting, and whining.

✔ Have a command lesson two to five times a day for three minutes. Go through all the commands he knows. If he's growling, skip the Down command until you get professional help.

✔ If your puppy will obey the Down command, repeat it throughout the day, positioning your dog rather than repeating yourself.

✔ Avoid stare downs unless you initiate them, in which case make sure your dog breaks eye contact first.

✔ Regulate the feeding to twice a day. Do not give food rewards or treats until your aggression problems are history.

✔ Once a day, enforce a 30-minute quiet time (either by stationing or anchoring) without toys or attention.

If your puppy growls during any of these efforts, such as getting him to move out of your way, don't push it. Stop everything until you get professional help. Your problem is serious.

Spatial aggression (object guarding)

A dog who shows aggression while eating, sleeping, grooming, or being medicated by a family member, stranger, or other dog professional (veterinarian or groomer) is showing spatial aggression. Spatial aggression is usually tied in with dominant, territorial, or psychotic aggression.

If you see this type of behavior, don't freak out, hit your puppy, or scream. These reactions only reinforce his defensive notion that you've come to steal his prize. To help your pup accept you as less threatening, follow these steps, which use the food dish as an example:

1. **Do not make a power struggle out of the feeding ritual.**

2. **Shake a plastic cup with some small dog biscuits (essentially, a treat cup) and reward your puppy with one; keep doing this until your puppy connects the sound with a reward.**

3. **Approach your puppy once a day with the treat cup while he is eating a meal; if he growls as you approach him during a meal, stop and toss him a few treats before you leave.**

4. **Repeat Step 3 until you can stand over him and drop treats into his bowl.**

5. **At this point, approach his bowl speaking happy praises but *without* shaking the cup. When you get to his side, toss a treat into the bowl and leave.**

6. Next, try kneeling down as you shake the cup and toss a treat into his bowl.

7. When you kneel and toss a treat into his bowl without tension, try placing the treat into his bowl with your hand.

8. After you offer your puppy a handful of treats, try stirring the kibble with your hand. If you're successful, continue this once every other day for a week.

9. Next, after offering a handful of treats, try lifting the bowl. Give it back immediately and leave. Repeat once a month only.

10. Repeat this entire process for prized objects, like bones or squeak toys.

Dogs notice fear. If you're afraid, your puppy knows it and will be suspicious. Call a professional immediately.

I cannot guarantee you will not get bitten in the process. Be your own judge; proceed as your puppy is comfortable and seek help if you need to.

Territorial aggression

Dogs who act aggressively when strangers approach their homes are territorial. This problem is encouraged by the following:

✔ When delivery people approach and leave the home territory, the puppy thinks that he drove them away, and his aggression is reinforced.

✔ When the owners are home and react to a territorial response by yelling or physical handling, the dog perceives their heightened response as backup. Job well done.

✔ When a dog reacts aggressively in a car or on a tie out, he is warning all intruders to stay away. Because they do, he considers himself victorious, and his territorial aggression is reinforced.

✔ When dogs are isolated during greetings or visits, they may develop *Frustrated Territorial Aggression (FTA)*. FTA is not a good thing. In a normal group of dogs, the leader permits or denies entry to a visitor, who is then "sniffed out" by the rest of the pack. Isolation frustrates this normal process and encourages a more aggressive response the next time the doorbell rings.

To prevent territorial aggression, assert yourself by keeping your puppy off the furniture and through a regimented training program, including the following commands:

✔ **Wait:** through thresholds and doors

✔ **Heel:** on walks once your puppy has mastered the learning phase

✔ **Sit:** for all greetings — inside the house and out

Also discourage all marking behavior. (Your puppy should eliminate in one area.)

If things are already out of hand, purchase a chin lead (see Chapter 5) and lead or station your puppy during arrivals. This collar reduces the negative restraint around the neck and places the puppy's body in a submissive posture.

Handling an aggressive dog on a chain collar is like holding an angry man's arms behind his back. It creates fury. Using a chin lead reduces this tension and communicates structure and discipline passively.

To make associations to visitors more positive, try these things:

- ✔ Use a treat cup or peanut butter jar to help your puppy associate outsiders with a positive reward.

  Peanut butter jar? Yes, peanut butter. Most dogs love it. Get them their own little jar and tape a bell to it to help them associate a special sound. When people come in, encourage them to offer the jar to your puppy *after* he has settled down.

- ✔ Eliminate all yelling and verbose or physical corrections because they add more negative energy to an already tense situation. To calm your puppy, you must set the example.

If your puppy is threatening anyone, get help immediately. A territorial dog is a dangerous dog.

While guard and herd dogs are more commonly known for this type of aggression (again detectable in puppyhood), you can find this kind of aggression in any breed.

Protective aggression

Does your puppy feel responsible for you? Even outside of his territory, does he react aggressively if anyone approaches? If your pup's acting like your guard wherever you go, you have a serious identity crisis to deal with. He thinks it's his job to protect you. You must let your puppy know you're the boss:

- ✔ **Buy a chin lead.** Both you and your puppy need training. You must learn how to assert dominance over your puppy.

- ✔ **Train your puppy.** Keep him behind you at all thresholds and when meeting new people.

- ✔ **Call a professional if you need help.**

It is not uncommon for dogs to develop this sort of relationship with a young child or a passive, inexperienced owner. The dog perceives the owner — man, woman, or child — as weak and in need of protection.

Predatory aggression

Predatory aggression is another instinctive behavior from times when dogs were wolves and hunted for survival. Most dogs still possess a chasing instinct. Although we have suppressed the drive to kill in most breeds, some (Nordic breeds and Terriers especially) instinctively chase and, in some instances, kill small game.

If you have a chaser on your hands, you have your hands full. Their instincts are strong. Focused play gives them an outlet, but you need to be present with other animals or children to discourage interactive chasing rituals. (For focused predatory games, refer to Chapter 28.)

Fear-induced aggression

Every litter has its shy puppies — mama's boys or girls who depend on her wisdom for safety. In human homes, these dogs continue to be needy. Their timidity, which surfaces in new situations, may turn into overwhelming fear if you don't give them proper direction and support. A puppy in this situation may react aggressively during adolescence.

Although shyness is a temperamental trait, this behavior also has a learned element: Soothing a frightened puppy doesn't alleviate the fear; it reinforces it.

If your puppy shows the early signs of fear with company (flight, approach-avoid, or protective barking from behind your legs or furniture), you need to be understanding and patient. You cannot correct a fearful puppy; doing so only increases his fear. You can't soothe him either, because your attention just reinforces this behavior.

A large part of the problem is that the puppy feels no one — not even you — has control of the situation. To help prevent this problem, you must assert yourself as the one who's calm, in control, and in charge of the situation. Here are some extra tips:

✔ Keep your puppy on lead when you expect company. Hold your puppy's lead while acting confidently in new situations.

✔ Encourage everyone to ignore your puppy until he approaches.

  When strangers or caring professionals back away from a threatening dog, the dog gets the message that aggression works.

✔ Use your treat cup or peanut butter jar to encourage a more positive association to situations.

When seeking a professional, find one who uses a soft and positive approach. Threatening this type of dog often creates more fear.

Dog-to-dog aggression

Aggression between dogs occurs when they perceive their territories as overlapping (which can happen anywhere because some dogs think that their territory is very extensive) or when there is a hierarchical struggle in a multi-dog household. This type of aggression is often exaggerated by well-meaning owners who scream or pull back when their puppy shows aggression. Such a reaction only adds to the tension.

Outside disputes

This problem usually results from lack of early socialization. If you have this problem, you must assess how serious it is. A class might be the perfect solution. You must learn to assert yourself and act like a dominant leader when you meet another dog.

The next time around, enroll in a puppy class immediately. In my Puppy Kindergarten classes, I allow ten minutes of off-lead play, which lets the puppies socialize with each other and with people.

Inside disputes

Whenever a home has two or more dogs, the dogs develop a hierarchical relationship. The leader is the one pushing the other dog out of the way when attention is offered and dominating over toys or food. In addition, your leader is the one racing to be out the door first.

Disputes arise when you undermine their organization by paying more attention to the underdog. The lead dog is frustrated and the underdog is confused. To calm things down, pay more attention to the Top Dog. Feed, greet, and play with him first and most. Spend time training him. The other dog will follow. If they fight, praise the Top Dog and ignore the other. I know it sounds cruel, and it's hard (I had to do it), but trust me. It works. If you're having difficulty, bring in a professional.

Psychotic aggression

I very rarely come across a psychotic dog or puppy, but they do exist. Most, although not all, dogs with this problem are the result of poor puppy-mill type breeding. Psychotic aggression is identified by erratic or fearful aggression responses in very atypical situations, and these traits are seen at a very young age. Following are the two categories of psychotic aggression:

- ✔ **Erratic viciousness:** At unpredictable intervals, this puppy growls fiercely from his belly. It may happen when his owner passes his food bowl, approaches when he's chewing a toy, or even walks by him. At other times, the dog is perfectly sweet — a "Jekyll and Hyde" personality.

- ✔ **Fear biters:** This puppy shows dramatic fear in or a startled bite response to non-threatening situations like turning a page of the newspaper or the movement of an arm. They can act extremely confused or threatened when strangers approach.

Many well-educated dog people use the term "fear biter" incorrectly. There is a big difference in a dog/puppy that bites out of fear and a fear biter. Don't automatically assume the worst if someone labels your dog with this term.

Don't panic if your puppy occasionally growls at you or barks at the mailman. A lot of puppies growl when protecting a food dish or toy, and the guarding instinct is strong in many breeds. These are behavioral problems that you can cure or control with proper training. Even many biters can be rehabilitated. The situations I'm speaking of involve *severe* aggression — bared teeth, hard eyes, a growl that begins in the belly, and a bite response you'd expect from a trained police dog. These personality disturbances are seen very early, usually by four months of age.

This type of aggression is both frightening and tragic because nothing can be done to alter the dogs' development. Their fate has been sealed by irresponsible, greedy people. If you suspect that your puppy might have either of these abnormalities, speak to your breeder and veterinarian immediately and call a specialist to analyze the situation. These puppies must be euthanized. In my career, I've seen only six cases, and all were purchased from unknown or suspicious breeders.

Getting Control of the Digging

Digging is often a puppy's favorite pastime — especially for puppies in the Terrier, Sporting, and Nordic Groups. Digging is also a great way to alleviate boredom, a reaction to stress (a move, a new baby, repair people in the home — see Chapter 26), or a cry for company, especially with the 8–11 month crowd.

All puppies go through a phase when they can't stand being alone. They fuss, and fussy pups dig. Unfortunately, you cannot teach your puppy not to dig. Instead, you must give him a place that's all his own. Here are some suggestions:

- Pick one area where your puppy can dig to his heart's content, around your house or in a park if you live in an apartment or a condo.
- Bring toys and treats to hide when you begin to dig. And don't forget the garden gloves.
- Go to the area with your puppy each day, instructing "Go dig!"
- Have a dig-fest. Dig with your puppy and cheer him on.
- If you catch your puppy digging somewhere he shouldn't be, correct him with "No!" and then tell him (escorting him to the right spot, if necessary), "Go dig!"

Spraying your puppy with a hose or setting mouse traps is cruel, and I don't encourage it. Putting the dirt back into the hole is confusing — now you're digging in the same spot, too.

Are you a gardener? Well, if you let your puppy watch, guess what? Monkey see, monkey do. Garden alone. Place your puppy indoors when you garden. It's just too tempting after seeing you dig in one area all day. Dig together in a more acceptable spot.

Most puppies dig if you leave them outside while you're home. They love to dig while you watch; it's a sure-fire attention-getter. Try to structure the indoor environment so that he can be in the house when you're around.

Nipping the Garbage Grabbing in the Bud

Garbage grabbing is the perfect eye catcher. It's very rewarding — and very annoying. Prevention is the best way to solve this problem: Keep a lid on your garbage and keep it locked away under the cabinets. No table treats before or after your meal. I know, the eyes are pleading and the scraps will go to waste, but if your puppy can have it in his bowl, he'll want it in the trash, too.

If your puppy is still rummaging around, try practicing one of the following setups:

- **Ten-foot line.** Place your pup on a drag lead (see Chapter 5) and toss something irresistible into the trash. The second he starts to show interest, step on the line and shout "No!" Rush up to the garbage can and kick and scream at it. Do not yell or look at your puppy. Go back to whatever you were pretending to do and repeat the process from the top. If your puppy ignores the temptation, give him a hug.

- **Sound off.** If your puppy is sound-sensitive, construct a *pyramid of penny cans*. Place ten pennies each in six cans and arrange the cans with three on the bottom, two in the middle, and one on top. Tie a string to the middle can on the bottom row and either attach it to the can or hold it. When your puppy shows interest in the trash, pull the string and shout "No!" at the can.

- **Balloon pop.** The last thing to try is the *balloon pop*. Blow up a few balloons and pop them one at a time with a pin with your puppy present. As each one pops, act afraid yourself. Don't pay any attention to your puppy; trust me, he'll be watching. Then tape the balloons to the edge of the garbage can and leave them there a couple of weeks.

Is your puppy an angel when you're in the room but crafty when you leave? Smart puppy. Your timing is probably off. If you're correcting him after he's stolen something, he considers your correction as Prize Envy and figures he'll take the item he wants when you're not around to challenge him for it. Try any of the following approaches:

- Set up a bitter-tasting lure by soaking a paper towel in Tabasco sauce and putting it in the trash. Repeat this trick until he loses interest in the trash.

- Set up the penny-can pyramid and booby trap him when you've left the room.

- Set up a mirror so that you can keep your eye on the garbage can even when you're not physically present. When you see your puppy approach the can, storm in, say "No, Sir!" and yell at the can.

Stopping the Swallowing of Socks (And Other Inedibles)

Chewing sticks, rocks, and socks is perfectly normal. Eating them, however, isn't. If your puppy is into swallowing everything in sight or has a hard time passing up the kid's underwear or shoes, you are dealing with obsessive-compulsive behavior.

I call it Prize Envy. When your puppy grabs something he shouldn't, you think, "Bad dog, give it back!" Your puppy, however, sees your body language from a puppy's perspective. He thinks you're racing forward to steal what he's found. If he wants to keep it, he had better split or gulp it — whatever "it" is. Some split. Others gulp. To stop this behavior permanently, you may need to seek professional help. Until then, follow these guidelines:

- Do not chase angrily after your puppy for anything.

- Place favorite treats in small party cups and distribute them around the house. If your puppy picks up something he shouldn't, grab a treat cup and encourage him to come to you and exchange the object for a treat.

- If you both notice something tempting on the ground, don't dive for it. Remember, you're setting the example. Try to distract your puppy and then remove the object calmly.

- Pick up around the house. If there's nothing to steal, there's nothing to swallow.

If you own a puppy with this problem, you have to keep a close eye on him. If you think your puppy has eaten something non-digestible, call your veterinarian immediately. These items can block the intestine and, if left untreated, kill your puppy.

Getting Through Separation Anxiety

Separation. Puppies hate it. If they had their way, they'd follow you to the ends of the Earth. But, alas, they can't. Puppies suffering from separation anxiety may chew destructively, soil the house, bark excessively, or act out other destructive behaviors. They don't do these things out of spite; puppies can't think that way. What you're seeing is anxiety, canine style. A puppy who exhibits this problem falls into one of two categories – the Passive Pup or the Top Dog (see Chapter 4).

Separation anxiety demands a multi-approach solution that starts with training. Training gives the Passive Pup a sense of identity and the reassurance that a competent leader is on the job. For the dominant Top Dog puppy, training places him in a subordinate, carefree pack position. If you need help training, get it. In the meantime, follow these ground rules:

✔ Never correct your puppy after the fact. Never. Corrections are not connected to the destruction; they're connected to your arrival, which makes your puppy more anxious the next time you leave.

✔ Avoid theatrical hellos and good-byes. Lavishing your puppy with kisses, biscuits, and drawn-out declarations of devotion do not reassure him. They stress him out.

✔ Leave a radio playing classical music to cover unfamiliar sounds.

✔ Place your puppy in a dimly lit area to encourage sleep.

✔ Leave a favorite chew toy. Rub it between your palms for scent.

If you're leaving for over six hours, try to find someone to walk your puppy. If necessary, proof the house from destruction or buy an indoor pen (see Chapter 5). Indoor pens fold nicely to store when you're home and can be expanded before you leave to give your puppy space when you're gone for extended periods. Dogs get cramped if left in small kennels for longer than six hours and can develop Hyper Isolation Anxiety.

When you're home, temporarily decrease the attention you give your puppy by 50 percent. Do not give in to "pet me" solicitations. Although petting him when he asks may relieve your feelings of guilt, it just makes your leaving him alone all day harder for him. Going from lots of attention to no attention is too sharp a contrast. When he's alone, your puppy longs for companionship. Because watching the soaps or chewing fingernails isn't an option, he may settle for devouring your couch.

If possible, buy a kitten for your pup. Kittens are super companions, and they're great company for puppies if raised with them. Getting another dog is also an option, although I recommend that you wait until you've resolved this problem with this dog before you add another one to the mix.

Also try setting up practice departures:

1. **Station your puppy in a familiar spot.**

2. **Instruct "Wait" and leave the room for 15 seconds.**

3. **Return and ignore him until he's calm; then praise him lovingly.**

4. **Repeat this ten times or until he stays calm.**

Continue these short separations until he shows no anxiety. Then double the separation time and repeat the procedure. Continue doubling the departure time until you're able to leave the room for 30 minutes.

Once your puppy's comfortable at 30 minutes, go back to short separations but this time leave the house. Gradually work your way up to 30 minutes out of the house. Start over, this time getting into and starting your car. With patience, you'll be able to build his confidence and leave him for longer and longer periods of time.

There are USDA-approved drugs that help alleviate separation anxiety. If you need more remedial help, make an appointment to talk to your veterinarian. (And if you seek help, make sure you avoid trainers who encourage discipline.)

Dealing with a Tinkler

Do you have a tinkler? The most frequent question I've been asked is, "Do they grow out of it?" Well, yes and no. Yes, if you handle yourself properly; no if you don't. Tinkling isn't a conscious thing. Puppies do it because they are over-excited or anxious. Discipline only makes the problem worse.

When you come in, ignore your pup until she's completely calm. Next, extend a jar of peanut butter or shake a cup of biscuits as you pet her. Divert her mind. Kneel down to pet her rather than leaning over.

If your puppy is timid around certain people, have everyone (including yourself) ignore her. When you soothe her, it reinforces the fear. When your puppy approaches the person she's timid around, offer her treats. Use a shake cup or peanut butter jar. When she is calm, have guests kneel and pet her chest.

If your puppy piddles during greetings or play sessions, ignore her or stop the play until she has better bladder control.

Refocusing the Stool Swallower (Disgusto, I Know)

This delightful habit comes in two varieties: other creatures' stool and their own stool. Believe it or not, eating stool — theirs or someone else's — is a fairly common behavior.

Other creatures' stools

Stool from other creatures is actually quite a delicacy to your puppy. Deer duds, litter logs, goose goblets — they're all candies to suit your puppy's delight. Most dogs outgrow this behavior if you feed them a balanced meal twice a day and ignore their stool fetish.

Try to refocus your puppy on a favorite activity. If you're suffering from litter-box blues, put the litter box in an inaccessible area, get a litter box with a lid, or correct the box as outlined in section "Nipping the Garbage Grabbing in the Bud." There's only one thing to be happy about in this situation — be happy you're not a dog.

Puppy's own stools

Though eating stool is probably the most grotesque thing you could ever imagine, in dogland, it's just a handy way to keep the den clean. When your puppy was much younger, he watched his mother do it, and when he sees you cleaning up after him, he thinks — well, you get the picture. To halt this habit:

✔ Never clean up messes in front of your pup.

✔ Don't correct your puppy when he shows interest in his stool. If you fuss, he'll gulp.

✔ If your puppy shows interest, refocus him on a favorite game. "Get your ball!"

✔ Ask your veterinarian to give you a food additive that makes his feces distasteful. I know, what could be more distasteful than dog poop? But such things do exist.

✔ After your puppy finishes eliminating, spray the pile with something distasteful, like Bitter Apple, Tabasco sauce, or vinegar.

Giving a Timid Pup Some Confidence

Timid puppies look so pitiful. Like kids, you want to soothe them. But puppies are not kids; they think your soothing is a sign of *your* fear. Now you're both afraid. That's a big problem.

To help your puppy, you must act confident when she is afraid. You're the leader. Stand up straight. Relax your shoulders. Breathe deep. Smile. Whether the fearful item is a bag blowing in the wind, a sharp noise (like thunder), or an uncommon face, act calm, face the feared object, and ignore your puppy until she starts to act more like you.

If your puppy shows aggression when she's fearful, call a professional and do not knowingly put her in "threatening situations."

Dealing with a thunder-struck pup

Here's a list of do's and don'ts when you want to handle a puppy's fear of thunder. The don'ts first: Don't coddle your puppy. Don't permit him to hide between the sheets or climb onto the couch. Don't isolate him. All these things make the fear worse. Depending on how bad your situation is, *do* try one or all of these approaches:

✔ Turn on some classical music and play it loud.

✔ Lead your puppy on his Teaching Lead while you act completely calm. Set the example.

Show him how to cope with the situation. Let your puppy have his fears; just don't respond to them. When he calms down, pet him lovingly.

✔ Find (or make) a thunderstorm tape recording. Play it on low volume while you play your puppy's favorite game with him. Slowly increase the volume.

✔ Ask your veterinarian for tranquilizers to soothe your puppy before a storm.

Chapter 16

Me Thinks I Need Some Help!

In This Chapter

▶ How to handle nonprofessional advice

▶ What to look for in a puppy trainer

▶ Do-it-yourself training methods: books and videos

▶ The pros and cons of boarding school

▶ What a behaviorist focuses on

Finding the right help for training, if you need it, is essential. Training is a joint effort for you and your puppy. My clients would be the first to tell you that training is a blend of the right actions — from how you hold the leash to your tone of voice to the way you stand — that helps your puppy learn what you are trying to teach. When I train people to work with their puppies, I harp on the little things until my students do them instinctively. If my harping doesn't come through in the pages of this book clearly enough, get help — the right help, as described in this chapter.

Puh-leez Don't Listen to Neighbor Bob

It's funny, actually. As soon as people know you have a dog, they become experts. Promise yourself and your dog one thing: No matter what these self-proclaimed experts say, no matter how convincing they say it, and regardless of how many parlor tricks their dogs know, *don't try out their methods*. Each puppy is different, and what works for one may not be appropriate for another. Plus, the neighbor may be pulling advice out of thin air, without having done any reading on puppy training.

How about Vets, Groomers, and Pet Stores?

If you ask for training advice from a vet, groomer, or pet store owner, you may get an off-the-cuff, routine answer but not one that is tailored for your individual situation or dog. Instead of asking these other professionals for training tips and solutions, ask where you might find a reputable trainer or class in your area.

Free advice never pays. If you try a little of this and a little of that, guess who's going to suffer? You'll make your poor puppy crazy.

Finding the Right Puppy Trainer

Finding a good trainer — one who is well-rounded in his or her knowledge of dog behavior — can be a real lifesaver. Many clients call me at their wit's end, and I discover a wonderful puppy who's just dying to come out. In my experience, it's usually the owner who's confused. So I train the owner, and the puppy behaves. Training is often just as simple as that. If you need help training your pup, scout out professionals in your area to get some good leads and call today. You and your dog will be glad you did. The following sections look at a few of the training options that are available to you.

The Association for Pet Dog Trainers can provide a list of trainers in your area. You can contact the association at the following address:

APDT
P.O. Box 954
Benicia, CA 94510
www.APDT.COM.com

A personal trainer

I'm a personal dog trainer. I train more than dogs, though; I train people. When looking for a personal trainer, you're looking for someone to train you (as well as your dog). Following are some of *my* training ethics, which I recommend you look for in any personal trainer:

- Put yourself in your client's shoes.

- Know that the client is trying to do the right thing.

- Understand the dog's personality and listen to what the dog is trying to communicate with his behavior.

✔ Know when you can't help. Be honest with your client.

✔ Help your client understand why the dog is behaving inappropriately. Help the client think for his dog.

✔ Teach the client Doglish so he can communicate with his dog. (Turn to Chapter 8 for info on speaking Doglish.)

✔ Help the client structure his home.

✔ Teach the client patience, tolerance, understanding, and sympathy. After all, he loves his dog.

Not all trainers are in this profession because they love dogs first and foremost. Some of them are in it for the money. Beware.

A group trainer

Group training class can be a real blast. It can also be a dog owner's worst nightmare. So what's the deciding factor? (No, it's not your puppy — no matter how badly behaved he is around other dogs.) It's the instructor. When exploring different classes, talk to the instructor and get a feel for his/her style of training. Here are some questions you can ask:

✔ **How many dogs are in the class? Are the classes divided by age or class levels?** The class size should be limited (I limit mine to eight) and must be divided by age and experience. I offer Puppy Kindergarten classes for dogs under six months, Grade School for inexperienced pupils, and High School and College for advanced students.

✔ **Do you have a favorite breed of dog or do you have experience with a wide variety of breeds?** The answer can indicate a strong bias on the part of the instructor. Make sure your instructor is not breed-biased. Your puppy should be seen as a unique and special personality, not a stereotype. Your instructor should be versed in breed-specific tendencies, however, and help you understand your puppy's individual character.

✔ **What do you teach in class?** Basic commands are necessary: Heel, Sit-Stay, Come, and Down. Does the instructor spend time explaining how to build these commands in your life?

✔ **Are the classes indoors or outside?** Having access to both environments is best.

✔ **Are behavior problems discussed?** Bad behavior is often what encourages many people to train their dogs. The instructor should be as comfortable talking about problem behavior as he/she is with command training.

✔ **Do you have a make-up policy?** If not, can you speak to the instructor to find out what you've missed?

✔ **Is family participation encouraged? Can the kids come?** The instructor should help you understand how your puppy relates to your entire family and encourage them to participate in the training.

Using Books and Videos

Are you a do-it-yourself person? I'm all for it as long as you follow the right advice. Obviously, since you're reading this book, you have some faith in my methods, but not everyone suggests a positive approach to training. Be selective when choosing your reading material and call for some help if matters don't improve. You only train your puppy once, so do it right.

Going the Boarding School Route

Sending your dog off for training is an option, but it's not one I recommend. It does have its pros and cons, though.

Some pros include

✔ Your puppy's not around.

✔ You won't be part of your puppy's education.

✔ Your problems are solved — temporarily perhaps, but you'll have some immediate gratification.

✔ If you follow through, your puppy will respond to the training.

✔ Certain problems may disappear.

Cons include

✔ Your puppy's not around.

✔ You won't be part of your puppy's education.

✔ It's expensive.

✔ Problems can resurface or may get worse because of the structure provided in the training environment.

✔ Training is quickly forgotten if you don't follow through.

If you're considering this route, visit the facility first and remember that your dog isn't a machine. Sending him off to school isn't like dropping off the car for a tune-up. You must follow through.

Which is better — private or group training?

People often ask me what the best way to train is, group or private? Honestly, the best training is a combination of the two. A private consultation lets me see how things go on a day-to-day basis. Class gives me the opportunity to follow up on that session while the puppy learns around distractions.

Using a Behaviorist

A *behaviorist* is someone who teaches dogs and has a degree in veterinary medicine. Behaviorists focus less on dog training and more on problem-solving. If you seek out a behaviorist, be selective. They're very costly and may not be any more effective in modifying your dog's behavior than a good trainer who's done her homework.

Many behaviorists use drug therapy to modify dog behavior. Though I'm not an advocate of this, in some cases, drug therapy can be effective.

There is no law in the U.S. that prevents an unqualified, uneducated person to appropriate the term "behaviorist." Check to ensure that a person qualifying him- or herself as a behaviorist has a doctorate of veterinarian medicine.

Part V
Behaving in the Big League

In this part . . .

You've conquered basic training, and you're ready for the big league. In this part, you find out about off-lead training, taking your puppy out in public, and for the truly adventurous, various sporting events that you and your puppy can do together.

Chapter 17

Training Off the Leash

*N*o one can underestimate the pleasures of a well-trained dog. In Chapter 14, I cover leash-training techniques; please master those exercises before you begin the exercises described in this chapter.

To have off-lead control, you must earn it. Remember, dogs are drawn to leadership; act self-assured and confident (even if you don't feel it) so your dog will want to trust your judgment.

Getting Mentally Prepared

As you work toward off-lead control, don't get too bold. When you work off lead, you have less control. Your puppy has a choice: come or not. If he doesn't want to come and he's free to run, you may be standing there helpless. Off-lead work means constantly reading and re-reading your puppy and being aware that your puppy is reading you. To have control, you must look like a leader; be confident and self-assured so that your dog can trust your judgment. To further your mental preparation, keep these three steps in mind:

✔ **Stay cool.** Frustration makes you look weak. As you work toward off-lead control, your puppy may act confused and unresponsive. The reason is that guidance factor of the command sequence is gone. You used to give the command and guide her with the lead. Now you don't, and it feels awkward to her. Whatever her reaction, stay cool. Any corrections add to her confusion. Jazz up your body language and use some pep talks to encourage her toward you.

✔ **Stay focused.** Eye contact communicates control. Your puppy should be watching you. If the reverse is true, you're the follower. To avoid this, make sure you work in a confined area or on a long line so that you can ignore your dog when she disobeys. If you're near your house, walk inside. A graceful retreat is not a failure.

✔ **Step back.** Your puppy is responding off-lead beautifully . . . until someone rings the bell, a chipmunk runs across the drive, or another dog's around. Then everything's out the window, and you're back to being ignored. Let me tell you a secret: Off-lead control takes time. If your puppy is good but still having trouble in a stimulated situation, review on-lead exercises in distracting situations (see Chapter 14). Using a lead helps control the situation and at the same time conditions more appropriate behavior.

Using the Right Equipment

As you work toward off-leash obedience, you'll be practicing exercises that extend your control to farther and farther distances. Before you start, round up these items:

✔ **Flexi-Lead:** This retractable leash is invaluable for advanced work. The longer, the better. (Turn to Chapter 5 for more info on the Flexi-Lead.)

✔ **Indoor drag lead:** A 4–6 foot light leash worn around the house.

✔ **Short lead:** This lead should be long enough to grab but short enough not to distract your dog (8 inches is a common length).

✔ **Tree line:** Attach a 20-foot lead to a tree. You use this stationed area to practice distance Stay commands. You can use a simple canvas lead, or you can make your own out of a clothesline attached to a dog clip. You use the tree line for distance control with Wait, Heel, Down, and Come commands.

✔ **Long line:** Purchase a 30–50 foot canvas lead or use a clothesline.

Attach all lines to your puppy's buckle collar, not her training (choke) collar.

Off-lead puppies aren't created overnight. Training is a step-by-step process. You'll be using your new equipment to increase your puppy's focus but don't get itchy fingers. Just because she behaves well on her Flexi-Lead one day doesn't mean she's ready for an off-lead romp the next. Take your time. Although I explain how to train with each piece of equipment separately, use them interchangeably in your training exercises.

The Flexi-Lead

This leash is a great tool for distance training. It allows freedom to explore, while still leaving you in complete control. As a training tool, you can use it informally during walks to reinforce the following commands:

✓ *Name:* Call out your puppy's name enthusiastically: "Daisy!" If she looks at you, praise her. That's all that's required. Just a glance. If she ignores you, snap the leash, say "No," and then praise her once you have her attention.

✓ **Wait:** Begin to command your puppy to stop 3 feet in front of you with this command. If your dog continues forward, snap the leash and say "No, Wait." Increase your distance to 6 feet, 8 feet, 12 feet, 16 feet, and 26 feet in front of you.

✓ **Sit-Stay:** Use the Flexi-Lead to increase your distance control (see Figure 17-1). Increase your distance incrementally. (To accustom your puppy to the pull of the Flexi-Lead, pivot in front of her and slide the leash out a few times.)

✓ **Heel:** Use this command to call your puppy back to your side. Call out her name and then command "Heel" as you slap your leg. Praise your puppy as she responds; then walk a short distance before you stop to release her.

✓ **No:** Whenever your puppy's focusing on something she shouldn't be, snap the leash and say "No!" Immediately refocus her attention with a toy, stick, or command.

Figure 17-1:
Using the Flexi-Lead to work on distance control.

Photo by Sarah Hodgson.

An indoor drag lead

Use an indoor drag lead (made from a lightweight puppy lead or rope, between 4–6 feet long) to keep an eye on your dog in the house. Throughout the day, stand by the line and give a command (Sit, Down, Wait, or Come). If she looks confused, step on the line and praise her anyway as you help her into position. For example, if you command "Down," and she gives you a blank stare, praise her as you guide her into position. Your understanding will help her overcome her off-lead confusion.

If your puppy gives you some defiant canine back talk (a bark or dodge), step on the lead, snap it firmly as you say "No," and station and ignore her for 15 minutes — the canine equivalent to being grounded with no TV.

A short lead

After your puppy's reliable on the drag lead, use a short lead to reinforce your stationary commands: Sit, Stay, Down, Wait, Heel, and Come.

In addition to using the short lead around the house, do a lesson once a day. Bring your puppy into a quiet room and practice a command routine. Initially, hold the short lead but then drop it once you've warmed up. Slap your leg and use hand signals and peppy body language to encourage your dog's focus.

A 20-foot tree line

Tie this line to a tree or post. Secure all knots. Leave the line on the ground and follow this sequence:

1. **Warm up with five minutes of regular on-lead practice.**

2. **Stop your puppy next to the 20-foot line and attach it to your dog's buckle collar discreetly.**

3. **Remove her regular lead and place it on the ground in front of her. Keep your hands free.**

4. **Command "Stay" and walk 10 feet away.**

    Extend your distance as she gains control. Run your fingers through your hair and swing your arms gently back and forth to emphasize that the leash is out of your hands.

5. **As your puppy improves, practice an out-of-sight Sit-Stay. Practice Down from a Sit-Stay and practice a Down-Stay.**

   You can also practice the Come command but never call at a distance greater than the line can reach. If she falls for this and darts for a quick get-a-way, wait until she's about to hit the end of the line to shout "No!" Return her back into position and repeat the exercise at a closer range.

If your puppy disobeys, determine whether her response is motivated by anxiety, confusion, or defiance. If she's confused or anxious, do not issue a correction. Calmly return to her side and reposition gently. Repeat the same exercise at close range. If your puppy breaks defiantly, however, either shout "No" as she hits the end of the line or, if she's baiting you, return quietly and snap the lead as you say "No." Reposition and repeat the exercise at close range for quicker control. Good luck.

A 30-foot long line

Attach your puppy to the 30-foot long line and let her roam free as you keep a watchful eye. Engage her by playing with a stick or ball and investigate your surroundings together. Avoid over-commanding. Just hang out and enjoy some free time with your dog. Every five minutes, position yourself near the line and issue a command enthusiastically.

If you're issuing a stationary command — like Sit, Wait, or Down — stop abruptly and stamp your foot while giving the command and signaling. If you're issuing a motion command — like Come or Heel — run backward as you encourage your puppy toward you. If she races over, help her into the proper position and give her a big hug. If your puppy ignores your command, quickly step on the line and say "No." (Don't scream; just speak sternly.) After your correction, give your dog the opportunity to right her reaction before lifting the line to snap it or reel her in. End your session with a favorite game.

Alphabet Soup: FAQs about OLT

Before I address frequently asked questions (FAQs) about off-lead training (OLT), let me warn you: It only takes one mistake to lose your puppy. Until she's an off-lead expert, she may get confused. Or she may turn into a little comedian and bound away from you just for fun. So practice all initial training in an enclosed area. Keep it safe until she's reliable.

You may be wondering many things at this point. Here are a list of questions I'm asked most often:

When will I know that I can trust my dog off lead?

You should feel it. It's never a smooth road in the beginning; some days you get a quick and happy response; other days feel more like your first day of training. Stay cool, though. Frustration is a sign of weakness, and you'll lose your dog's respect. Keep your dog enclosed as you practice so that if she starts to act cocky, you can retreat immediately. And don't hesitate to go back to the long line or Teaching Lead exercises for quick review.

I get so frustrated when my puppy ignores me that sometimes I feel like hitting him. Is it ever okay to hit him?

Feeling like hitting is fine. Actually hitting him isn't. If you hit your dog, you erode your relationship and diminish his off-lead trust. If you're really angry, walk away calmly. Remember, a graceful retreat is not a failure.

My puppy breaks every time I leave him in a Sit-Stay on his Flexi-Lead. What can I do?

Increase your distance slowly. For example, if your puppy gets up every time you walk out 15 feet, practice at 10 feet for a week, then at 11 feet, then 12, and so on. In addition, don't face your puppy as you walk out. Walking backward invites a Come response. Instead, walk out confidently, back toward your puppy, and pivot at your final destination. Remind him "Stay."

There are times when my dog crouches and barks at me. How can I make her stop?

Don't look at her. She's trying to turn all your hard work into a game. Ignore her until her antics subside. Work her on the Teaching Lead at short distances if she's being impossible.

Don't the lines get caught around trees and doors?

Yes, they do. Clip all lines to the buckle collar and never leave your puppy unsupervised.

When I place my puppy on the short lead, I can't get near her. Should I just give it up?

You need to work on your drag lead for another week or so. When you try the short lead again, place it on *with* your drag lead and correct her by stepping on it when she darts away.

No off-lead practice in an unconfined area. Your puppy's a fragile jewel that you must protect.

Practicing the Emergency Down Command

Chapter 14 covers the Down command. But for off-lead safety, you need to take it a step further. The Emergency Down command is a high-fired version of the Down command that will have your puppy hitting the dirt in mid-pace. It can be real life-saver. I used it to stop one of my pups who was dutifully fetching a ball that was rolling onto the street.

In the beginning, your puppy may be a little confused; so be patient and positive throughout your training sessions. Don't start practicing this exercise until your puppy has mastered the Down command (see Chapter 14).

1. **Stand next to your unsuspecting puppy.**

2. **Suddenly command "Down" in a very life-threatening tone and point toward the ground.**

   Use the type of tone you'd use if a loved one were about to walk off a cliff.

3. **Kneel down quickly as you bring your dog into position.**

4. **Act like you're being bombed, too.**

Soon your dog will catch on and act independently. Once she does, begin extending your distance from her.

Eventually, this exercise could save your dog's life if, for example, you were ever separated by a road and her life was threatened by an oncoming vehicle. It's true. The Emergency Down really does save lives. Once I was leaving my training classes with my husky, Kyia, when a tennis ball slipped loose and started rolling toward the road. Kyia, sweet thing, wanted to help and ran innocently to collect it. In a panic, I shouted "Down" and she dropped like a rock. What a good girl.

The Emergency Down exercise is very stressful. Limit your practice to one out-of-the-blue Emergency Down sequence a day.

Chapter 18

Going out in Public

Training's biggest reward is the freedom it gives you to take your puppy everywhere. A well-behaved puppy is a welcomed social guest, a plus at parades and picnics, and an added fan at after-school sporting events.

Your puppy won't transfer lessons from the living room to public appearances automatically, however. You need to teach him how to behave in social situations. This chapter covers this type of training.

Don't be foolish. Wait until your puppy has received all appropriate vaccinations to go socializing. Susceptible to many airborne viruses, a young puppy is at risk for life-threatening illness.

Preparing Yourself in Advance

Before you jump right to taking your dog out in public, you need to prepare yourself. The first trip out can be a real embarrassment. You'll be self-conscious, your puppy will be too distracted to listen, and you'll feel compelled to tell everyone, even those who aren't paying any attention, that "he's so much better at home." How do I know? I've been there.

The first-time outing blues

The first outing may be utter chaos, but don't be discouraged. Even I had the "first-outing blues" with my Shayna May. As I tried to steady her by my side, I walked straight into a light post. Ouch. When people gathered to pet her, she jumped to lick their faces. But that first day passed, and Shayna learned that her manners were expected everywhere, whether greeting Aunt Carolyn at the door or ten school children in the park. The eventual compliments overshadowed my initial embarrassment, but I didn't start out with perfection, and you probably won't either.

Before you hit the streets, practice in selective areas so that you can devote all of your attention to your puppy. Eventually, being in public will seem effortless, and you'll both be welcomed everywhere. But your first trip out may be a real shocker. Are you wondering, "If it's such a nightmare, why bother?" Here are three reasons:

- ✔ It gets easier.
- ✔ A well-mannered dog is fun to share.
- ✔ Being out enhances your puppy's focus. You'll be the one looking confident in new, unexplored territories.

In short, going public requires some effort, but before you get started with your pup, keep in mind a few universal rules:

- ✔ **Keep your dog on his Teaching Lead.** His leash reminds him of good behavior. No fancy stuff or showing off, please. There are too many dangers.
- ✔ **Use lots of encouragement.** Cheerfulness is contagious.
- ✔ **Paws behind heels.** Remember, you lead and he follows.
- ✔ **Keep the communication flowing.** Commands provide structure.
- ✔ **No elimination in public.** Take care of that activity at home. (Bring a bag just in case of accidents.)
- ✔ **Know when to say "No"** — to both your puppy and other people.

I know going out in public sounds daunting, but once you get the hang of it, it'll seem natural. It's all about leadership.

Introducing Your Pup to People

Stop shaking. Meeting people doesn't have to be a hair-raising experience. If your puppy is good on the leash, knows his commands, and is friendly, you've got what you need. Before you venture into the social scene, though, read over the following disclosures. If you identify with any of them, follow my specific instructions and skip the rest of this section:

- **First disclosure.** If you're having aggression problems, the only person you must introduce your puppy to is a trainer/behaviorist with a specialty in aggression rehabilitation. How do you find such an expert? Ask your veterinarian. It's better to be safe than sued.

- **Second disclosure.** If you notice your puppy getting nervous or tense around unfamiliar people, join a class or work under private supervision. Don't push the issue alone.

- **Third disclosure.** If you don't believe that you have what it takes to train your puppy, you don't. Confidence is contagious. Hire some extra help if you need the support.

Five rules to follow

When you're debuting that puppy of yours, follow these five key rules:

- **Rule #1.** Make sure your puppy is familiar and comfortable with the setting before you attempt to introduce him to anyone. Don't greet people your first day out.
- **Rule #2.** Feet ahead of paws. Correct all attempts to scoot forward.
- **Rule #3.** Tell admirers what you're doing: "We're in training."
- **Rule #4.** Stay more focused on your puppy than the admirer. Correct all attempts to break.
- **Rule #5.** Put faith in your own knowledge. Just because everyone has advice doesn't mean it's right. "I don't mind if he jumps" doesn't hold water. *You* mind. Period.

Introducing the wild one

How you handle introducing your puppy depends on none other than your puppy. If your puppy is overly enthusiastic, you need to tame his expressiveness. Keeping him focused on you is the key.

Ask people to wait until your wild one is calm. Enforce a Sit-Stay, keeping your feet ahead of his paws. Place your left hand, fingers down, along his waist and below the ribs. Using your right thumb to brace his collar, hold him steady in case he jumps. If the person still wants to, he can pet your puppy. Remind your puppy to Stay and don't let up your vigil until the person is gone. Whew — what a workout.

Introducing the scaredy cat

Ask your greeter to wait until you and your puppy are in position. Place your puppy in a Sit-Stay and kneel down at his side. Put your left hand on his waist and your right hand on his chest, holding his head up for confidence as the greeter pets him.

Having problems?

If your puppy is a little cautious when people approach, before you start out, place some treats in your pocket (or, if your puppy likes peanut butter, bring along a jar). Ask the person to wait until you and your puppy are positioned. Enforce a Sit-Stay, keeping your feet ahead of his paws. Once he's steady, ask the person to give him a fist full of treats without attempting to pet him. If he seems comfortable, pet him together as you hold his head upright with your left hand. If he still seems nervous, quit while you're ahead. You'll get there.

As he gets more confident, wean him off his treat dependency. Use one with every other person, then every third person, and so on.

Introducing Your Pup to Other Dogs

Are you shaking? Envisioning your puppy hurling himself at the end of the lead? Well, wake up! You're just having a nightmare. If you've had some stressful encounters in the past, try to put them behind you. Memories cloud control. Wipe the slate clean and have faith in what you know. When introducing your puppy to other dogs, you just need to get control of the situation and then lead the greeting by giving the Go sign.

Getting control — first and foremost

If you see a dog when you're out and about, don't approach it immediately. First, get control of your situation:

1. **If your puppy acts excited, snap the lead firmly and remind "Heel."**

2. **Continue in your original direction and pick up your pace.**

3. **Don't look toward, approach, or follow the other dog.**

4. **If your puppy continues acting wild, speed up and keep snapping.**

5. **Praise him for focusing on you.**

6. **Never give in or let up.**

What if the training tables are turned?

Suppose that you and your puppy are out taking a walk, and you're approached by someone who's out teaching her puppy socialization skills. And that someone wants to have her puppy greet yours as a training exercise. Are you obligated?

No. If you're not in the mood or your puppy's too hyped, just say no. If you're game, however, get your puppy in control behind you and then release with "OK, go play!" Call him back to Heel when playtime is over.

Giving the Go sign

Once you have your puppy under control, you can permit a greeting by saying "OK, go play!" Before you do, though, make certain the other dog is friendly and the other owner is respectful of your training efforts. When play-time is over, instruct your puppy "Heel" and move on.

If your friend has a dog and you want to get the dogs together to play, let them meet each other on neutral ground, such as an empty playground or field. Doing so prevents a fierce territorial reaction. When they first meet, you should expect a lot of bluffs, such as growling, mouthing, and mounting. Don't choke up on your lead. This behavior is natural, and your interference often prompts a fight. Stay calm but observe closely. The dogs must determine a hierarchy. Once that's accomplished, they'll settle down. If you're certain a fight has begun, separate them with the leashes. Don't handle fighting dogs.

If you're approached by an off-lead dog, don't hesitate, don't look at the dog, and don't let your puppy look at the dog. Just walk quickly away from the area. Discourage any confrontational attempts your puppy makes by snapping the leash and walking faster. Both of you should avoid eye contact. An off-lead dog defends his territory. If you leave without confrontation, he'll stop the chase immediately to harbor his fighting reserves for a more threatening foe.

Car Ride! Oh Boy Oh Boy!

The first step in shaping your perfect public partner is getting him to the destination with your sanity intact. If some of you are chuckling, it's no wonder. Most puppies are less than cooperative in the car. Jumping from seat to seat and barking at passing strangers is the norm.

Put yourself in your puppy's paws. To him, your automobile is a window box with wheels. And while passing cars, pausing for bicycles, and braking for squirrels is part of your normal routine, it pushes his chasing and territorial instincts to the max. Whether he barks or bounces, the predator whizzes away. Conclusion? He's victorious — the champ. Not only do they run away, but they run fast. You haven't even gotten out of the car and your puppy's already pumped. See where the problem starts?

Negative corrections don't work. Yelling is perceived as barking — backup, collaboration style. Besides, discipline and driving don't mix. To solve this problem or to train a pup to behave, you need to follow some simple routines.

Getting your pup into the car

Follow this routine every time to get your puppy into your car:

1. **Lead your puppy to the car with the Heel or Let's Go command.**

2. **Open the door and command "Wait." Pause.**

3. **Say "Go to your spot" and direct your puppy to a prepared car station or into a crate.**

4. **Secure your puppy (see Chapter 5 for options) and tell him "Stay."**

Now you can proceed. Things always go more smoothly when they're organized.

Getting your pup out of the car

Eventually, the time comes to get your pup out of the car. Again, from your dog's perspective, the situation is pretty exciting — new sights, smells, and faces. If he doesn't notice you or listen to commands at first, don't take it personally. Getting him focused is the challenge at hand:

1. **Before opening the door to let him out, instruct "Wait."**

2. **If he jumps forward, catch the car lead, say "No," and snap it back.**

3. **Re-instruct "Wait" and pause until he's calm.**

4. **Put on his Teaching Lead and say "OK" as you let him exit.**

5. **Immediately instruct "Heel," bringing him to your side.**

6. **Instruct "Wait" as you shut the door.**

7. **Proceed with "Heel."**

   Now you're walking in style.

Attach the clip to the buckle collar or chin lead. Do not clip the car lead to a training collar.

Dealing with car fear

Cars really frighten some dogs. The cause usually goes back to being transported at an early age, but this fear can result later in life, too. If your puppy is afraid of the car, avoid pacifying or being overly forceful. Both reactions reinforce fear. If you must take him somewhere, pick him up, if possible, or take him to the car while he's napping. Speak or sing softly. Have the car already pulled out with classical music playing on the radio. Equip his area with a familiar blanket and a favorite toy. For further suggestions, see Chapter 27.

Dealing with car sickness

Some dogs just don't like riding in the car. The motion upsets their inner ear and, like cats, they prefer to stay home. Because staying home is rarely an option, you need to condition your dog to the car slowly:

1. **Designate a place for your puppy in the back seat or cargo area.**

2. **Pull your car out into the open and, with all the doors open, use the car as a playground.**

   Climb in and out of the car with your puppy, encouraging her interest with favorite toys and treats.

3. **After a romp, take a break in the car, giving your puppy water and food if it's mealtime.**

4. **Play "Find the Car" games with your puppy.**

   Tell your puppy "Find the Car" and run over to the car, treating your puppy for following you. Work this routine until the car is something the puppy enjoys being around.

5. **With the engine running, repeat the preceding steps.**

6. **After a playtime, secure your puppy (in a crate or on leash) to his area and go for a short spin in and out of the driveway; repeat this step until your puppy is comfortable.**

7. **Slowly extend your trips, stopping for a cheerful game or two along the way.**

If, during this time, you must take your puppy on an extended trip, don't feed or water him for at least two hours before. Exercise him before you leave, spread sheets over his area, bring paper towels, and pray.

Having problems?

Does your dog refuse to hop into the car? If he's a tiny tot, his reluctance is understandable. If, on the other hand, you have a 120-pound Great Dane, *you're* the one being taken for a ride. You have to make a stand not to lift him ever again. If you do, you're forcing him into a state of learned helplessness. Lead him to the car, taking some of his favorite treats along — dog or human — and try baiting him in. If this makes little impression, get in the car and, as you bribe him, pull him gently forward. Still no luck? Bring a friend along, pass the lead to her through the car, and have her gently pull as you encourage him forward. If he still resists, physically walk each limb into the automobile one at a time but under no circumstances lift.

"Okay, I'm There — Now What?"

When you get to your destination, the first five minutes is three-fourths of the battle. Whatever practice location you've picked — a park, town, friend's house, or building — first impressions really count. If you take control immediately and give understandable directions, the rest is a tail wag.

Suppose you've just brought your dog into a Heel after shutting the car door. Instantly, your dog probably has one of two reactions: He'll either become wild or a scaredy cat.

Controlling the wild one

If your puppy is the wild type, his nose will twitch a mile a minute, he'll pivot toward every new stimulation, and he'll pull to investigate every blade of grass. Here's a way to control your Huck Finn:

- ✔ Enforce Heel. Keep his paws behind your ankles at all points.

- ✔ Tell strangers to back off until your puppy's trained. It's embarrassing, I know, but you have to. You don't want Buddy jumping up and giving someone a scratch, even by accident.

- ✔ Reinforce your requests. If you ask for a Sit-Stay, get a Sit-Stay.

- ✔ Take all commands back to the introductory stage, no matter how well you're doing at home. Initially practice only Heel and Stay commands.

Influencing the scaredy cat

If you have a passive or scared puppy, the experience of arriving at a new place may seem overwhelming. His tail may disappear, his body may lower, and, when stimulated, he'll try to hide behind you. If you bend to soothe your scaredy cat, you reinforce his reaction — and soothing him is so tempting, I know. Just keep saying to yourself over and over, "Soothing reinforces fear. Soothing reinforces fear." Instead of soothing him, try the following:

- Look confident and stand tall like a good leader puppy. Soon he'll mimic you.

- Bring some treats and a favorite toy — something he can focus his attention on. (Withholding these items at home makes the new adventure seem really exciting.)

- Use Heel and Stay commands often; familiar sounds soothe anxiety.

- If he's too nervous to listen, enforce a response without corrections.

- Stay calm and positive. Deflect any admirers until he's feeling safe.

Having problems?

Having some trouble once you get where you're going? Here are some questions I often get, along with my advice for handling the situations:

Heel! Are you joking? He does it great at home, but he's a maniac everywhere else.

Here are two remedies for an out-of-control Heel:

- **The side step:** Whenever your dog focuses on something to your left, take a giant step to the right, snap the lead, and remind "Heel." The bigger or older the dog, the sharper the snap. Repeat until your dog's alert to you. Praise that.

- **The kick back:** If you have a charging brute on your hands, place your left hand on your left thigh. The second he moves forward, remind "Heel" as you thrust your left leg back. Don't kick him, though; just move your leg in the opposite direction as you remind "Heel." Repeat until he stays behind your leg.

If you're still having problems, consider a different collar or try holding the lead behind your back.

My puppy starts barking the second I let him out of the car! How can I get him to stop?

He's obviously a very excited guy. Start practicing in empty parking lots. Bring along a travel mister pump filled with white vinegar or Binaca mouth spray. If he starts barking, spritz in front of his nose and say "Shhh." You must be sneaky about the spritz, though; he can't know where it's coming from.

My puppy's so afraid, she freezes and won't move. I've never seen her this bad. What can I do to help her?

Try coaxing her forward with her favorite treats or peanut butter and praise. If she's terrified, get some help.

Going inside Buildings

Pick a building you might visit with your puppy: the veterinarian's office, hardware store, pet shop, or your kids' school. Your puppy's behavior in those buildings depends on who enters the building first. If your puppy leads you, he's in charge. If you lead your puppy, then you're the head honcho. Whoever *starts* in charge *stays* in charge.

1. **Bring your puppy to a Heel as you exit the car.**

2. **As you get to the threshold, brace your arm behind your back.**

   Puppies sense when they're going somewhere new. Say "Shhh" if he starts getting excited.

3. **Pause before you open the door and command "Wait."**

   Don't open the door until he's settled down.

4. **Re-command "Wait" as you open the door.**

5. **If your puppy lunges, snap him back sternly and say "No!" Then pause again until your puppy is calm.**

6. **Say "OK" as you lead him through.**

Follow and practice this routine, and your puppy will soon become very comfortable inside buildings.

Some dogs are nervous when they enter new buildings. If your puppy is, don't reinforce his anxiety. If your puppy's showing fear, show confidence. Don't pet him or reassure him things will be okay. Instead, take along some treats to encourage him as you approach the building. Stand tall and ignore his caution. If he puts on the brakes, kneel down and encourage him inside.

Meeting Up with Curbs

Whether you live in a city or not, eventually you'll run across a curb. Applying my usual psychology, some restraint is in order here.

1. **As you approach the curb, make sure your puppy is in a "Heel."**

2. **At the curb, instruct "Wait."**

3. **If your puppy continues, snap the lead and say "No, Wait," pulling him behind your ankles.**

4. **Say "OK" as you lead him across.**

5. **Remind "Heel."**

Meeting Up with Stuff Your Pup's Afraid Of

When you go out, you may run into objects or obstacles that are pretty scary to your dog. How you handle the situation determines his reaction. If your puppy's nervous and you soothe him, you're communicating fear, and he'll grow more cautious. On the other hand, if you act confident by investigating the new object on your own, you'll highlight your courage and impress your puppy. He'll follow your lead, and after seeing no harm came to you, he'll grow more confident. Following is advice on how to handle specific hurdles:

✔ **Grates:** Take you puppy's favorite treats and go sit on a grate. Encourage him to the perimeter. Slowly encourage him forward and praise him as he attempts to take his first steps. It may take weeks to see him walk over a grate calmly.

✔ **Stairs:** One of the cutest miracles I get to perform is teaching pups to handle stairs. I'll tell you my secret. Once your puppy is large enough to handle stairs, avoid carrying him. Instead, brace his rib cage securely in your hands and help him to manipulate his body to do the action. Don't forget to praise him while you do. If yours is really frightened by the whole flight, carry him to the bottom few steps and ask someone to kneel below to coach him forward.

✔ **People in uniform:** Some dogs fear people in uniform. To help him overcome his fear, act very friendly toward uniformed people. Ask them to help you socialize your puppy as you give them some treats to offer to him. If they're willing, ask them to kneel and avoid eye contact until he's sniffed them out. Another great trick is to rent a uniform from a costume shop and dress up in one yourself.

How to brownnose your vet

I'll let you in on a secret. Veterinarians love a well-behaved dog. It makes their job a lot easier. To impress your vet:

1. **Bring your puppy's favorite chew toy in case you have to wait.**

    When you get to the office, your puppy will probably be excited or afraid.

2. **Instruct "Heel" at the car. At the entrance, command (and enforce) "Wait."**

3. **Say "OK" and remind "Heel" as you check in.**

4. **If you must wait, place him in a Down position next to your side and give him his favorite chew.**

5. **Instruct "Wait" as you go into the examination room to keep him calm and focused.**

Some puppies aren't wild about receptionists and aren't too impressed by the DVM. Set up a practice run and ask the receptionist to meet you outside. Give her your puppy's treat cup (place some yummy treats in a plastic cup) and ask her to avoid making eye contact with your puppy. If your puppy is tense, avoid confrontation. If your puppy wants to approach, have the receptionist reward him with treats.

✔ **People of a particular sex:** Some dogs fear people of a particular sex. This problem results from any number of circumstances. Generally, they all fall under either inappropriate or lack of socialization with a particular sex. If this happens at home, place your puppy on his Teaching Lead during arrivals and follow the directions given for uniformed people. If the problem doesn't improve or if you notice any aggression, seek professional help.

✔ **Children:** If your puppy is afraid of children, act like a child with your puppy. For example, poke him or pull his ear like a child would do, squeal in a high-pitched voice, and stare at him at his level by kneeling or crawling. Once he's socialized to these patterns, he'll be more accepting when the children do it. If your puppy's nervous around babies, borrow a friend's blanket (for the aroma) and wrap a doll in it to carry around the house, including your puppy in all the fuss. Also, practice your Heel and Sit-Stay commands around the perimeter of a playground but don't let the children approach. If you try these suggestions but the problem doesn't improve, find a private trainer who has experience with this problem.

Condition your puppy to the sound of his treat cup. Allow kids to take the cup and toss treats to your puppy. If he's enthusiastic, let the children toss treats toward him. You can let him take treats gently from the children.

If your puppy tenses up, his eyes grow cold, or he starts to growl, do not work him around children until you are under the supervision of a professional trainer. Don't become another statistic. Dogs that bite children are often forcibly euthanized.

Going on an Overnight Visit

Taking your dog with you on an overnight visit can be either a lot of fun or a disaster — depending on how you handle the situation. Do some pre-departure planning; pack a bed, a crate, chew toys, treats, leads, and a small portable radio (yes, a radio; it drowns out any unfamiliar sounds and soothes his anxiety while you're gone).

When you arrive, greet everyone calmly or leave your puppy in the car with the radio playing. Enforce a Sit for greetings and a Wait at all thresholds. When you go to your room, set up the crate or sleeping station. Offer your puppy his treats and toys. Set up the radio next to his area.

Find an easy-listening station. Heavy metal can be a little jarring.

If possible, avoid crating your puppy immediately. After setting up the bedroom, lead him around the outside perimeters and play a familiar game. If you must go, place your puppy in his area with a chew toy and turn on the radio. Make sure you depart and arrive calmly. No overly theatrical guilt-trip scenes, please.

If children are in the household where you're staying, before you go, take a cup of Cheerios, shake it, and toss your puppy a handful. Repeat this activity until your puppy recognizes the sound. Tell your friends to have an identical box waiting for your arrival. When you first get there, let your puppy check the place out and then encourage the children (or the parent and the child) to shake the treat cup and offer fists full of cereal as your puppy is introduced to the new smells and the activity around the kids.

If you anticipate or sense any aggression, leave your puppy at home or, if he must come, keep him apart from the children. Get professional help immediately.

Chapter 19

Great Adventures for Performing Types

In This Chapter

▶ Agility competitions and obedience trials

▶ Good citizenship programs

▶ Competitions that focus on dogs' natural instincts

▶ Specialty programs

▶ Flyball and Frisbee competitions

*I*s your puppy into performing? A real ham? Love to be the center of attention? Has he mastered all the basics and is still eager for more? Well, you're not alone. Most dogs love to have a special activity and a time to let all their natural juices run wild, whether the activity be pulling a sled, running through an obstacle course, chasing a ball or Frisbee, or simply sharing their love with groups of new people.

If you want to take part in an extra-curricular activity, scan this chapter with your dog at your side. Here you can find so many available options that you're sure to come across something you and your dog will love to do together.

To get the most from these activities, you must socialize and teach your puppy basic obedience first. Although you can start teaching your pup the skills needed to participate in the competitions and events covered in this chapter, don't pressure him at a young age. Remember that many of the activities covered here are designed to encourage competition *after* your puppy has matured.

Agility Competitions

Agility is the Grand Prix sporting event in the dog world. At first sight, an agility course looks like a gigantic playground. The course obstacles include things like long open and closed tunnels, a tire frame for the dog to jump through, an A-frame for him to navigate across, a see-saw, weave poles, jumps, and much, much more.

Agility fever is very catchy. To find a dog or Agility Club in your area, call or write to the American Kennel Club (add "Attn: Agility" to the address) or the U.S. Dog Agility Association, Inc. (see the "Who to Contact" section at the end of this chapter).

AKC Obedience Trials

Obedience trials don't take a dog's physical appearance into account. Although the dogs must be purebred to enter this ring, the only thing that wins brownie points is good temperament and mindful behavior.

Although mixed breeds are barred from AKC competitions, they do have their own activity club with similar rules and certifications. For more information, write to the Mixed Breed Dog Club of America (see the section "Who to Contact" at the end of this chapter).

To earn any of the obedience titles, a dog has to compete a certain number of times, earn a certain number of points, and get more than 50 percent of the points on each of the required exercises. The required exercises vary, depending on what title you're going for.

Though the instructions for this type of training are beyond the scope of this book, many other books have been written specifically about preparing for the obedience ring. If you have a well-mannered, friendly, obedient dog resting nearby, and your eyes are lighting up at the thought of a little friendly competition, this type of activity might be just the challenge for you.

For more information regarding obedience regulations, write to the American Kennel Club and include "Attn: Obedience Regulations" in the address (see the section "Who to Contact" at the end of this chapter).

Canine Good Citizenship Programs

The Canine Good Citizenship Program (CGC) is a noncompetitive training and acceptance test designed to recognize and certify dogs and their owners as responsible citizens of their community. Although this test is promoted by the American Kennel Club, it is not limited to purebred dogs. Mixed breeds are encouraged to gain certification as well. Presented as more of a program than a competition, this test measures a dog's social skills and public manners. The goal of the CGC test is not to eliminate participants but to encourage pet owners to learn the skills necessary to train their dogs to be safe members of our society.

The commands a dog must respond to in order to take part in this test are "Heel," "Sit," "Down," and "Stay." The test is comprised of ten evaluations, including things like accepting a friendly stranger, sitting politely for petting, and walking through a crowd.

I am a certified CGC evaluator and give this test to my High School (dog High School that is) graduates. It's a fun way for everyone to measure their success. If you think you and your dog are ready for this evaluation, you can contact the American Kennel Club in North Carolina (see the section "Who to Contact" at the end of this chapter; refer to the address that includes "Attn: CGC").

Outlets for a Pup's Natural Instincts

Is your puppy a breed who's job description won't let her rest? Well, the American Kennel Club offers organized breed-specific activities that you can take part in.

Earth trials

Do you have a Terrier whose instincts to chase, bark, and dig are driving you crazy? If so, these trials might be the perfect outlet for all his natural instincts. The breeds allowed to compete include all purebred dogs from the Terrier Group, as well as Dachshunds.

At the test sight, a tunnel is rigged with a caged hooded rat to serve as bait. The dogs are tested in different classes, which vary in the length of the tunnel and the amount of time allotted for a response.

Dogs are scored on (what else?) their spirit, which is measured by their barking, lunging, and biting capabilities. Poor rat. If you think this is something you and your dog would be interested in, you can write to Patricia Adams, the Entry Trial Secretary (see the "Who to Contact" section at the end of this chapter).

Herding trials

Though there are still farms that utilize the instincts of the traditional herding, guarding, or all-purpose farm dog, most of the dogs from the Herding Group are coveted as cherished pets and family members. However, some of these dogs still take their genes very seriously. You'd notice them in a minute. They're the ones herding their owners from the kitchen, rounding up the schoolchildren as they get off the bus, and staring longingly as the Discovery channel airs a special about the sheep of the Scottish highlands. If you find yourself feeling woeful for your little herder, perhaps this activity is for you.

Training a herding dog does not have to start in puppyhood. Although many instincts appear in a young dog, some dogs don't show any herding talent until they're older. If you are interested in pursuing this activity, remember that you are encouraging your dog's instinct to herd or guard, not to chase or kill. Rough handling or tugging games can spoil a good herding dog.

The American Kennel Club sponsors competitions and awards titles for both beginning and more experienced contestants. To get more information about Herding Trials, you can write to the American Kennel Club (include "Attn: Herding" in the address), the American Herding Breed Association, or the Livestock Guarding Dog Project (see the section "Who to Contact" at the end of this chapter).

Field trials

If you're a hunting enthusiast and you have a dog that fits the bill, then these events might be for you. The AKC sponsors separate Field Trials for Basset Hounds, Beagles, Dachshunds, Pointing breeds, Retrievers, and Spaniels. Each event brings man and dog back together for the task that the dog was originally bred to do.

If you are interested in finding more information regarding these trials, be sure to specify your breed when you write the AKC for the Trial Rules and Standard Procedures. Make sure to include "Attn: Registration and Field Trial Rules and Standard Procedures for Pointing Breeds/Retrievers/Spaniels/ Dachshunds (specify breed)" or "Attn: Beagle/Basset Hound Field Trial Rules and Standard Procedures" in the address. You can also write to the United Kennel Club (see the section "Who to Contact" at the end of this chapter).

Lure coursing

The goal of lure coursing, which was set up in 1972 by the American Sighthound Association, is to "preserve and further develop the natural beauty, grace, speed, and coursing skill of the Sighthound." The breeds involved include the Afghan Hound, Basenji, Borzoi, Greyhound, Ibizan Hound, Irish Wolfhound, Pharaoh Hound, Saluki, Scottish Deerhound, and Whippet. These dogs all have one thing in common. They love to run after game, and they love to run fast. (**Note:** To be entered in competition, a dog must be registered in a recognized organization such as the AKC or the National Greyhound Association.)

In lure coursing, the dogs run in trios after a lure (usually a white bag with or without fur covering it), and judges score the dogs on speed, agility, skill, enthusiasm, and endurance.

For more information, write to the American Kennel Club (include "Attn: Lure Coursing" in the address) or the American Sighthound Field Association (see the section "Who to Contact" at the end of this chapter).

Specialty Programs

Some activities don't require any pedigree to join the fun. The following activities are open to dogs of all breeds and mixes. But don't be fooled. Even though these programs are open to everyone, it doesn't mean just any dog will do. Each of these activities requires certain characteristics and drives. Will you and your dog fit in? You'll have to be the judge. . . .

Therapy dogs

Using dogs in therapeutic situations is an activity very close to my heart. Much like music or art therapy, dogs can ease interactions between two or more people in a variety of situations, such as long-term care facilities and institutions. It is now proven that interacting with animals lowers blood pressure and facilitates interpersonal relationships.

If you have a dog who is social and loving, yet calm and well-mannered, you may find this activity very rewarding. Although many facilities welcome volunteers, it is best to take a class or work with someone who is familiar with the rigors of the therapeutic situations before committing yourself. Even the most even-tempered dogs can startle or feel stressed when faced with an unfamiliar experience. By exposing your dog to every possible situation that might occur, he'll be better able to cope with unexpected predicaments.

To get more information about outreach programs and certifications in your area, contact your local shelter or write the Delta Society, which has a national center researching Pet Assisted Therapy and a certification test for trained dogs (see the section "Who to Contact" at the end of this chapter).

Sled dogs

When most people think of sledding, they think of a husky-type dog with a thick coat and curly tail. This sport, however, is not restricted to any particular breed. When I was five, I went to a local nature preserve to witness a sledding event and saw a sled pulled by two Poodles and another with a trio of Doberman Pinschers. So, for all you snow enthusiasts who have dogs who get a charge out of taking you for a walk, grab a pencil and read closely. Dog sledding is a blast, and although I wouldn't encourage any of you toy owners to hitch up, it's not limited by breed.

Believe it or not, the 1,040 mile Iditarod race from Anchorage to Nome, Alaska, is not the only competition in town. There are also sprint race competitions that vary in number of dogs and distances run.

Serious advocates start training their puppies at three months. However, if you have an interest, don't be discouraged if you have an adult dog. Most dogs love to learn new tricks, and most are more than willing to pull you. For information about competition and training programs, write to the International Sled Dog Racing Association (see the section "Who to Contact" at the end of this chapter).

Tracking dogs

Dogs' noses are analogous to our eyes. Tracking to them is like a land survey to us. However, to train your dog to follow a specified trail is no simple feat. Tracking is advanced obedience work and requires a lot of encouragement and patient repetition. Anyone who has trained a tracking dog will tell you, however, that the final result is worth the effort. A rapport between a handler and good tracking dog is built on solid trust. Tracking dogs have been used by the police and individuals to find lost people when all other modern technological techniques have failed.

Training must start with good communication. *Positive retrieves,* where the article is within sight, are the best starting point. As a dog's ability and enthusiasm increase, articles can be hidden from sight in tall grass or around corners (this is known as a *positive blind retrieve*). Exposing a dog to different weather conditions and locations is important in creating a reliable tracking dog. To find out more about training a tracking dog, refer to specific training books.

Contact the AKC for more information about the test and the courses. Be sure to include "Attn: Tracking" in the address (see the section "Who to Contact" at the end of this chapter).

Breed-Specific Working Titles

Many national breed clubs have designated individual working titles for activities for which their breed was originally bred. For example, the Newfoundland Club of America sponsors clinics and competitions where dogs can earn Water Dog (WD) and Water Rescue Dog (WRD) titles. This club also awards drafting (cart pulling) titles — Draft Dog (DD) and Team Draft Dog (TDD) — for a team of Newfoundlands.

Many other breed clubs sponsor events not yet recognized by the American Kennel Club. The Dalmatian Club of America offers road titles. The Alaskan Malamute offers titles for weight pulls. To discover what your breed club has to offer, write your national club, which you can find through your breeder or by contacting the American Kennel Club (see the "Who to Contact" section for the AKC address).

Fun and Games

Do you have a high-energy dog that's only interested in high-speed fun? The following sports are open to dogs of every persuasion. The only requirement? Energy and plenty of it.

Flyball

Flyball is a real heart-pounder. This game is quite unlike anything else in the dog world. Although the majority of enthusiasts remain in Canada and the north Midwestern United States, I have a strong feeling its popularity will be growing.

To play the sport of Flyball, you need a team of four spirited dogs with a slight obsession for tennis balls. The team races together on a relay-type system. The goal of each dog is to run 51 inches, over four jumps to the Flyball box, pick up a tennis ball, and run back over the jumps to the start-finish line. As one dog returns, another is sent until all four dogs have run.

Frisbee training for humans

This information isn't for your dog, dear readers. It's for you. If you can't toss the Frisbee predictably, your dog will give up on you. So find yourself a good 9¼-inch diameter disc, prop this book open, and start with lesson number one:

✔ **The grip:** Place your thumb on the outside edge and curl your fingers under the lip. Don't white-knuckle the thing. A firm grasp will do. Carry it around the house for a couple of days. Now you're talking.

✔ **The stance:** With your feet shoulder width apart, point the shoulder of your tossing arm at the object you're aiming for. Although you end up shifting your weight forward, always keep some weight on each foot.

✔ **The toss:** The toss must be smooth and sharp and even. A thrust back with your elbow and a snap of your wrist projects the disc forward. Make sure your shoulder stays aligned with your target, your head is up, and your eyes are looking out ahead of you.

What dog breeds make the best competitors? No breed taller than 8 inches is barred from competition, although the breeds most frequently seen include Border Collies, Doberman Pinschers, Jack Russells, Shelties, Miniature Poodles, and mixed breeds.

If the idea of such heart-stopping fun is raising your eyebrows, you'll want to contact the NAFA and get its rule book and information about its training and competition locations (see the section "Who to Contact" at the end of this chapter). Good luck.

Frisbee

To play Frisbee with your dog, he has to know how to catch (the *fly*) and retrieve (the *return*), and *you* have to know how to throw (see the sidebar "Frisbee training for humans").

To train your dog for the fly, follow these steps:

1. **Treat the disc as a dinner plate.**

   It looks like one anyway, right? For a week feed your dog on the disc, picking it up after each meal to prevent chewing. Wash and hide the disc until the next feeding.

2. **Practicing inside initially, teach your dog playfully with the disc, saying "Get it."**

   When he grabs the disc, tug *lightly* to ensure a secure grip before you get him to release it by offering food or tremendous praise.

3. **Now play keep away.**

   Show your dog the disc and run a short distance before allowing him to grasp it. To see whether your dog is sufficiently in love with the new object, turn it upside down and slide it a short distance away from you on the floor. When your dog grasps it, praise him tremendously. (Initially, your dog probably won't want to give the disc back to you. That's okay; worry about the good retrieving skills after you've nailed the grab.)

4. **Try the keep-away game with a new disc that hasn't been used as a dinner plate.**

   Your dog might react totally different. Keep the praise high every time he grasps the disc.

Are you sure he loves it now? Then you're ready to teach the return:

1. **Place a ten-foot light lead or rope on your dog during Frisbee time.**

2. **When he grabs the disc, encourage him to come back.**

   If he returns with or without the disc, praise him wildly. If he decides not to, snap the lead and reel him in. Again, you're concentrating on the return, with or without the disc.

3. **After your dog is cooperating, try the return off leash.**

   If you practice outside, stay within an enclosure.

4. **Next, practice with five or six discs, encouraging your dog to return to you before you toss the next one.**

You can find a great resource for Frisbee at `www.skyhoundz.com`. I've got the video; it's a blast.

Who to Contact

American Herding Breed Association
Linda Rorem
1548 Victoria Way
Pacifica, CA 94044

American Kennel Club (AKC)
260 Madison Avenue
New York, NY 10016
(212) 696-8200
www.akc.org

American Kennel Club
Attn: CGC
5580 Centerview Drive, Suite 200
Raleigh, NC 27606-3390
(919) 233-9780

American Sighthound Field Association
Lester Pekarski
P.O. Box 1293-M
Woodstock, GA 30188

Delta Society
P.O. Box 1080
Renton, WA 98057-9906

International Sled Dog Racing Association
460 S. 43rd St.
Boulder, CO 80303

Livestock Guarding Dog Project
Livestock Guard Dog Assoc.
Hampshire College
P.O. Box FC
Amherst, MA 01002

Mixed Breed Dog Club of America
Attn: Phyllis Massa
1937 Seven Pines Dr.
St. Louis, MO 63146-3717

North American Flyball Association
Mike Randell
1342 Jeff Street
Ypsilanti, MI 48198

Patricia Adams/Entry Trial Secretary
Dogwood Cottage RD2
Box 38A
Franklinton, NC 27525

United Kennel Club
100 E. Kilgore Road
Kalamazoo, MI 49001-5593

U.S. Dog Agility Association, Inc.
P.O. Box 850955
Richardson, TX 75085-0955
(214) 231-9700

Part VI
Ensuring Fitness and Health

In this part . . .

There's more to raising a puppy than providing good training. There's health and well being to keep in mind. Diet, exercise, and daily hygiene are things your puppy can't discuss with you; he depends on your foresight to keep him in good condition. In this part, I discuss puppy nutrition, how much exercise your puppy needs, and how to stay on top of good hygiene and health. And I take a look at what to do if an accident happens.

Chapter 20

Even Puppies Have to Watch What They Eat

In This Chapter

▶ The differences among commercial dog foods

▶ What's involved in a homemade diet

▶ Wet versus dry food

▶ The six essential elements of dog food

▶ Diet allergies

▶ Special diet considerations

*B*roken down, aren't all dog foods basically the same? No, Virginia, all dog foods aren't the same. The only true similarity is in the percentage of organic components required to meet a dog's daily allowance, which is governed by the FDA. Foods differ on what ingredients are used to reach the *minimum daily requirement (MDR)*. To pick the right food for your dog, you need to learn how to read ingredient labels. You also have to consider *your* puppy. Formulas that agree with one don't necessarily agree with the other. As you pay more attention to your puppy's diet, you'll discover that the most costly, aggressively marketed, or cleverly labeled food isn't necessarily the best.

Feeding your puppy the wrong diet affects his health *and* his behavior. The wrong diet can increase your puppy's susceptibility to disease, infection, and possibly nervous/aggressive disorders.

From Plate to Palette: All about Dog Foods

You have a myriad of choices when it comes to what to feed your pup. Store bought or homemade? Premium brand or run-of-the-mill? Wet or dry? When nearly every brand on the market claims to be the best, how do you decide? Well, brace yourself, dear reader. I've done some good investigative reporting to get the scoop on just what makes one puppy food different from the rest.

Cheap versus designer foods — What gives?

Many brands of dog food are on the market. In this section, I give you the scoop on just how one dog food differs from the other. I divided the foods into three groupings: pick-me-up-anywhere brands, premium labels, and holistic feed. Figure 20-1 illustrates how much food a mid-sized dog must eat to meet her daily nutrition requirements.

Figure 20-1: How much food a mid-sized dog needs to eat to meet daily nutritional requirements.

PICK UP ANYWHERE

PREMIUM BRAND

HOLISTIC FEED

Photo by Sarah Hodgson.

The origins of commercial dog food

Before the Second World War, dogs ate our leftovers — a tradition since the moment the first dog was domesticated from the wolf. With the war came economic strain and a weakened work force. One result of this situation was the development of commercialized dog food. Animal parts unfit for human consumption, otherwise discarded as wastes, were processed as dog food. Yummm. The first commercial bags were sold in the grocery stores; many of these same brands can be found today. In the early 70s, specialty pet stores were introduced, and with them came the study and preparation of higher quality foods. Now a third ranking of foods, known as holistic formulas, is available.

✔ **Pick-me-up-anywhere brands:** You can find these brand names just about anywhere. A piece on *60 Minutes* describes how these widely commercialized foods garnish their meats: They select from the 4 D categories — dead, dying, diseased, or decaying. How's that for appetizing? In addition, much of the fat in these brands is indigestible, requiring more bulk feeding to meet daily nutritional requirements.

✔ **Premium labels:** Found in specialty pet stores and animal hospitals, premium foods originated to improve the quality of ingredients offered to pets. The grade of meat is up, and the food contains a higher quantity of usable fats.

✔ **Holistic feed:** These foods can also be found in specialty pet stores. The word holistic translates into "human grade everything": human grade meats, often hormone and steroid free, digestible fats, and a grain carbohydrate mix of the highest standard. Though this type of dog food often costs more and can be challenging to find, it is calorie rich, requiring less bulk to meet the daily nutritional requirement. And theoretically, if *you* got really hungry. . . .

When searching for the right diet, pay close attention to your dog: How's his digestion? Foods with low-quality ingredients don't absorb as well and can give your dog loose stools. Check the nutritional label to ensure you get a blend of high-quality proteins (from dairy and meats) and low quality (from vegetables and grains). A good diet should help your puppy produce two to four compact, inoffensive-smelling stools a day.

What about the homemade diet?

Yes, you can still feed your dog human food, but you have to make sure it's balanced. Followed responsibly, the home diet can be modified for your puppy's age, breed distinctions, and individual needs. Some dogs, regardless of breed, suffer from commercialized dog foods; the natural diet can solve problems related to this condition. The drawback to feeding your dog naturally is that you *must* commit yourself to prepare balanced meals and to shop for products regularly to ensure freshness.

If you want to try a homemade diet, refer to *The Holistic Guide For A Healthy Dog,* by Wendy Volhard and Kerry Brown, DVM, Macmillan Publishing, 1995.

If your dog gets into baker's chocolate, beware. It contains a chemical that is poisonous to dogs. In large quantities (one ounce per pound) it can kill. (Turn to Chapter 24 for more information about common household poisons.)

Which is better — dry or wet?

What's the difference between dry and wet food? Cost in shipping and cost to the consumer. Wet food contains 65–78 percent water; the weight of the can and water increases the cost of shipping. No studies have proven either wet or dry to be nutritionally superior. So the choice is up to you. Many of the veterinarians I consulted suggest a combination of the two.

Dry food requires careful storage. If you let it sit around too long, the vitamins may start degrading or the whole bag will acquire mold or pantry moths.

The Essential Components of Puppy Food

To pass regulatory standards, foods must contain six essential elements: *protein, fat, carbohydrates, vitamins, minerals,* and *water.* But that's where the similarities end. Though the requirement is set by law, each label can choose whatever ingredients to fill that requirement. For example, some foods use soy to meet the daily protein requirement; other foods use meat or animal protein. It's like the difference between eating ten soy burgers to get my daily requirement of protein versus a good wholesome piece of chicken. Well, perhaps I'm exaggerating, but you catch my drift. For dogs, animal protein beats soy hands down. The following sections look at the essential components in dog food one at a time.

Proteins (21–26 percent of the food)

Protein is the source that determines the quality of the dog food. When you read the label, you see one or more protein sources: meat, animal, and grain protein. Here's the translation:

✔ **Meat protein:** Meat protein consists of organ meat or muscle meat. This type of protein is the closest to human quality and is superior to other protein sources.

✔ **Animal protein:** Animal protein consists of any part of the animal that contains protein — hair, hoof, lip, and eyelashes included.

The *crude protein* measurement for a puppy food totals all protein obtained from the animal protein source, as well as the protein found in the grains.

✔ **Vegetable or grain proteins:** Reconsider foods that lead off with soy or glutameal protein. First of all, you have to feed a lot of this food to your dog to meet his daily requirement, and what goes in must come out. Second, unusable protein stresses the kidney. Anything that spells out "gluten" can be translated into hard-to-digest, low-quality (though inexpensive to the manufacturer) protein.

Some puppies are allergic to grains found in dog food. The most common allergies are to corn, wheat, and soy. Certain grains also may contain fertilizer residue, which can cause an allergic reaction. If your dog refuses to eat his food or his digestion seems abnormal in any way, consult your veterinarian and bring along the labels from your puppy's food to help her identify any possible aggravating ingredients.

Here are some interesting tidbits about protein:

✔ The need for protein changes throughout your puppy's life and whenever there is temperature or emotional stress on his system. When stress occurs, your puppy uses more protein.

✔ Ever wonder what the difference is between active, low active, lite, puppy, and performance is? You guessed it: the percentage of protein.

✔ More protein is not better. High-protein diets are used for show or working dogs. If you have a sworn couch potato or a dog who must spend hours alone, feeding her a high-protein diet (which, broken down, equals energy) makes her jittery and hyper.

Carbohydrates (42 percent of the food)

Some dog food manufacturers meet the MDR for protein by using primarily vegetable matter. Vegetable sources of protein also contain high levels of carbohydrates. The problem is that dogs don't digest carbohydrates the way people do. Human digestive systems are much more complicated. We start digestion in our mouths, where we chew and savor our food. Dogs, on the other hand, chew and gulp; their digestion starts in their stomachs.

Knowing this is important because carbohydrate digestion is a slow process that's not cut out for gulping. Foods high in carbos can cause digestive problems in dogs, such as bloating, upset stomach, constipation, and too much stool. Make sure you pick a diet that contains more animal protein than vegetable protein. How? Pick a food that has two or more animal sources of protein listed in the first five ingredients.

Is your dog susceptible to bloat? If he inhales his food, you can slow him. Take a large pan, place heavy rocks in the bottom, and add his food to create quite the eatable obstacle course. Be sure the rocks are too large to eat.

Fats and preservatives (15–20 percent of the food)

Fats are the most costly ingredient in dog food, primarily because they're harder to extract and preserve. The fat in the diet gives your puppy stable, even-tempered energy. In addition, fat keeps your puppy's skin and coat healthy, mobilizes digestion, and stabilizes temperature — keeping her warm when it's cold and cool when it's warm.

Sources of usable fats include chicken fats, sunflower or canola oil, fish oil, and lactose-free dairy products.

Once a puppy loses her baby teeth, she loses the enzyme needed to process the milk chemical lactose. Although a dog doesn't know the difference between lactose and lactose-free, her stomach sure does. Lactose produces gas and loose stool.

Here are some tidbits to keep in mind when researching fats and preservatives in your puppy's diet:

  ✔ Many foods have begun to add tallow fat to meet their minimum daily requirement. Used in the production of candles, this fat is inexpensive *and indigestible*. When a brand claims a "new formula" make sure the change does not include this unusable ingredient.

  ✔ Supplementing fat in your puppy's diet is often unnecessary. If your vet encourages you to increase fat content, use pressed safflower oil — approximately 1 teaspoon for small dogs; 1 tablespoon for large dogs. This oil has a high concentration of linoleic acid and is least likely to cause an allergic reaction.

  ✔ In commercial puppy foods, check the label to see what preservatives are used. Ethoxyquin is a recognized carcinogen.

Vitamins (1 percent of the food)

Vitamins do two things: They unlock nutrients from food, and they provide energy. That's it in a nutshell. There are two types of vitamins: fat soluble and water soluble:

- ✔ The fat soluble include vitamins A, D, E, and K. These vitamins are stored in fatty tissue and the liver.

- ✔ Water soluble include vitamins B and C; they're flushed through the body daily — either used up or excreted.

  Should you supplement vitamin C? Not everyone agrees. The argument for supplementing is that vitamin C strengthens the elastic tissues, making them more resilient to stress. Although no formal studies prove this, there are no negative effects.

The need for vitamins varies depending on your puppy and his lifestyle. The suggested rations to meet the minimum daily requirements are averaged for all dogs. The truth is, the MDR was set using Beagle-sized puppies living a sedentary life in a laboratory. Take that — and the fact that vitamins are a rather unstable lot, easily destroyed by light and heat — into account, and you can see that investing in a good vitamin supplement is a smart decision. Ask your veterinarian for suggestions.

Vitamin deficiencies can lead to poor growth, digestive disorders, elimination problems, stool eating, a weak immune system, greasy, stinky coats, Addison's Disease, thyroid malfunction, aggression, timidity, and sterility.

Some foods have a long list of vitamins. Keep in mind that only 1 percent of the food is sourced from vitamins. Though the list may look impressive, less is more.

Minerals (1 percent of the food)

Minerals are a lot like their cohorts, the vitamins. They help the body in its normal daily functions like circulation, energy production, and cell regeneration. Minerals come in two varieties: elemental and chelated. Elementals come from the earth; they're less easy to digest because they can't be broken down. Chelated are found within organic matter and break down easily.

Though mineral deficiencies are more common than vitamin deficiencies, do not supplement your dog's diet unless your veterinarian directs you to do so. Adding minerals to your puppy's diet can cause an imbalance that is harmful to his health. (To discover more about how specific minerals affect your dog's health, refer to *The Holistic Guide for a Healthy Dog,* by Wendy Volhard and Kerry Brown, DVM, Macmillan Publishing, 1995.)

Here's another reason to not use dog food high in soy protein: The absorption of iron, a mineral necessary for good circulation, is aggravated by a diet high in soy protein.

Water

Did you know that your dog can live three weeks without food but will die within days without water? Water is necessary for all digestive processes, as well as temperature regulation, nutrient absorption, and as a transportation medium, shipping things between organs and out the body.

How much water your pup needs depends on her physical activities and the type of food she eats. Panting is your dog's means of sweating. If your dog is panting, she needs a drink. Dry food also encourages thirst. Because dry food contains only 10 percent moisture, your dog needs about a quart of water for every pound of dry food she eats. Canned dog food or home-cooked diets, on the other hand, contain more water (keep in mind, though, that this does not necessarily make them a superior food source).

If you're using water from the faucet, have it tested or do it yourself to ensure it's free of harmful contaminants. Faucet water has been known to contain bacteria, viruses, lead, gasoline, radioactive gases, and carcinogenic industrial components that can cause chronic health problems. Wal-Mart department stores carry a $4.00 water testing kit that tests hardness and measures chlorine, pH, nitrate, and iron levels.

Cushing's Disease (a disease causing hyperactive adrenal glands) can be caused by drinking too much chlorinated water.

Food Allergies

Dieting allergies are being diagnosed with increased frequency. Symptoms include an itchy face, chewing on paws, and Inflammatory Bowel Disease, which leads to diarrhea.

Hypoallergenic diets utilize a single protein and a single carbohydrate source. The protein chosen is usually one that is not in other types of dog food (such as lamb, venison, rabbit, or fish). Rice is often the carbohydrate of choice for hypoallergenic diets.

Even your pup's dishes may contain allergens. To be on the safe side, use stainless steel dishes for both food and water and wash with anti-bacterial soap or bleach.

For more information on allergies and how to deal with them, check out Chapter 22.

Special Nutritional Situations

All puppies are different. One formula just can't suit everyone. Learn as much as you can about the nutritional needs of your puppy — talking to your veterinarian, breeder, and educated pet store professional — to find the diet that is most suited to your pup's needs. This section covers some thoughts to keep in mind.

If you have a large breed puppy who's prone to growing quickly, don't be surprised if your breeder or veterinarian suggests feeding him an adult food.

Some puppies have specific ailments that require a prescription diet. Your veterinarian can guide you in your selections and provide appropriate foods to keep your dog well. These diets have a guaranteed analysis that breaks down each ingredient to ensure you're getting the identical food sources in every bag/can.

Hip dysplasia is a serious growing abnormality where the hip doesn't properly align. Dogs can develop this condition in either of two ways: The first way is purely genetic. If a dog is blueprinted for this condition, he will get it regardless of diet. The second way a puppy can contract hip dysplasia is situational. Over-excited play stretches ligaments and tendons. If this occurs in the midst of a growth phase, the added stress can scar the tissue, which grows over time and will hasten hip dysplasia. The point? Feeding an adult lower protein diet manages the growth spurts.

As your puppy ages, he'll need a different balance of nutrition to keep him going. Like us, older dogs need less protein and fewer calories.

Chapter 21

Proper Puppy Exercise

*O*ne common misconception about dogs is that leaving a dog outside all day is good for him. "He needs fresh air" couldn't be further from the truth. If you leave your puppy out all day, you end up with a neurotic creature digging in the yard and barking until the neighbors complain. Although true that proper exercise outside leads to a calmer dog inside, "proper exercise" is the key phrase. Proper exercise involves you.

Consider the Age of Your Pup

A puppy's tissues are soft. His bones are growing. He's as awkward as an infant trying to take his first step. Stairs frighten him. Although taking your brand-new companion with you on your five mile jog would be nice, it wouldn't be safe. Too much exercise stresses your puppy's growing body. Your puppy would get distracted and quit; she might demand to be carried. You'd notice a limp. Sure, you want to keep your puppy in shape — an obese puppy is an unhealthy puppy — but puppies aren't born ready to run endless miles. Let yours develop first.

Until a puppy is four months old, you should play with him (preferably on a *long line*) instead of walking him. Any of the games mentioned in Chapter 28 will do.

Play on grass or dirt surfaces. Keep pups off the pavement, except if you're going out to potty them; hard pavement is too stressful on their bones and tissues. Tile floors are also a real nightmare for puppies because they're so slippery. Lay carpet strips down until your pup gets older.

Don't Just Watch — Be an Exercise Companion

Puppies don't like to exercise alone. They need a companion to frolic and play with. Unless you have a couple of dogs, you need to exercise your puppy two to four times a day for 5–20 minutes, depending on her age and breed. I know this sounds like a lot of exercise, but once you get into it, it'll feel like recess in the third grade. Remember the bell? Yes!

When you bring a young puppy home, she has five needs: food, water, elimination, sleep, and *exercise*. Exercise is a need. When it's time to play, you have no choice: You must get involved. Because a walk down the street can be frightening to a new puppy (cars, big dogs, and so on), games like those described in Chapter 28 are the best way to tire her out.

Avoid games like tug-of-war, wrestling, chasing, or teasing. These games frustrate pups, communicate confrontation, encourage nipping (especially on clothing), and make you look more like a playmate than a leader.

Factor in the Size and Breed

Size is another factor in determining how much and what kind of exercise your pup needs. Breed is, too. A German Shorthaired Pointer — a large puppy bred to run around in fields looking for birds — needs more exercise than a teacup-sized Poodle. Yes, common sense would tell most people that, but I'm surprised how many people buy a breed for its looks without realizing the amount of exercise their new puppy needs. See Table 21-1 to find out the energy level of your breed (for more information on breed groupings, flip to Chapter 2). Your breed's energy level determines the amount of interaction needed and how often:

Energy Level	*Amount of Interaction Needed*	*How Often*
Very high	20 minutes	2–4 times daily
High	15–20 minutes	2–3 times daily
Medium	10–15 minutes	2 times daily
Low	5 minutes	1–2 times daily

Table 21-1	Breeds and Their Energy Levels	
Breed	*Bred To*	*Energy Level*
Pointers	Course fields all day, point, and retrieve	Very high
Retrievers	Stay by master's side, retrieve on command	High
Spaniels	Flush and retrieve birds	High
Setters	Run afield, point, flush, and retrieve fowl	High
Sighthounds	Pursue fast-moving game	High in spurts; then low
Scent hounds	Follow and trail game	High
Large game hunters	Challenge large game	Medium
Sled/Draft	Pull sleds long distances and pull carts to market	Medium to high
Guarding	Guard territory	Medium
Personal protection	Protect home and master	Medium
Rescue/Water Dogs (in general)	Rescue man	Low
Portuguese Water Dog		High
Sheep herders	Herd sheep	Medium to high
Livestock driving	Move sheep and cattle from field to field	High
Terriers	Hunt barn pests	Medium to high
Fighting breeds	Originally bred to fight each other or other species	Medium
Non-Sporting	All vary historically	Medium
Dalmatian	Currently bred for companionship	Very high
Toy Group	Companionship	Low

If your puppy doesn't work off his energy outside, he'll work it off inside. If you don't run him, he may demolish your couch. Is it spite? No, just energy and boredom.

Know the Difference between Puppy Play and Puppy Fights

If you're taking your puppy on a play date, get ready for some wild mouthing and jumping action. I know it looks vicious, but this is how puppies play. Have you ever seen a dog swing another around by his scruff? As long as he does it in the spirit of fun, it's okay. The question is how can you tell whether it's fun or fighting? Here are some telltale signs:

✔ Fights usually start during the introduction. If two dominant dogs meet (usually same sex, although not always), they do a lot of *bluffing* — hackles raised, chest out, head up, throaty vocalizations, tail just above the rump or under it, and eyes locked. If one dog doesn't back down (by breaking the stare, lowering his head, or doing a play bow), they may fight to determine dominance.

✔ If two dominant dogs are playing and one gets too rough, the other may not back down. The vocalization turns from a roughhousing tone to an aggressive one quickly.

✔ Some dogs fight off their playmate when they've had enough. If your puppy looks tired and bothered, separate him from other dogs.

✔ If you have a dominant puppy, leave a nylon lead on his collar while he plays so that, if things get out of hand, you have something to grab. Encourage the other dog owner to do the same.

✔ If a fight starts with an unleashed dog, grab the base of one dog's tail while another person grabs the other dog. Back away from each other simultaneously to separate them. Don't reach for their collars; either dog may unintentionally bite you.

An alternative means of separating a fight is to pour or spray water or Bitter Apple on the dogs' heads. Please note that the water is meant only to stun the dogs so you'll be able to separate them without getting bitten yourself.

Following are a few other things to keep in mind:

✔ More often than not, people create dog fights. Yes, people. Left alone, dogs usually work out their differences and establish a hierarchy. All out fights occur when people step in screaming and yelling. Dogs respond to the added tension and go for blood. Sometimes, the best way to settle a dispute is to leave the room.

Never correct a Top Dog who's in a fight with another dog. Confrontational play helps the dogs decide who's king (or queen) of the mountain. You cannot balance their play. Remember, dogs respect a hierarchy; mess with it, and you're asking for trouble.

✔ Dogs know the difference between another grown dog and a puppy. Everyone is more tolerant of puppies. Don't be surprised, however, if a grown dog pins a pup or growls a warning. It's nature. Don't interfere. The grown dog is teaching the pup a lesson on respect and self-control.

Considerations for Pups with Hip or Elbow Dysplasia

Normally, the head of the femur grows into the joint socket and rotates freely as your puppy moves around. But hip dysplasia affects many dogs, both purebred and mixed. In a moderately dysplastic puppy, the femoral head angles outward and the bone thickens, leaving a gap in the joint. This gap creates slips in motion, causing discomfort and instability. Severe hip dysplasia is extremely painful. With the femoral head degenerated and practically dislocated, motion is crippled, and pain is constant. Your veterinarian can inform you of surgical options.

Swimming is a wonderful exercise for puppies with this condition. Not everyone is fortunate to have a pond or pool in the backyard, but if you look hard enough, you may be able to find one. Long swims and leash walks on grass/turf (no cement) can build muscles and strength slowly.

If you have a setback and the limping starts again, talk to your veterinarian, ease off exercise, and start back slowly when you're given the go ahead. Your puppy is physically handicapped. He needs you to take care of him.

Elbow dysplasia is similar to hip dysplasia, but the trouble occurs in the elbow joint. Elbow dysplasia is more common in large breed pups between 6 and 14 months. Signs of pain include lameness in the forelimbs.

Protocol for these puppies is either bed rest or surgery. I know, restricting the movement of a high-energy puppy is a great big headache, but try to imagine how your pup feels. Being a confined youth isn't easy. Be compassionate and patient. If possible, take your puppy swimming.

A note about osteoporosis

Avoid all-meat diets, which are high in protein and phosphorus but low in calcium and vitamin D. This unbalance stimulates the pituitary gland in dogs' systems and causes osteoporosis. The condition results in skeletal deformities, such as stunted bone growth, spinal aberrations, and joint pain.

What you can do for your pup

If your puppy has a skeletal disorder, like hip or elbow dysplasia, you must deal with it. Begin by following this check list:

- Neuter your puppy — don't pass on this problem — and talk to your breeder. If he's responsible, he'll eliminate that breeding combination.

- Feed your puppy a balanced diet and avoid high calorie, rapid-growth diets, which can aggravate the disorder. The tissues, bones, and muscles must grow together evenly.

- Avoid supplementing the diet, especially with calcium. Ask for your veterinarian's suggestion.

- Keep your puppy's weight down. Too many pounds on a stressed joint is a bad thing.

- Eliminate contributing environmental factors like long jogs. Also correct jumping habits. Are stairs stressful? Talk to your veterinarian.

- Buy cozy bedding. Buy heating pads too.

- Carpet any area your puppy travels frequently. Slippery floors don't provide good traction.

- Avoid leaving your puppy out in the cold. Keep him in a warm, dry environment, especially at night.

- And last, but not least, massage that joint. (Avoid putting pressure on the joint itself.) Get blood flowing to the muscles, especially if your puppy's on bed rest.

A dog can be born with a predisposition for dysplastic disorders, but you can avoid the worst effects by controlling your dog's diet and avoiding stressful exercise. See the sidebar "What you can do for your pup" for more advice on how to deal with these disorders.

Keeping an Injured Pup Still

Some puppies are under doctor's orders to keep still. A spinal injury, a broken bone, a bad cut, or a genetic disorder may require what, in veterinarian circles, is known as *strict cage rest*. I can tell you from experience that enforcing this rest is a bigger problem for you than your puppy. He can't understand the doctor, and as he heals, he wants to move about as usual. It's your job to keep him immobile until he gets his doctor's clearance. You can wreck a good surgical job or bone realignment by giving your puppy too much freedom too fast. Here are a few ideas to keep your puppy's mind busy when his body must be still:

✔ Provide him with his favorite chews — pig's ears, hooves, bones, a rope toy. Go ahead, spoil him rotten.

✔ Buy a Kong toy or hollowed-out bone and stuff it with peanut butter.

✔ Massage his muscles to increase blood flow and keep them healthy. The massage feels good, too.

✔ Play calming music to help relieve the stress of being confined from outside activities.

✔ Talk to your puppy. He loves the attention and the distraction of listening to your voice.

You're going to have to be the strong one. Your puppy will want to run around before doing so is safe. Follow your veterinarian's orders to the letter.

Chapter 22

Staying on Top of Good Hygiene and Health

Staying on top of good health can prevent a lot of disease and heartache. One way to accomplish this is to keep your dog clean and groomed. Not only does regular grooming make your puppy look and feel good, but it also lets you discover any ailments before they get serious. Brushes, nail clippers, toothpaste, cotton balls — these are just some of the paraphernalia you'll use to keep your puppy in tip-top shape. Of course, the other way to stay on top of your pup's good health is to make sure you join forces with a caring vet who can help your puppy grow into a healthy dog.

Brushing Puppy: A Dream or a Nightmare?

Grooming can be a complete nightmare or a delightful, interactive time with your dog. Whether grooming is a chore or a treat is determined in puppyhood. Keep the first brushing episodes fun and end on a positive with a treat or favorite toy. Following are some suggestions to make your puppy's first associations with grooming pleasant ones:

✔ Find a soft bristle human/puppy brush. (Avoid the wire-bristled brush for now, at least. You can eventually work toward using a brush of your choice; talk to a groomer to decide what brush is best for your dog's needs.)

✔ Spread peanut butter or chicken broth in your puppy's food bowl or provide a delectable chew for distraction.

Show the puppy the seasoned floor when the puppy is in a quiet mood.

As the puppy enjoys the diversion, draw the brush over her body softly.

If you follow the preceding suggestions, your puppy will take the experience in stride, and soon you'll both be looking forward to the time together.

If your puppy growls fiercely at any point while you're brushing him, stop everything and call a professional right away.

A Lifetime of Easy Bathing

I remember dog baths back when I was a kid. I had a big Husky-Shepherd mix named Shawbee. To say she hated her bath is an understatement. She dug her heels in the minute we'd turn her down the hall. Restraining her in the tub was no picnic either. Four hands had to be on her or else she was hall bound, shaking suds as she ran down the stairs and out the door. It was quite entertaining.

Here's a way to prevent this scenario: Make *Tub* a command and practice tub exercises long before you give your puppy a bath. The trick works so well, your puppy might start jumping into the tub on command.

1. **Say "Tub," run to the tub, and treat your puppy (without actually putting her in). Repeat, repeat.**

2. **Next, lay a towel on the bottom of the tub or sink for traction, place some toys around it, and rub peanut butter into the basin at your puppy's nose level.**

   You're going to practice without water.

3. **Help your puppy into the tub; then play for five minutes and take her out.**

   Love and treat her calmly. Sit on the tub's edge. And remember, no bath, no water.

4. **Repeat Step 3 until your puppy looks forward to tub togetherness.**

5. **Next, run the water as you're playing but let it drain (don't fill the tub).**

6. **Once your puppy allows the water to run with her in the tub, let the tub fill to hock (ankle) depth.**

   If your dog squirms, stop the water, sing softly, and offer some treats as you scratch her back lovingly.

7. **Proceed gradually until you're able to tub and bathe peacefully.**

I know these steps sound like a lot, but think of it as one week's adventure. After all, it's a training exercise — and a small effort for a lifetime of easy bathing.

Stick with one bath a month at most. I never bathe my dogs more than a few times a year, although I water my dogs down if they need a mud-rinse. The reason? Dogs don't have pores to produce oil. If you bath them constantly, their coats become dry, dull, full of dandruff, and brittle.

"WHAT Have You Been Into?"

If you think dog smell is a bad odor. . . .

Getting skunked

Few dogs learn to avoid skunks; my childhood dog Shawbee never did. I remember the long nights spent trying to get the skunk juices off her face and the smell off her fur. I wouldn't wish this experience on my worst enemy. If your puppy is given the opportunity to hunt a skunk, you're in for a hearty surprise (not to mention a stinking one).

Fortunately, the skunk is nocturnal. You can avoid them by keeping your puppy on leash during evening walks.

Sure, I've tried tomato juice, spaghetti sauce, ketchup, V8 — let me spare you the anticipation. Not only does the juice combine to create a new noxious odor, but your puppy also turns pink in the process. Here are a few other remedies that may give you better results:

✔ On the market is a product called Snuck Off (by Thornell Coop). Snuck Off is a definite improvement on the age-old tomato remedy and a lot less messy, but don't be surprised if your puppy still emerges with a lingering odor.

✔ Here's another a remedy that I fortunately haven't had to try but I've heard works wonders. It's an odd concoction, but according to my client, "It's miraculous!" Bathe your dog with the following mixture:

> 1 quart of three-percent hydrogen peroxide
>
> ¼ cup baking soda
>
> 1 teaspoon liquid soap

And then follow the bath with a water rinse.

✔ I also hear that a feminine douche, used as a rinse, works miracles. Just don't stock up all at once — they might commit you!

Rolling in dead carcasses and feces

If you don't know what *rolling* refers to, if your dog has never rolled in the feces or carcass of another animal, consider yourself lucky. Even blessed. For those who must endure this pastime, understand that although the behavior seems totally gross, it is like bathing in perfume to a dog. Charming analogy, I know.

Yes, puppies often roll more than adult dogs (the curiosity factor), but the hard truth is, once a roller, always a roller.

A dog that rolls is not "bad." It's a selfish thing: a desire to smell doggoned delicious — not a plot to stink up your home. Discipline and after-the-fact corrections won't stop it. The only way around rolling is to monitor your dog's walks, teach the No command so that you can stop it as it happens, and bathe your dog when you aren't in time to stop it.

Giving Puppy a Manicure

Puppies take no pride in their nails. None. I'm not sure they even think about them until you try to cut them. Then there's a big sob story. If you have a pup who struggles every time you take the clippers out, you know what I'm talking about. If you have a pup who hasn't seen the clippers yet, lucky you. You can prevent this problem before it begins.

The best kind of clipper looks like a guillotine. Seriously. I can't explain it any better than that. When you're clipping your puppy's nail, you want to clip the very tip, just at the point it starts to curl (see Figure 22-1). Front nails grow faster than hind ones. If you have a dog with a dew claw (a nail that rides high on the back paw), don't overlook it. If nails grow too long, they can crack, break, or become ingrown. You need to clip your puppy's nails about once a month.

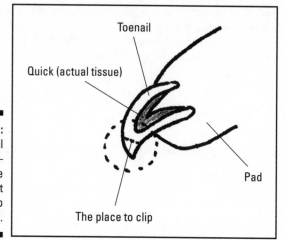

Toenail

Quick (actual tissue)

Pad

The place to clip

Figure 22-1:
Clip the nail
at the tip —
right where
the point
starts to
curl.

If you're reading this before you've cut your dog's nails, consider yourself blessed. To avoid having a clipper-phobic dog, make paw-handling part of every positive interaction, from petting to treating.

1. **Initially, just handle your puppy's paws, nothing fancy.**

   If you're in the car and come to a red light, turn to your puppy, handle her paws, and tell her "Good girl." Have as much hand-on-paw contact as possible for a week or two; no clipping.

2. **Next take out your peanut butter (or broth) and swipe some across the refrigerator at your dog's eye level. As she licks, rub her paws with the clipper.**

   Don't cut the nails just yet. Open and shut the clippers to acquaint her with the sound.

3. **Now try one cut — just one.**

   Place the edge of the clippers over the top of the nail and squeeze the handle quickly.

   White nails show the nail bed, which you must avoid. If your puppy has dark nails, you need to take extra precaution. If you're concerned, ask your veterinarian or groomer to give you a lesson.

4. **The next day, try two nails and then three.**

Do not correct your dog if she protests. Be understanding and slow down. Again, it sounds like a production, but in the long run, you'll be glad you took the time. Anyone who has cut his dog or frightened him by being too rough can tell you having a clipper-phobic dog is a disaster.

God forbid you cut into your puppy's *quick* (the tissue part of the nail). Aside from being excruciatingly painful, the cut will bleed for hours because the quick has lots of veins and nerves. To prevent excess bleeding, purchase a clotting solution from your veterinarian. It works like magic.

Taking Care of Puppy's Face

Although puppies don't worry over their looks, their facial features shouldn't go unnoticed.

Puppy's eyes

Soulful, sweet, comic — your puppy's eyes express it all. It's up to you to keep them healthy, bright, and clear.

- ✔ Do not let your puppy hang her head out the car window. Sure, it looks refreshing, but one pebble can knock out an eye. Leave the windows open a crack if you must or station your puppy far enough away to keep her face clear of open windows.

- ✔ Be careful. Watch your puppy's head when playing interactive games like stick toss and soccer. Eyes are very tender.

- ✔ If you have a long-haired breed, clip the hair surrounding the eye.

- ✔ Don't squeeze shampoo on your dog's head or spray flea repellent directly at your dog's face. Cover her eyes as you apply any products with your fingertips.

- ✔ Does your dog have morning eye crust? It's not so bad as long as you wipe it clear everyday. Use warm water and a soft rag or tissue. Built-up crust can be painful, irritating, and a pretty gruesome sight.

Avoid dogs and cats with mange, ringworm, or other skin irritations. Make sure that the pets your puppy hangs out with are healthy.

If you notice that your puppy's eyes are tearful, full of mucous, swollen, or itchy, see your veterinarian. She could be suffering from conjunctivitis (which is very contagious), a cold, internal parasites, or an allergy. If your veterinarian prescribes eye medication, administer it carefully.

- ✔ To apply drops, swipe something tasty on the refrigerator (peanut butter or broth) 30 degrees above your dog's eye level. Pull back the upper lid until you see the white of your dog's eye and administer the medication.

✔ To apply ointment, set up the same situation, but pull the lower lid down and squeeze the medication along the lower lid. Be careful not to poke them. Stay very calm and positive to help your puppy relax. If your pup puts up a big fuss, ask for drops so that you can keep the applicator further from her face.

Your puppy has a third eye lid. If you lift the lower lid carefully, you see a pinkish lid that closes independently. This lid protects your puppy's eye from dust and other particles that are picked up near to the ground. This third lid can become infected. Note its healthy color and take your puppy to the veterinarian if this lid gets inflamed.

Puppy's ears

I'm mesmerized by this body part. I can literally lull myself into a trance petting ears. And it doesn't seem to matter what shape — uprights, floppy, short, cropped. Dogs seem to love the ear massage as well. Ahh, bliss.

But ears need more than massaging to keep them healthy. The ear can play host to all sorts of bacteria, mites, and yeast infections. You must take good care of that flap to prevent these microscopic suckers from moving in and settling down. Because they do best in moist, damp, waxy environments, you need to keep the ear dry and clean. Different dogs require different cleaning schedules (from every couple weeks to daily). As a general rule, floppy ears require more care than uprights because of limited air circulation. If you have a hairy-eared breed, you may be instructed to pluck the hair out of the way. Talk to your veterinarian or groomer for personal instructions. Excess hair can trap wax and make one big mess that cries out for parasites. (Refer to Chapter 23 for information regarding ear mites.) Following is some general information about caring for your puppy's ears:

✔ Clean the outer ear flap. Ask your veterinarian to recommend a commercial ear solution that helps prevent infection. Using a cotton ball soaked in the solution, swipe the outer flap. Don't go too deep; the ear is very tender, and going in too deep can be painful. Repeat this process until the cotton comes up clean.

Do not use Q-Tips or poke into your puppy's ear canal. You can do irreparable damage.

✔ Prevent water from entering the ear. If you're bathing your pup, put a large piece of cotton in the opening ahead of time and wipe the ears out with a dry piece when you're finished.

Ear infections are quite common. Signs of infection include a red/swollen ear, discharge, head shaking, ear itching, or a bad odor. What a drag. Get your puppy to her doctor immediately. Left untreated, infections can cause fever, depression, irritability, and loss of balance. Your veterinarian will prescribe an ointment that you administer at home. Here's how:

1. **Wait until your dog's a little sleepy.**

2. **Bring her to the refrigerator and swipe some peanut butter or margarine at her eye level.**

3. **As she's licking the refrigerator, gently squeeze the amount of ointment specified by your veterinarian into her ear canal.**

4. **Massage her ear as you praise her warmly.**

Puppy's nose

There's not too much to say about the nose. Back when I was growing up, you used to feel it to determine how your dog was feeling. If it was too hot, the dog had a fever. If it was too dry, the dog was depressed. It may sound crazy, but that's what I was told. The truth is, dogs' noses can heat up in a warm environment and can get dry when the air lacks humidity. If you want to know whether your dog's running a fever, take his temperature, rectal style. Oh joy. . . .

Dogs' noses can get discolored. How? Sometimes from the sun. When your puppy hangs in the sun, protect that nose with sunblock 45. Other times, an allergic reaction to a food dish or household detergent causes discoloration. In such a case, use stainless steel bowls for your dog's dishes and clean with environmentally safe products.

Puppy's mouth

You must take care of your puppy's teeth. Though dogs are less prone to tartar buildup than we are, they're not immune. Sure, they have more concentrated saliva, and they chew bones and things, but this doesn't take the place of dental care. Without a little help from "friends" (that's us), they'll suffer from tooth decay, cavities, abscesses, periodontal disease, and tooth loss. To keep your puppy's teeth healthy:

- **Feed your puppy dry food.** Crunchy is better.

- **Start brushing your puppy's teeth once a week.** Use special dog toothpaste. (Avoid human toothpaste; fluoride and dogs don't mix.) Read the label for instructions. If your dog is adverse to the brush, use your finger or a finger brush. If your dog growls, quit immediately and call a professional.

If you have a young puppy, acquaint her with this procedure early on. Rub your fingers along her gums throughout the week and praise her calmly as you brush.

✔ **As your dog gets older, you may opt for a yearly professional cleaning.** To clean your dog's teeth, your veterinarian needs to anesthetize her; then he scales each tooth separately and finishes with polishing. Good dental care prevents disease and decay.

Some puppies put up an enormous struggle. For these critters, your veterinarian may suggest an oral spray that breaks down tartar.

Taking Puppy in for Regular Checkups

Puppies, like kids, need vaccinations and regular checkups. Once you've found a veterinarian you're comfortable with, get out your appointment book and schedule regular visits to ensure that your puppy gets all the protection she needs.

Choosing a good vet

Choosing a veterinarian is one of the most important decisions of your dog's life. And, unless you live in rural America, you have several to choose from. Following are some concrete guidelines to make finding a good vet easier:

✔ **Ask other pet owners.**

✔ **Visit the vet both with and without your pet.** Call first to let the office know you'll be arriving to check the place out and meet doctor and staff. If you bring your dog, take along some favorite treats and encourage the staff to feed her. Her first recollections will be very good.

✔ **Look around.** Is the environment clean? Well organized? How does it smell? Do they let you tour the hospital? If so, that's a good sign.

✔ **Ask the doctor some questions.** Where did he study? How long has he been practicing? Are there certain diseases he doesn't (or won't) handle? Does he have references for serious ailments or procedures, such as total hip replacement or ultrasound?

✔ **Trust your opinion.** Do you get good vibes?

✔ **Trust your puppy.** Does her personality do a 360 when you enter the door? If she's miserable, try a different doctor. If she's still miserable, you know it's all in her head.

A word about rabies

Rabies is a very serious virus. I cannot stress proper vaccination enough. The following story brought it home to me.

Crash wasn't a dog. He was a kitten. A tiny creature whose black-and-white coloring looked more like a surrealistic painting than any sort of genetic code. He was a young animal, killed by a mysterious virus that is still far too rampant in our country. In his story, there is a lesson for all animal lovers.

Crash was rescued from the roadside by a good friend of mine named Mo. Crash was taken to the veterinarian, where his scrapes were treated, and Crash was sent home with Mo, who nursed him patiently back to health over the next month. Crash updates were given every few days. He went from a drowsy, shell-shocked, frightened animal to a lively, humorous, and otherwise normal little kitten. But then mysteriously everything fell apart. He had trouble walking, his head jerked and pulled to one side, and he no longer responded to the liquid antibiotics he had been on since his rescue. Mo and Crash made their last trip to the hospital.

Crash did not make it through the night. When he died, his head was severed and sent in to be analyzed. It was confirmed: Crash had rabies. It was a sorry ending for a creature who already had shared and experienced so much love.

Unfortunately, no test exists to determine rabies in an already infected but symptom-free animal. If you pick up a stray, early precautionary measures and a six-week quarantine are advisable to avoid possible infection. With your own pets, prevention is the key. Yearly or tri-yearly vaccines must be updated to prevent pointless deaths and the spread of this deadly disease. Though nothing could have been done to save Crash once the disease entered his system, a loving home and early veterinarian care could have prevented this trauma. Responsible pet ownership is the only way to prevent the disease from entering our pet population.

Getting yearly vaccinations

First vaccines should be given as puppies are weaned off their mother's milk. Unless a puppy is orphaned, which would require more medical intervention, a puppy's first vaccine should begin at six weeks. If a series is recommended, follow-up shots are given two to three weeks later. These shots are called *boosters*. After the puppy reaches doghood, vaccines need to be given annually, in general.

Vaccines aren't guaranteed 100 percent. Some dogs are allergic to them. Other antibodies don't build up enough of a defense. Post-vaccine illnesses are tragic. Keep your puppy at the animal hospital for a half hour after initial vaccines and learn the signs and symptoms of each in case she should get ill.

Dealing with allergies

I suffer big time in this arena. I think I'm allergic to more things than I'm not. Funniest allergies? Dogs and cats. As I write, I'm being kept company by my beautiful 11-year-old cat, Kashina, who's fascinated with my typing. While monthly shots have salvaged my career, dogs with allergies are less fortunate. Canine allergens include wool, dust, molds, pollen, cedar chips, propylene glycol (a rawhide treat preservative), pesticide chemicals, house and garden plants, weeds, and food products. Dogs with allergies suffer from swollen paws, itchy gums, sneezing, and eczema. The worst part is that dogs can't articulate what's wrong, so pinning down the culprit is difficult. If you suspect your dog has allergies, talk to your veterinarian. She can test to determine what's bugging your puppy and give him medication to relieve his symptoms.

Here's a checklist to follow if you suspect your puppy suffers from allergies, noting all seasonal and environmental changes:

- ✔ Use detergent soap designed for babies' diapers when washing your puppy's bedding.

- ✔ Check out the sprays used in your home, yard, and garden. Do not use any products toxic to your pet.

- ✔ Use bleach and water (¼ cup of bleach per gallon of water) to clean your dog's areas. Many dogs are allergic to commercial disinfectants.

- ✔ Don't overuse cleaning or parasite products. Flea sprays, powders, and dips are very toxic.

Spaying or Neutering Puppy

A female dog is prevented from reproducing by an operation commonly called *spaying*. Her ovaries (those egg-producing sacs) are removed. This operation requires your gal to be anesthetized, and recovery takes 5 to 14 days. A male dog is prevented from fathering puppies through an operation called castration. Basically, his testicles are removed from a small incision and his sacs sewn up before you can say "Boo." Your dog is anesthetized for the procedure and is back on his feet in 5 to 10 days.

If you're not planning to breed your dog, have your dog spayed or neutered. Here's my argument: wild dogs have three needs. They need to eat, driving them to hunt and kill for survival. They need shelter; it's the den thing. And they need to reproduce. Hormonal drives can override all else; a hungry lost dog can block out all other concerns when presented with an opportunity to mate.

When to spay or neuter

Yet another controversial topic. Though I've always neutered my dogs when they were between seven and eight months old, you need to discuss this matter with your veterinarian. Some veterinarians will alter dogs earlier, stressing that it be taken care of before a female dog's first heat (which I tend to agree with); others prefer to alter dogs later. Listen to all arguments, think about what you find out, and decide what makes most sense for you.

With the domesticated dog, you take care of the first two by offering your dog food and shelter. But the need to reproduce remains and can be quite frustrating. A dog will leave the warm, safe perimeters of home to go out and look for a mate. Therefore, either enter a responsible breeding program if you decide to breed your dog or alter him (that is, have your dog spayed or neutered).

I've loved every dog who lived under my roof, but none of them were picture perfect, and consequently all were either spayed or neutered. It didn't change their personalities. They didn't get fat. Trust me, altering is not like a lobotomy; it simply removes the need to scope and fight for mates. Here's a list of some other, more scientific arguments for altering your dog:

- According to the Adoption Option, approximately 4–6 million dogs are euthanized in animal shelters each year. Don't add to the problem. If you're not breeding your dog responsibly, have him altered.

- Having your dog fixed reduces the chance of breast, ovarian, uterine, or cervical cancer for females and testicular cancer or prostrate infection for males.

- Male dogs are less likely to mark the home or fight with other male dogs and are more likely to stay close to home.

If you adopt your puppy from a shelter, you may be required to neuter him. Some shelters offer to do the procedure for you; others recommend you to a low-cost facility. Neutering can cost anywhere from $50 to $250, depending on the individual dog's sex and health.

Getting a Puppy Health Insurance Plan

Just when you thought everything was insured. Now you can get a plan for your dog. Be very careful in selecting your carrier, however, or you might get stuck paying out of pocket for ailments you thought were covered. Here are some questions to ask when you're out shopping for a good policy:

✔ How long has your company been in business?

✔ Are you licensed within your state?

✔ Is your policy accepted by the state commissioner's office?

✔ Will I be able to choose my own veterinarian?

✔ Will you cover care if my veterinarian refers me to a specialist?

✔ What's the yearly deductible? Is there a cap on specific illnesses or accidents?

✔ What does the policy not include (worms, checkups, dental care, heartworm tests, and so on)?

✔ Are there any conditions or diseases your policy doesn't cover?

✔ Do you cover ultrasounds, CAT scans, bone scans, intensive care, reconstructive surgery, or medications?

✔ Do you cover preexisting conditions?

✔ How do I pay the premium? Monthly, biannually, annually?

✔ Will you cover my dog throughout her lifetime, or is your policy limited by age?

✔ Under what situations would you terminate a policy?

✔ What is involved in signing on?

Make sure you read the fine print before you sign anything. No plan covers 100 percent of everything. Health insurance for your dog can be a real lifesaver in an emergency or if your dog gets extremely sick, but you don't want to pay for a policy only to find it doesn't cover all services necessary for her recovery. Please ask your veterinarian to recommend a good carrier.

Some western states offer HMOs, which provide a whole range of services for a monthly fee and a small co-payment. Operating on the philosophy that preventive care is the best guarantee against illness, these plans cover routine checkups, lab testing, medicine, and hospital care. Ask your veterinarian for more information.

Chapter 23

"Eewwww!" (The Parasites Chapter)

Gee-whiz. How can I make this chapter entertaining? It's a hard task considering the fact that I'm completely bug phobic. Thinking about any bug — flea, worm, tick, or otherwise — nesting on or in my dog really gives me the creeps. Visualization is definitely not advisable.

In this chapter, you find out more than you want to know about parasites, including how to recognize them. In addition, I discuss methods to annihilate these critters from your puppy's body, as well as offer good prevention tips.

What Exactly Is a Parasite, Anyway?

A *parasite* is a creature that lives off another animal. Parasites can feast on skin and blood, or they can leech on inside your puppy's intestinal tract, eating your dog's leftovers. If your dog itches one spot too much and starts to pull her hair out, she may get a *hot spot* (officially known as *acute pyotraumatic dermatitis,* which is not due to a single underlying cause). Go to the doctor immediately and treat the problem before the area becomes infected.

Getting Rid of the Blood Suckers (External Parasites)

External parasites live for blood — your dog's, to be precise, although some settle for a human snack if the mood strikes them. The following sections go through these varmints one at a time.

Fleas

Fleas are an age-old problem, and they generally hang out in the lower portion of your puppy's body, behind the shoulder blades. One sure fire way to detect a problem is to buy a flea comb and brush your dog's rear with it. If you pull out some "dirt," put it on a paper towel and add a few drops of water. If the dirt turns a reddish color, you're holding flea excrement. Oh joy.

Contrary to popular belief, fleas don't live on dogs; they feed on them. Fleas live in carpets and grass, so treating the problem involves all-out war.

Treating your puppy

I'm obsessive about flea prevention. I use every home-spun herbal remedy known to man — from brewer's yeast and garlic, to menthol, eucalyptus, and citronella — and I've never had an out-of-control flea problem. (If you don't feel like pressing your own garlic, you can find commercial pills for brewer's yeast and garlic that work just as well.)

Talk to your veterinarian about safe options for your puppy. Your vet may recommend collars, oil pouches, or other products during flea season. Be sure to use these remedies only as frequently as the label instructs.

Do not spray, rub, or squeeze flea prevention products near your dog's face or scrotum. Most products are toxic. Talk to your veterinarian first and discuss safe treatments.

Ask your veterinarian about flea tablets or preventive powder. Although these remedies don't take care of the fleas you have now, they do sterilize the fleas, putting a cramp in their reproductive cycle. Insect growth regulators are not new, but their internal (systemic) use is. They have extraordinarily low toxicity and are useful in preventing house and bedding infestations.

Dogs can be allergic to flea saliva, a condition veterinarians call *Flea Allergy Dermatitis*. Itching is intense and can lead to hair loss and self-mutilation. Sometimes the itching gets so bad that your dog creates a hot spot, and a bacterial infection develops.

Treating your home and yard

Home isn't so sweet when you share it with fleas. A full-blown flea infestation is like a scene from a horror show — bugs hopping onto your skin from every direction faster than you can bat them away. My suggestion? Treat your home the second you discover a flea problem.

- ✔ Ask your veterinarian for advice.

- ✔ Vacuum, vacuum, vacuum. You not only pick up the adults, but you scoop the eggs and larva from their nests, too. Make sure you toss the bag after you vacuum, though; adult fleas are wonderful acrobats.

- ✔ Treat your dog's bedding by washing it with an anti-flea detergent from the pet store or throw it out.

- ✔ Talk to your veterinarian or pet care professional about the pros and cons of different products. And don't forget to check the flea product label; it should be FDA approved. Follow the instructions for personal safety.

- ✔ Treat all rooms in your house. Fleas love to travel.

- ✔ If your home/yard treatment's toxic, make sure all creatures, two-legged and four, are out of the house for the day (this is a good time to take your pets in for a flea dip).

- ✔ Open all windows when you get home; then vacuum again and toss the bag.

- ✔ Select a product that treats all life stages and repeat the treatment as suggested.

Yards are very tricky and can be expensive to exterminate. A good freeze takes care of all parties involved, but if you can't wait — or you have mild winters — talk to your veterinarian about your options.

Ticks

Ticks are another blood sucking parasite. Like fleas, ticks prefer furry creatures, but they settle for humans in a pinch. Unfortunately, ticks are found all over the world and can carry airborne diseases.

Ticks, like fleas, develop in stages: eggs, larva, nymph, and adult. Eggs are laid in a damp shady environment. As they develop from stage to stage, they have several hosts and can pick up a bacterial infection from any one of them. Adult ticks feed on blood.

Removing a tick

Ticks love to climb. Their favorite area is around your dog's head. Removing a tick is no picnic. When they feed, they insert barbs into the skin like fish hooks. If you try to pull a tick out, you end up with a headless blood-filled sac, and your dog ends up with a nasty bump on her head. To remove a tick, follow these steps:

1. **Stun the tick with a cotton ball soaked in mineral oil for 30 seconds.**

2. **With special tick-removing tweezers you can buy from a pet store, press down on the skin on either side of the tick.**

3. **Squeeze the skin surrounding the tick tightly and grasp the head (see Figure 23-1).**

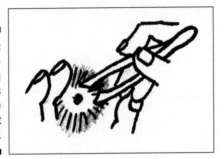

Figure 23-1:
Use tick-removing tweezers and squeeze the skin next to the tick.

4. **Lift up and out.**

   This step can be painful (give your dog a spoonful of peanut butter or some biscuits while you take care of the removal business).

5. **Wash your hands when you are done.**

Deterring ticks in the first place

You can do a lot to prevent ticks from feasting on your dog:

✔ Ask your veterinarian to recommend a tick collar. Secure the collar snugly around your dog's neck. Also ask your veterinarian to recommend a repellent.

Do not spray around your dog's eyes. To treat your dog's forehead and ears, place the product onto a glove and massage in those hard-to-reach areas. Don't forget your dog's paws.

Tick products are very toxic. To prevent your dog from licking himself after treatment, keep him occupied with his favorite game until the product dries. If you have a pup, discuss safe treatments with your veterinarian.

✔ Walk your dog in the open sunshine. Ticks love to hang out in shaded, woody areas.

✔ Inspect yourself and your dog after every walk. Run a flea comb, which you can purchase at any pet store, over your dog's coat after every outing. Ticks take a while to burrow, and a flea comb picks them up.

✔ To protect yourself, wear light colors and tuck your pant legs into your socks. To protect your head, wear a cap.

It's hard to kill these (blood) suckers. They're drown-proof, squish-proof, and squeeze-proof. I find the best way to kill a tick is to burn them or drop them into a jar of bleach, rubbing alcohol, or vodka (for lower toxicity). (Keep the jar out of the reach of the kids.)

Mites, mange, and lice

These bugs are quite content hanging around on or in the skin or coat of your dog, living on skin, hair, or blood. Before treating for these parasites, make sure you get a diagnosis from your vet.

The quick scoop on tick diseases

Feasting on blood from birds on up through the food chain, ticks often carry diseases. Here are the four most common:

Rocky Mountain Spotted Fever: Ticks carrying this disease (Dermacentor ticks) are most common in the southeast United States, although RMSF has been diagnosed as far north as Long Island. It causes failure of blood clotting mechanisms, rash, fever, loose and bloody urine and stool, nose bleeds, and respiratory difficulty.

Canine Ehrlichiosis: This nasty condition is transmitted by a Rhipiecphalus tick (although deer ticks are also in question). It causes severe anemia, fever, bruises, and bleeding disorders by attacking the white blood cells.

Canine Babesiosus: This disease is more common in Europe than the United States. This organism attacks the red blood cells causing severe anemia.

Lyme disease (Canine Borreliosis): Lyme disease has spread to over 47 states. It can affect most mammals and is transmitted through the common deer tick. (Nearly 50 percent of all adult deer ticks carry the disease.) Once the organism gets into your dog's system (or yours, for that matter), it seeks out joints, causing painful inflammation, fever, loss of appetite, and lameness. Left untreated, your dog's kidneys, heart, and neurological processes may be in danger.

Your veterinarian will run a *titer* (measures level of antibodies or immunity) to determine whether your dog has been infected with any of these diseases and needs treatment.

Ear mites

Ear mites nestle in your dog's ear and feed on the outer layer of skin. The first sign of ear mites is your dog's behavior; she'll scratch her ear intently, shake her head, and walk funny. You can check for ear mites by examining your dog's ear canal; if it's filled with brown wax and crusty around the edge, take your pup to the vet. Your veterinarian can make a quick and certain diagnosis and get her on the road to recovery. After your dog gets a professional flushing from her doctor, you need to follow up with daily drops and cleaning procedures.

Lice

Lice live on hair shafts. This condition is species-specific, contagious, and common in shelters, pet stores, or any other crowded area. Lice secure themselves to your dog's hair shaft and hold on for dear life. Symptoms include itching and hair loss. Left unchecked, anemia can occur. Fortunately, treatment is easy. Talk to your vet.

Mange mites

These nasty creatures are related to ear mites, although they're more free-ranging, often localizing along the spine, legs, head, or underside. There are three different types of mange mites:

✔ **Cheyletiella or "Walking Dandruff":** These critters hang out along your dog's spine and create a lot of flaking as they munch the skin. The surest sign? Intense scratching and nibble-biting along the spine. Your veterinarian can confirm suspicions and offer treatment and advice.

✔ **Demodectoc mange:** Demodex mites are usually transferred from a mother dog to her pups during nursing. Under normal conditions, these mites exist at a harmonious level; however, if a puppy gets stressed or is malnourished, they can multiply and create either a localized infection (the infected area loses hair and becomes itchy, red, and bald) or a widespread infection (creating large, inflamed, bald patches). Talk to your vet for a diagnosis and treatment.

✔ **Sarcoptic mange:** Otherwise known as *scabies,* these crab-shaped bugs burrow into your dog's skin and tunnel around laying eggs and sipping blood. Their favorite spots are the head region, legs, and underside. The surest sign is a dog that literally can't stop itching all over. Again, see your vet for confirmation and treatment.

As much as you'd like to control the itch with anti-inflammatories, don't. Drugs such as cortisone lower an already weak immune system and have other side effects.

Internal Parasites — Gross Me Out!

Internal parasites are much more of a health hazard to dogs, especially puppies, than external parasites. They can really mess with their developing systems and deplete the necessary balance of nutrients.

If you have young children, take extra precaution. Some of these parasites can be transmitted. Walk your puppy in an untrafficked area and carry a poop bag for immediate cleanup.

Heartworms

This nasty worm is transmitted by mosquitoes (and, therefore, is more prevalent in warmer climates) and lives in the chambers of the heart and the lungs. Left unnoticed, heartworm disease is fatal. This is one parasite that's better to prevent than cure. You have two preventive options:

✔ **Daily preventive pills:** These pills are less expensive than the monthly version and come as chewables or tablets. They must be given consistently to be effective. (Daily preventives are also available as a syrup.)

✔ **Once a month preventive pills:** These medications are prescribed according to weight. If you have a pup, be sure to ask your veterinarian how to accommodate for his growth. Though these pills are more expensive, busy people often prefer them.

If you forget to give a daily for more than a week, or one monthly pill, consult your veterinarian before you resume medication. Pills can be dangerous, even fatal, if given after the worm has entered the heart.

Follow your veterinarian's prescription. If he says to use the heartworm prevention year round, do. And you must still have an annual test done; prevention's never 100 percent.

Other internal critters

Coccidia lay their eggs in stools. Dogs become infected by eating other dogs' stools. Intestines playing hotel to these creatures become inflamed, which leads to loose, watery stools, bloating, vomiting, weight loss, and strained elimination. Fortunately, diagnosis is easy and treatment is quick and effective. See your vet.

Giardia are water loving creatures found in most outdoor water sources. Once ingested, they feast on the inner lining of the small intestine, creating inflammation, which leads to loose, mucous-coated stools, bloating, and weight loss. Easy to detect, early prognosis is key. See your vet.

Hookworms not only feed off your dog's food, but they also suck her blood. Dogs pick up hookworms by eating the feces of infected animals. A young pup can become infected nursing on mom or even coming in contact with worms who creep through their tender skin. Symptoms include bloating; excessive gas; smelly, loose stools; a skinny dog with a large appetite; bloody stools; and a dry, brittle coat. See your vet.

Roundworms float inside a dog's body — in the liver, through the heart, and onto the lungs. In their final stage, they settle in the small intestine where they feast on your dog's dinner. Dogs who have a case of roundworms are plagued with an insatiable appetite; loose, smelly diarrhea; gas; and bloating. See your vet.

Tapeworm true story: I remember asking my brother why a piece of rice was crawling out my dog's rear end. Turns out it wasn't rice; it was a tapeworm. *Yuck.* Truth is, that's how most people discover their dog is infected: the "white rice" diagnosis. Other telltale signs include incredible appetite and noticeable weight loss, rectal itching, abdominal pain, and indigestion. Dogs pick up this parasite by eating fleas that serve as the tapeworms' intermediate host. See your vet.

Whipworms live and reproduce in your dog's large intestine, causing inflammation and the following: bloating and cramps; bloody or mucous-coated stools; a dry, brittle coat; smelly diarrhea; and a major appetite. Dogs become infected by eating worm-ridden stools (an especially popular activity for pups!) or by stepping in feces and licking their paws. See your vet.

Hookworms and roundworms aren't strangers to humans. Children fall victim to these parasites if their play area is frequented by free-ranging pets (cats as well as dogs). Not only can they be transmitted fecal-oral, but the worms can enter through the skin. It's not unheard of for a responsible owner to forget to wash his hands after cleaning up stool or for a child to play with a dog's elimination. If you suspect you or a child has hookworms or roundworms, call your doctor immediately. To prevent these problems, clean up after your dog (and cat!), wash your hands after cleaning, and check your child's play area twice a day.

Chapter 24

Accidents Happen

● ●

In This Chapter

▶ What you can do to prevent accidents

▶ Puppy first aid: Treating a pup in trouble

▶ Preparing a first-aid kit in case of emergencies

● ●

*N*obody wants an accident to happen. No one wants to see his puppy get hit or cut, be poisoned, or suffer from the heat. But things *can* happen, and you need to be prepared. Learning what steps to take before you get your puppy to the animal hospital can save his life. This chapter covers the steps you need to follow in an emergency. Remember, though, that none of the suggestions in this chapter take the place of seeing your veterinarian immediately.

An Ounce of Prevention . . .

Puppies are insatiably curious creatures. Take a look at your house from your puppy's point of view: "Plants, certain objects, cords, and dropped items get a giant reaction from my parents if they're within hearing distance. What fun!" Try to prevent as many emergencies as possible.

Puppy-proof your rooms

Walk (or better — crawl) around your house and look at it from your puppy's perspective. What looks tempting? You can use duct tape to secure wires, and you can clean off coffee tables and clear book shelves for the time being. I know, I know . . . you don't want to rearrange your living space, but puppies are like babies; they get into everything for the sheer fun of discovering something new.

Take care of cords and wires

Hanging there like a snake, an electrical cord or a telephone wire can be quite tempting to attack and chew. The damage can range from a sharp to lethal shock to a mild to third-degree burn. If you notice a severed cord, check your puppy's mouth for burns (and see the "Treating burns" section later in this chapter).

Prevent lamp cord electrocution! Tape all cords hanging four feet from the ground to the wall and pin floor cords to the baseboard.

Take care of small indigestibles

Though it may seem odd to you, some puppies love to swallow what they chew; especially if you're trying to take the object away from them forcefully *(Prize Envy)*. Problem is, not all things pass through a puppy's intestines. Some get stuck in the intestines, initially causing vomiting, gagging, dry heaves, and coughing, which can go on for days. If that's not cause enough for alarm, the puppy stops eating and drinking. If the intestine is blocked and nothing is done, it ruptures.

Treatment depends on how soon you get your puppy to the veterinarian. If the object is large enough, it may be identified on the exam table; otherwise, an X-ray will be needed. To remove the foreign object, the doctor may order surgery. The sooner you get your puppy to the doctor, the better the prognosis.

Pick up. Puppies love to carry things in their mouths. If you chase them or get uptight, they often swallow their find to hide the evidence. Keep all rooms free from swallowables.

Know what's poison to puppies

Puppies love to investigate things with their mouths. Are they naughty? No, they're just curious. Sometimes, however, what they put in their mouths can be poisonous; if they swallow it, they could be in big trouble.

Put all dangerous substances out of the reach of your pet, just as you would put them out of the reach of children.

Common household poisons

The section "Treating a pup who's been poisoned," later in this chapter, lists several common household poisons and tells how to treat your puppy if he gets into anything poisonous. Here, though, are a few especially big hazards to your puppy:

✔ Household garbage

Household garbage is one of the most common sources of inedible ingestions (toxins) for puppies. Keep a lid on it.

✔ Anti-freeze

✔ Chocolate

✔ Lead

✔ Rat poison

Poisonous plants

Inside or out, plants can entertain your puppy for hours, but not all plants are dog-friendly. Some are deadly. See the following list of harmful plants:

Indoor plants	Outdoor plants
Cactus	Azalea bush
Dumbcane	Daffodil flower bud
Marijuana	Honeysuckle
Mistletoe	Horse chestnut
Philodendron	Lily of the valley
Poinsettia sap	Morning glory flower
Tobacco	Rhododendron shrub
	Rhubarb
	Skunk cabbage
	Tulip bulb
	Wild mushroom

If your puppy is carrying a plant in his mouth, do not race toward him; otherwise, he perceives your actions as Prize Envy and may gulp the evidence. Approach calmly and stare at the floor, not into his eyes. "Plants aren't for puppies, silly."

Puppy First Aid 101

If your puppy has an accident, stay cool. If you lose it, he'll get nervous and go to pieces. Be a rock of confidence. Be mentally tough. Organize. Think. If necessary, get him to the hospital as quickly and efficiently as possible.

The key in an emergency is to stay calm. Keep your head on straight. If you've done the proper preparation, you'll be fine.

Restraining a hurt pup

Even the most beloved pet may bite when he's in pain or confused. If he doesn't bite you, he may go for the vet or one of the technicians, so restrain your puppy for their sake. The simplest restraining technique requires a bandanna or a rope (the bandanna being more comfortable). To restrain your puppy, follow these steps (and see Figure 24-1):

Figure 24-1: Restraining your hurt pup to prevent a possible bite.

1. **Fold the bandanna into a long band.**

2. **Drape the center of the band across the top of your dog's nose.**

3. **Cross the two ends underneath your dog's chin.**

4. **Tie the ends securely behind your dog's ears.**

5. **Check the crossing point underneath.**

    If it's too loose, your dog will paw it off; if it's too tight, you'll choke him.

Transporting a hurt pup

Transporting a dog who has internal injuries is tricky business. He'll be restless and want to move. It's your job to make sure he doesn't. If you suspect a broken bone, spinal injury, or internal bleeding, transport your puppy on a firm surface, such as metal or plywood. Otherwise, placing your puppy on a sheet or towel is acceptable. Don't cover his face, or he may panic.

Be ready. Place a dog-sized board aside for emergencies.

How puppies experience pain

Dogs can't articulate pain. They can't intellectualize it, meditate on it, or separate themselves from it. Pain is pain. An intense feeling. A state of being. Pain puts dogs in a vulnerable state. It confuses their thought process and their physical organization. Their only drive is to protect themselves and alleviate their distress. Add that state of mind to your puppy's natural temperament, and what you get is a fairly predictable reaction. For example, my dog Shayna May is a big baby. Although she acts tough, when in pain, she seeks me out, desperately looking for help. Another more dominant, independent dog may bite his owner when she tries to help. A really shy dog might pee on his own leg. Though dogs experience pain in the same way, they deal with it differently.

Performing artificial respiration and CPR

As horrible as it is to see your puppy lying there after a fire, a car accident, choking, ingesting poison, or electrocution, it may not be too late to save him. So be quick and think clearly when performing the following steps:

1. **Check for a heartbeat.**

   See the instructions that follow for administering CPR.

2. **Check for any obstructions in the mouth; clear his mouth of any blood or mucous.**

3. **Pull out his tongue to make sure the airway is clear.**

4. **Shut his mouth gently.**

5. **Pull his lips over his mouth and secure them by wrapping one hand under his chin.**

   For breeds who have pushed-in noses, wrap your mouth around the nose.

6. **Create an airtight funnel to his nose with your free hand.**

7. **Inhale and then exhale air smoothly into your puppy's nose.**

   Stay calm.

8. **Repeat every five to six seconds.**

If you cannot feel your puppy's heartbeat, you must pump his heart for him by performing CPR (cardiopulmonary resuscitation). To give CPR, follow these steps:

1. **If you have a large pup, lay him on his right side. If you have a small one, place a hand on either side of his chest.**

2. **Compress the heart area of the chest in short bursts, one compression per second.**

3. **Exercise one breath every six seconds.**

You'll know when you've saved your dog. He'll come back to life.

If your puppy is in cardiac arrest, try to have two people working: one pumping the heart and one breathing.

Stopping the bleeding

Bleeding comes in three forms:

- ✔ **The everyday cut and scrape:** This injury is no big deal. Twice a day, wipe the area with hydrogen peroxide to keep it safe from infection, and it should heal just fine.

- ✔ **A continuous or oozing stream:** This type of bleeding requires medical attention immediately. Raise the body part above the heart if possible and apply bandages one on top of the other to soak the blood as you press down on the area to slow the flow.

- ✔ **A gushing spurt and flow:** This type of bleeding is serious — very serious. Your puppy can go into shock quickly and die if she loses too much blood. Place bandage on top of bandage, elevate the limb if possible, and put constant pressure on the incoming artery. Drive to the nearest animal hospital.

If you suspect internal bleeding, get your puppy to a hospital immediately. Internal bleeding is a life-threatening situation. White gums, a distended abdomen, a bloody cough, or vomiting spells are indications of internal bleeding.

Find your puppy's pressure points. While he's sleeping, feel for the pulse near the hip and elbow joints. These arteries regulate blood flow and, in an emergency, can be pressed to slow them down. You can also use ice packs to slow the flow of blood, but use ice packs only for oozing cuts and scrapes.

Dealing with a pup in shock

A dog can go into shock if he experiences a sudden loss in blood, a trauma, or electrocution. A dog in shock shows the following symptoms:

- ✔ A fast heart rate (the heart tries to make up for a drop in blood pressure)
- ✔ Rapid breathing pattern (trying to increase oxygen flow to the body)

- Dilated pupils and glaring stare
- Unconscious or semi-conscious behavior

Shock is life-threatening; it causes blood pressure to drop dramatically, which prevents oxygen from circulating in the body. Without oxygen, your puppy will die quickly. If you suspect your puppy has gone into shock, stay calm, keep him still, lay a blanket over his body, and get to the nearest veterinarian immediately.

Treating bites and stings

Outdoor dogs run the risk of meeting creatures who aren't all that friendly. Insects sting, snakes bite, porcupines quill, and life goes on. However, for the concerned dog owner, the suffering that's involved can be heartbreaking.

Bug bites and stings

Most bug bites are no more of an annoyance for a dog than they are for us. A bump, scratch, and a bit of swelling doesn't alter the day too dramatically. But if a dog is allergic to the bite or sting, the reaction can be severe or even life-threatening. Symptoms of a mildly allergic dog include fever, joint pain, muscle ache, swelling, vomiting, and diarrhea.

A severely allergic dog goes into respiratory failure that can be fatal within minutes. This reaction is called *anaphylaxis* and requires immediate veterinary attention. If you know your puppy is sensitive to insect bites, ask your veterinarian to prescribe a bee sting kit that can counteract the reaction in an emergency.

Snake bites

Though most snakes bite when they feel threatened, most bites aren't poisonous. How can you tell? Poisonous snakes have fangs that make holes in the skin. Here are some other general guidelines:

- Most native North American snakes that are solid colored or have stripes running the length of the body are non-venomous.
- Be careful of snakes with diamond backs, stripes running *around* the body, or those with blotch patterns. In North America, poisonous snakes include rattlesnakes, water moccasins, cottonmouths, coral snakes, and copperheads.

A puppy who tangles with a poisonous snake usually doesn't have long to live. The first thing that happens is he swells up like a balloon. Within hours, he'll go into seizures, fall into a coma, and die.

A porcupine run-in

If your puppy runs into a porcupine, he'll end up with a face full of quills. These nasty darts are hooked on the end. Have a veterinarian remove them.

Do not try to pull porcupine quills out yourself. The end of the quill hooks into your puppy's tissue. Aside from being painful, ripping out the quill can cause a serious infection.

If you suspect your puppy has been bitten, follow these steps and get him to the nearest animal hospital immediately (and bring the dead snake, if possible):

1. **Stay calm. Don't stress your puppy.**

2. **Limit his movement. Movement circulates the venom.**

3. **If possible, place a tourniquet above the wound. Suction via a snakebite kit, if available.**

4. **Flush the wound with hydrogen peroxide or water.**

Treating burns

Curiosity strikes again. Puppies can get burned from a variety of chemicals and household appliances. As with human burns, dog burns have three degrees:

✔ **First-degree burns** are superficial; the top layer of the skin peels and gets red and sore.

✔ **Second-degree burns** go deeper, damaging many layers of skin. These types of burns can result in bleeding, blistering, or oozing. Your veterinarian can prescribe medications and ointment to lessen the pain.

✔ **Third-degree burns** are really nasty. They burn away every layer of skin right down to the tissue. These burns can be life-threatening if more than 50 percent of the body has been harmed. Third-degree burns often cause shock and require immediate veterinarian care.

Burns also come in three varieties: thermal, chemical, and electrical.

✔ **Thermal** burns are caused by a reaction to intense heat. Fire, automobile parts, hot pipes or appliances, and scalding water are just some of the things that can cause a thermal burn.

✔ **Chemical** burns result when strong chemicals contact your puppy's skin. Ammonia, cleaning products, battery acid, bleach, gasoline, and paint products are examples of chemicals that are harmful to your pet.

✔ **Electrical** burns result when your puppy contacts a surface that transmits electrical current. Car batteries and electrical cords and outlets are a few examples.

If your puppy gets burned by chewing on electrical cords and is in pain, apply ice to the burns and give him ice water. Then take him to his veterinarian, who'll prescribe antibiotic oral gel to prevent infection and may recommend a dietary change until his mouth is back to normal.

Severe electrocution is often life-threatening. If your puppy is electrocuted, he will show signs of shock and may need CPR on the way to the animal hospital.

Your reaction should be calm and immediate. Here are some things to keep in mind:

✔ Take your puppy to a quiet area and calm him.

✔ Steadily pour water over the area; if it's a chemical burn, continue to pour water for 5–10 minutes.

✔ If the burn is superficial, keep it clean and rub it with an anti-bacteria ointment twice a day. More serious burns demand immediate medical attention.

Treating a choking pup

Choking usually occurs when your puppy is chewing or playing with a toy and is suddenly challenged, startled, or takes a deep breath. If you're not around or you don't react quickly, choking could be fatal. One way to prevent choking in the first place is to think smart: Don't give your puppy toys smaller than his face.

If your puppy chokes on something, keep calm and stay focused when following these steps:

1. **Bring your puppy into a standing position, even if someone must hold him there.**

2. **Try to reach in and dislodge the object.**

   Be careful — you could jam it in further or get bitten if your dog's panicking.

3. **If you can't dislodge the object, try a modified version of the Heimlich maneuver.**

   Clasp your hands together underneath your dog and pull up into your dog's abdomen — just behind the sternum (see Figure 24-2). Repeat this five times vigorously.

Figure 24-2:
This vet is
demonstrat-
ing the
modified
Heimlich
maneuver.

4. **If all else fails, get your dog to the veterinarian immediately.**

Treating a pup who's been poisoned

Puppies love to check out everything with their mouths. Sometimes, though, what they put in their mouths can be poisonous, and if they swallow it, they can be in big trouble.

If your puppy has something bad in his mouth, don't race toward him angrily. You'll look like you want the prize, and he may gulp it to hide the evidence. Instead, walk into the next room calmly and start shaking a treat cup or gathering your car keys — anything to get his mind on something else fast.

You can't always be there to watch your puppy. You can, however, watch for signs that he swallowed something poisonous, which include vomiting, bowel discharge, muscle trembling, and increased salivation.

Ask your veterinarian how to induce vomiting in an emergency. If your puppy swallows something harmful (but non-corrosive), get him to throw it up quickly.

Table 24-1 lists common household poisons and abbreviations for what to do if your puppy gets into one. Here's what those abbreviations mean (source: *Puppy Owner's Veterinary Care Book*, James DeBitetto, DVM, Howell 1995):

- **IV:** Induce vomiting (if the dog swallowed the poison in the preceding two hours) by giving hydrogen peroxide (several teaspoons for a small dog or tablespoons for a large dog) or syrup of ipecac (1 teaspoon or 1 tablespoon, depending on dog's size).

- **L:** Use a laxative (if it's been more than two hours since the poison was swallowed). Give mineral oil (1 teaspoon for dogs under 25 lbs., 1 tablespoon for 25–50 lb. dogs, and 2 tablespoons for dogs 50 lbs. and over).

- **W:** Wash off skin with water and vinegar.

- **M2M:** Give mouth-to-muzzle resuscitation, as described earlier in this chapter (see the section "Performing artificial respiration and CPR").

- **VI:** Take dog to vet immediately.

- **VA:** Schedule an appointment with the vet some time in the next week.

- **VO:** Give a dose of vegetable oil and water to block absorption.

If you have to take your puppy to the vet for poison treatment, try to find the substance and bring it with you to the animal hospital.

Table 24-1	Common Household Poisons and Treatment Codes
Poison	*What To Do*
Acetone	IV, VI
Ammonia	V, VO, VI
Anti-freeze	IV, VI
Bleach	IV, VA
Carbon monoxide	M2M, VI
Charcoal lighter fluid	IV, L
Chocolate	IV
Deodorants	IV, VI
Soap	IV, VA
Furniture polish	IV, L, VI
Gasoline	IV, VO, VI
Ibuprofen	IV, VI
Kerosene	IV, L, VO, VI
Lead	IV, L
Lime	W

(continued)

Table 24-1 *(continued)*

Poison	What To Do
Insecticides	W, VI
Paint thinner	IV, W, VI
Phenol cleaners	W
Rat poison	IV, VI
Rubbing alcohol	IV
Strychnine	IV, VI
Turpentine	IV, VO, VI
Tylenol	IV, VA

If your puppy should get a topical substance stuck on his fur, do not try to remove it with turpentine or gasoline. Vegetable oil works best.

You can call a 24-hour poison center if your puppy has swallowed something poisonous: 1-900-680-0000. With this 900 number, your phone bill will be charged.

Treating heatstroke

Dogs don't have pores. They can't sweat. The only way they can release heat is through the pads in their feet and by panting. Dogs can suffer from heat-stroke if left in poorly ventilated areas, such as a car, kennel, or tied out, or if over-exercised on a humid day. If you notice shallow breathing, a rapid heart rate, and high temperature, cool your puppy gradually with wet towels, a cool bath, or ice around the neck, head, and groin; then take him to the veterinarian.

Heatstroke is preventable; never leave your puppy in a poorly ventilated environment and make sure water is available on warm days. Leave an extra set of keys in the glove compartment. If the dog must be left in the car, leave the car running with the air conditioning on and doors locked.

Please don't take your puppy with you on hot days. A car, even with all the windows down, can overheat within an hour. What a horrible way for a dog to die — locked in a hot automobile, just wanting and waiting for his caretaker to come back.

Puppy First-Aid Kit Essentials

Here's a first-aid kit for dogs. Set these things aside in a safe place or take them with you when you travel with your puppy:

- Strip of cloth to use as a muzzle
- Gauze pads
- A sheet or towel that can be used to carry your puppy in a supine position
- A rope or bandanna to muzzle your puppy
- A few strips of cloth to tie around a bleeding wound
- A tourniquet rod (use only in severe emergencies)
- Hydrogen peroxide
- The poison hotline number and a list of all poisonous plants
- Bacitracin
- Ice packs
- Snakebite kit if you're in snake country
- Towels to wet in case of heatstroke
- A rectal thermometer
- A towel and water jug (to be kept in your car) in case you get stuck

If a Trip to the Vet Is Necessary

You've done all you can do. Now the situation is in more experienced hands. If you insist on observing procedures, do it quietly. Stand back in a corner of the room, stay out of the way, and be quiet. Honestly, I'd prefer the waiting room. Getting emotional not only distracts your veterinarian, but it also upsets your puppy. If your veterinarian asks for your help, do exactly what she says: no more, no less.

Part VII
Dealing with Life in the Real World

In this part . . .

*H*aving a puppy is a big responsibility. Your puppy will quickly become a part of your neighborhood with her own fan club. To make sure that your puppy stays welcome, take to heart the chapter on being a good neighbor.

You also have to consider your puppy's reaction to life changes. If something stresses you out, it will stress your puppy, too — guaranteed. And since vacations and week-end getaways are a part of life, forethought to your puppy's comfort should come way in advance of your departure.

Chapter 25

Being a Good Neighbor

"It's a beautiful day in the neighborhood . . . ," except for the pounding rhythm of a barking dog! I love my neighborhood dearly, but on a quiet summer day when my neighbors leave for the beach and tie out their eight month old Beagle (bless her little soul), I'd like to move to Barbados. It's not the Beagle's fault. Once I went over after three hours of the street dog serenade, only to find her water bowl empty. I gave her a fresh bowl of water and a chew bone, which kept her busy the rest of the afternoon. Ahhh . . . peace and quiet.

You need to keep a lot in mind to be a good dog neighbor; this chapter can help.

Leaving Your Puppy at Home Alone

To be a good neighbor, you need to keep your puppy quiet when you're away from home. No puppy enjoys being left alone; she's sociable by nature. Don't be surprised if she thinks of some activities to pass those lonely hours — digging, chewing destructively, or *barking*. Is there anything you can do?

Yes. You have a lot of options when you leave your puppy alone. She can stay inside or outside. You can confine her in a room or let her roam around. You can tie her up or fence her in. What's best? Put yourself in your puppy's paws. Outside is okay; there's fresh air and sunshine. But being confined outdoors can be stressful because of all the activity that the puppy *can't* get to. Most puppies would rather remain inside with a cozy blanket and bone to chew.

Preparing for your departure has lasting benefits. Before you leave, do the following:

✔ Exercise your puppy for 10 minutes.

✔ Follow play time with a 2-minute training session.

✔ Leave a couple of chew toys and scent them by rubbing them in your palms.

✔ If you leave your puppy indoors, leave her in a dimly lit, confined space with an old shirt or blanket and a radio playing soothing tunes.

✔ If you leave your puppy outdoors, provide her with access to a shaded area and plenty of fresh water.

If your puppy suffers from separation anxiety and is a gulper (eating things she shouldn't), crate or enclose her in a small space with a large bone and no bedding. She might eat the bedding otherwise.

Neighborhood Puppy Manners 101

High-class neighbors get along. They know when to accept what won't change and make the best of it. Low-class neighbors bicker and fight. They make a mess. They're loud and intimidating. The question is, which of the two do you want you and your puppy to be? The choice is yours, but if it's high class you want, it's high class you'll get — just follow these steps (turn to Chapter 14 for details on these commands):

✔ Instruct "Heel" as you parade around the neighborhood; teach your puppy to follow your lead.

✔ Use the Wait command to teach your puppy to wait at curbs and while you visit or window shop.

✔ Teach the No command to discourage your puppy from everyday temptations like cars, joggers, and other animals. (You can introduce the concept of No after your pup's 16 weeks old.)

If your dog's lunging at the end of the leash, trying to get at whatever has his attention, it's too late to discourage him — you need to catch him before he even starts to show interest. For this or any other soft spot, you need to keep your antennae out; then you can correct him before he's even noticed the thing he loses control over.

✔ Have your puppy eliminate on your own property. As they grow into adulthood, puppies recognize boundary limits with their noses. Help your dog learn where her territory ends. In case of an accident, carry a bag with you to remove the evidence from your neighbor's lawn and dispose of it properly.

Five Signs That You're a Bad Neighbor

A neighbor has returned your wandering pup more than once.

Your dog barks outside (and when you leave).

Your dog torments other neighborhood dogs on walks.

Your puppy visits neighbors' yards, re-landscaping, retrieving their papers, and eliminating on their lawns.

Your neighbors appear afraid of your puppy.

Dealing with the Neighborhood Dogs

Most dogs like to think they own their neighborhoods. The problem is, every block usually has more than one dog. Left to their own devices — free ranging, so to speak — the dogs establish a hierarchy and get along fine. But they're not free. Leashes and other confinements cause territorial frustrations.

The leash *should* be used to communicate leadership — human leadership, that is. Puppies, however, don't always listen to that message. Some puppies think they walk their owners. A confident puppy leading its owner wants to approach other dogs. When this dog is suddenly restricted by a choking feeling around the neck or chest, he gets very defensive. He pulls harder and gets more intense. As he grows up, he threatens from afar.

A cautious puppy, on the other hand, feels intense panic when approached by another dog. Because no one has communicated leadership to this pup, it collapses in a state of panic, often scurrying back and hiding under its owner's legs. Although this may seem endearing, a puppy hiding under your legs is like a child clinging to his mother's skirt. These puppies need training to learn that you are there to direct them in *all* situations.

Resist the temptation to soothe a frightened puppy. Your intentions are pure, but, because a puppy views soothing as submissive and fearful, you're only reinforcing your pup's concern. Act brave and calm and speak in directional tones.

When your puppy approaches or is approached by another dog, follow the suggestions in the "Neighborhood Puppy Manners 101" section and remember:

- Do not look at the other dog.
- Walk by the dog at a brisk pace.
- Keep your dog behind you at all times.

What if you want to let your puppy play? Keep your pup at your side while you cross the street or the puppies approach each other. Then release your dog on a loose lead with "OK!"

If you and your on-lead puppy are approached by an angry off-leash dog, walk swiftly from the scene, correcting your dog from facing off to the aggressor. If either of you makes eye contact, you may be attacked.

Dealing with the Chasing Instinct

Chasing is an instinctive behavior that goes back to wolf times when dogs had to hunt for a living. Even though we offer our puppies all the luxuries of retirement, many still think chasing (anything, but especially cats) is a great pastime.

Chasing the neighborhood cats

When a new puppy approaches a cat, one of two things happens: The cat runs, which leads to — you guessed it — a free for all. Or the cat stands its ground, often hissing or bating at a persistent pup. Regardless of the cat's reaction, you want to steer clear of the interaction. Yelling and chasing a wild puppy only backs him up. Stepping in and correcting a defensive cat makes the cat more reclusive and frustrated with your new addition.

If your puppy has already formed the chasing habit, don't fret. You can resolve things:

1. **Secure a light 6-foot nylon leash to your puppy's collar.**

2. **Focus on your dog's ears (ear perk is preliminary to the chase). To influence chasing, you must correct the thought process, not wait until the chase has begun.**

   Dogs' ears act like built-in radar. They can pick up sound in every direction. Unfortunately, if your puppy's ears are alert to every distraction, she's not focused on you. Some training is definitely in order.

3. **If your dog's ears lift when the cat saunters by, snap the lead and say "No!"**

   Do not look at the cat or the puppy. Eye contact means interest.

4. **Walk away from the cat (or other animal) confidently. Encourage your puppy along with "Let's go!"**

5. **Continue to snap and say "No" until your dog focuses on you.**

   Do not drag your dog away from the object. Snap and release.

Introducing your own cat and your puppy

Introduce your cat and puppy in a small room that has an elevated surface, such as a bathroom sink, for the cat to sit on. Bring the cat in first and pet it soothingly on top of the counter; offer it a treat as you let the puppy in the room. Stay calm as you distract your puppy with toys and chews. If your puppy gets excited, stay calm and see what happens. Use a spray mister or Bitter Apple to spray in between the two animals if necessary. Repeat this process until the two are more used to each other.

Chasing the neighborhood cars

Chasing cars is one scary problem. Young puppies are usually hesitant about cars until their fourth or fifth month, when fear turns to fascination and moving objects are best chased. To nip this problem in the bud, you need to think a few steps ahead of your dog. If your puppy is very young (under 12 weeks), act scared when you see a car. Whimper in puppy-like sounds and retreat to the road side. After you begin formal training (16–18 weeks), follow these steps:

1. **Instruct your dog "To the side" and run to the curb quickly.**

2. **Next, tell her "Wait" as the car passes, bringing her behind your heels.**

3. **If she looks at the car, say "No!" very sternly and snap the lead.**

Use this same technique with bikers and joggers. Correct your dog the second she *thinks* about chasing something. Once she's in motion, you're too late.

Chasing the neighborhood kids

They dart, they spin, they stare, they bark . . . *wow*. Those little two-legged creatures are just like puppies. This setup requires a few volunteers — little volunteers, that is. If you don't have kids, borrow some. Then practice these steps:

1. **Start inside. Place your puppy on a leash and go to an open room.**

2. **Ask the children to run in front of you. Watch your puppy.**

3. **The second you see that gleam in her eye, just as she prepares to bound after them, say "No!" sternly and snap back on the lead.**

   Correct the thought process.

Now for distance control. Using your long line or Flexi-Lead, repeat the procedure again. Tell your little volunteers to race around *in front* of you; no circling behind. Correct all thoughts of a chase by snapping back on the lead, saying "No," and praising your pup for resisting temptation.

Chapter 26

Adjusting Your Puppy to Stressful Changes

Change is a part of life. Although many changes are for the best, all changes are stressful. I'm not just talking about humans; dogs experience stress, too. The difference between their stress and ours is how they display it. Sure, I may pack in some extra calories when I'm feeling anxious, but I won't destroy the couch; your puppy might. And do you know what happens if you correct an anxious pup? He gets more stressed and destroys other things — perhaps your rug or bed, for example. Is he being bad? Not necessarily. He's just confused and worried. He needs your help to adjust. Other signs of stress are aggression, barking, hyperactivity, or extreme withdrawal.

Moving to a New Home

Moving is one of life's most stressful changes. First, the financial decisions may bring about more theatrical conversations than on the average day. Then you have the packing, shipping, and traveling back and forth. When the big day finally arrives, your energy is spent; you've reached a new peak of exhaustion. My heart aches for you, but it bleeds for your developing puppy. Chaos really throws him. Due to his biological nature, he depends on predictability to ensure his safety. Through this change, you may notice your puppy resorting to early puppy behavior; he may become hyper, demand attention, nip, jump, or chew. Forgive him now and help him cope. Following are some suggestions that you can use to help him:

✔ Play some classical music while you debate and discuss your big move. It'll calm everyone.

✔ Include your dog in your packing activities. Don't isolate him in the backyard. If he gets in the way, station him with a bone to chew and pet him when he settles down.

✔ If you're traveling back and forth to the new house, lead your puppy in the home using familiar commands like Wait and Let's Go. Create stations in your new home, using familiar toys and bedding (see Chapter 12 about using your Teaching Lead). If you're spending the day at your new house, don't forget to pack some dog food and water. Bring his familiar bowls.

✔ Keep your dog with you while you're unpacking. Let him sniff the collectibles as you remove them; he identifies objects with his nose and will feel happy to recognize something.

The first time you leave your puppy in your new home, he may stress out, resulting in destructive chewing or excessive barking. Confine your puppy in a small room or crate with one of your old shirts and a favorite chew. Do not correct your puppy if he demolishes something. Your corrections only increase the anxiety and destruction.

Do not let your puppy off leash in your new environment unless it's fenced in or he's secure on a long line. He'll be disoriented for a few weeks and may get lost if he wanders off. Was your old place fenced in? If your dog was accustomed to running free in a yard but can't now, you need to make up for the loss. Use a long line or a Flexi-Lead and discover some good games to burn off that energy.

Are you moving to a new climate? Going from extreme cold to hot or vice versa can be alarming for your pup. Perhaps a sweater will be in order in colder climates or a big bowl of water if the weather is suddenly blistering.

Bringing Home a Baby

A new baby in the house can be one of the coolest changes of a lifetime — for people, that is. Puppies, on the other hand, often feel shafted and shoved to the back burner. To ensure this doesn't happen to your four-legged pal, start planning for the new arrival before you're running to the hospital.

Before bringing baby home

Imagine you have the baby, a cute little creature, just weeks old. Your parenting instincts will be in full throttle. Now enters your beloved puppy. Is he used to lounging on the furniture or jumping up for attention? Can he order up a back rub by pawing, barking, or nudging you? Can you see a problem developing? He won't stop this behavior just because you're holding a new-born. Heaven forbid you shout at or isolate him; he'll grow leery and jealous of your new fancy. Fortunately, you can take a few steps ahead of time to ensure that nobody gets left in the doghouse:

✔ As early as possible, socialize your puppy with small children. Put some cereal (cereal has less calories than dog biscuits; kids can be very generous) in a cup and shake and treat until your dog associates the sound with a reward. Then invite some friends who have children over and ask them to shake and treat. Stay calm while they visit; keep your dog on a leash if you're uneasy. Dogs are very telepathic; your emotions come across loud and clear.

✔ Take your puppy to a playground. Keep him on a 6-foot lead and ask the kids to take a break and give your dog a treat.

✔ If your puppy is showing any signs of aggression, call a professional. Your reaction can make the problem worse. Petting or soothing reinforces the behavior, and disciplining makes your puppy feel more threatened.

✔ Establish an exercise schedule that will be realistic with your new responsibilities. Mornings may be rough — help your puppy look forward to afternoon romps.

✔ Establish a station in or just outside your baby's room and get your pup accustomed to settling on command. Tell him "Settle down" and secure him on a 3-foot lead if he seems restless.

✔ Walk through your daily routine with a stuffed doll. Allow your puppy to sniff it regularly. When changing your baby (both the doll and the real thing), practice the commands Wait and Stay. When putting your baby down for a nap, guide your puppy to his station saying "Settle down." When nursing your baby, give your puppy a special chew and place his mat/bed near your feet.

✔ Watch your words. Phrases like "What a good boy" must be changed to "What a great dog!" If the phrases you use for baby and dog are too familiar, your pup will get confused.

✔ New furniture rules. Dogs shouldn't be allowed on the furniture near a new infant. If you wait to spring this rule on your pup after the baby's home, the puppy may feel shafted. Lay down the law now. Keep a short leash on your puppy's buckle collar; if he hops up, snap him off with the lead handle and say "No." Remember, pushing is interactive and suggestive of a game.

If you must have your dog on the furniture, give him the luxury on command only. Tell him "Up" and pat the cushion when you want him there; use "No" with a leash correction if he comes up uninvited.

✔ Get your puppy used to one hour of the cold shoulder every day. Yes, I want you to ignore your puppy completely. You can break it up into two 30-minute or three 20-minute segments, but get your dog accustomed to life without your doting. If your puppy can get your attention wherever and whenever he wants it, he'll be upset when you're focused on the baby.

✔ Stop all confrontational games, like tug-of-war and wrestling, and eliminate all in-home chasing matches. Play games outside; teach your puppy calm household manners.

✔ Consider your child's toys and how they might compare to your puppy's favorites. Give your puppy a couple of objects to chew or play with and discourage him from picking up everything on the floor. Mark all the child's toys with mouthwash. Just a dot will do. If he goes for it anyway, pick it up and shout at the toy (not the dog). Soon he'll avoid everything that smells like mouthwash. Lead him to his object and praise him.

✔ Babies like to grab and pull, and your dog may be startled if their tug is the first. Grab and tug on your puppy's coat as you treat and praise him. Pull that tail. Hug him tight. What a wonderful puppy. Isn't this great? Don't forget to make some baby sounds too — go for the full effect.

✔ Don't give your dog shoes, socks, rags, plastic, or stuffed toys. He'll think anything in that category is fair game.

When it's time for baby to come home

The day will come. Your baby will break into the world, and your life will never be the same. To help your puppy adjust, follow these steps:

✔ Ask the nurse if you can bring home some bed sheets from the nursery. It may seem like a strange request, but I'm sure yours won't be the first. Place them in the baby's new room and around the area you plan to nurse. Praise your puppy for sniffing them but discourage chewing or tearing. (Keep your puppy on leash, if necessary.)

✔ Brush up on obedience lessons while Mom's in the hospital. Puppies love structure.

✔ Hire a dog walker if the house is empty. Isolation is stressful.

✔ Introduce puppy and baby on neutral ground. The hospital parking lot will do if the weather cooperates. Exercise your dog before the meeting and bring along some peanut butter to distract your dog's interest if you're nervous. Do *not* choke up on the lead or shout at your dog — it's unsettling and makes a bad first impression.

✔ If your puppy's too boisterous, give his leash a quick snap and say "No Sir." Spread some peanut butter on your hand and say "Kisses."

Figure 26-1:
Using butter
to teach
your puppy
to give the
baby kisses.

Photo by Sarah B. Gilman.

The butter trick also works as you establish a bond between your baby and your puppy. Dab some butter on your baby's hand and say "Kisses" (see Figure 26-1).

✔ Plan your homecoming. Keep your puppy on leash and let him welcome the baby, too. Use the same techniques as the first meeting to ensure a smooth arrival.

✔ Let your puppy drag a leash and use it to correct all mouthing or jumping behavior. Look at and praise your dog when he's calm.

✔ If your puppy is restless at his designated stations, secure the 3-foot lead and hook him up while you direct him to "Settle down."

Puppies like diapers, so don't be surprised if you find your dog nibbling on one. My suggestion? Get a super-secure diaper bin and spray a little Bitter Apple on the outside to discourage his interest. Last, but not least, correct *it* when your dog goes near: "Bad, bad diaper bin!"

Sometimes your puppy won't adjust well to the new arrival. Your dog may be too used to being the only child. If your dog growls at the baby, call in a professional to assess the situation.

New infant resentment syndrome (NIRS) is exactly what it sounds like. If your old faithful friend is suddenly excluded from normal daily activities, he'll feel resentful and may fix his alienated feelings on the new arrival.

Gaining and Losing a Housemate

Whether you're inviting someone in, shipping someone out, or mourning the loss of a loved one, it's a life-altering experience — one your puppy will feel almost as much as you.

Getting a new roommate

Getting a new roommate has a lot of perks. Expenses are cut in half, chores are split, and company is permanently installed. You probably won't take too long to adjust. Your puppy may be another story, especially if your new companion's sharing that sacred spot on the couch or your bed. To help your puppy adjust:

✔ Think ahead. Limit your dog's bed or couch time to invitation only. If he jumps up uninvited, say "No" and snap him down. (Keep a short lead attached to his buckle collar.)

✔ Create a special sleeping area next to your bed. Place an old shirt there to keep your pal cozy.

If your dog just won't stay off your bed, secure him on a short lead until he's accepted his new sleeping quarters.

✔ Limit your attention when your new companion is around. Encourage your dog to seek out the new arrival for some love.

✔ Ask your new companion to feed your dog.

✔ Let your companion know your house rules: no jumping, barking, pawing, or begging at the table allowed. If he/she is a spoiler, your dog will be confused, you'll be angry, and you'll need to refer to the next section.

Giving a roommate the pink slip

Dogs grow very accustomed to a pack and may suffer the loss of an extra companion, especially if that companion is a major care giver. To help your puppy adjust:

✔ Fill in the extra spaces. If your puppy was used to being fed and walked at 4 p.m., you need to be there or hire someone a few times a week until your puppy's adjusted to your schedule.

✔ Avoid spoiling your puppy to make up for the loss. More structure is in order, not less.

✔ Enroll in a training class. These classes are fun and give you both something to focus on.

✔ If your puppy loved to play a certain game with his missing companion, you play the game with him instead.

Mourning the loss of a loved one

I've lost two people very close to me in my lifetime. In both cases, I was in a trance for weeks. Emotionally, I had to drag myself out of bed. I lost my zest. Sure, my dogs felt confused by the passing, but I think they were more confused by my mental state. Here are some things I did to help them out:

✔ I asked a friend to walk them in the morning and had the neighbor's kid come by in the afternoon.

✔ I set my alarm clock to ring at their meal times.

✔ I set aside five minutes per day for an obedience lesson.

✔ I bought them new chews and tried to play kick the bottle (their favorite game) with them in the afternoon.

This is not an easy place to be in. Your world is forever changed, and yet daily demands continue — especially from those dependent on you. Get through one day at a time. Ask for help when you need it. And find life in the love you share.

Getting Another Puppy

Getting another puppy may seem really exciting to you, but your resident dog may be less than thrilled. Some dogs take to new paws on the carpet; others don't. To make the transition as smooth as possible:

✔ Introduce the dogs in a neutral place, like a park or parking lot.

If the meeting place is in the open, place both the puppy and new dog on 20-foot lines and stand back as they check each other out.

✔ Stay cool. If a loose lead is suddenly tightened, you're communicating tension. If your resident dog's unsure and you compensate by shouting every command in the book, your old pal will be a nervous wreck. Nervous dogs are likely to attack.

✔ Even a young puppy may do a lot of body and vocal bluffing at the initial meeting. Her hair may stand up, and she may even growl. Meeting anyone for the first time can be a little scary. If you interfere, the dogs may fight. Just stand back and ignore them; interact with them when the initial tension has subsided.

Some dogs just won't get along. If you're bringing together two dogs of the same sex or dogs who got used to being "only children," they may fight. Be prepared. Have two people handy to take the leads and run in the opposite direction.

When you add another puppy to your household, you've got your work cut out for you. The next year is going to be quite the balancing act. Resolving housebreaking, chewing, nipping, or jumping habits can be double the work load. You have to pay close attention and be very consistent. On the other hand, raising two dogs can also be twice the fun if you're considerate of their individual needs and train them to be more focused on you than each other.

Here are some hints for making the task easier:

- ✔ **A dog is a dog is a dog.** Truer words were never spoken. Certain similarities string them all together. However, like us, each dog has his own unique personality and temperament that affects the way he relates to his world. In a multi-dog household, everyone must be sensitive to the needs of each individual dog.

- ✔ **Let them establish their hierarchy.** Personality also affects the way dogs relate to one another. Groups of two or more dogs form a hierarchy, with the most outgoing, assertive dog assuming the Top Dog rank.

  Dogs don't base hierarchy on who came first. Nor do they base it wholly on who's the toughest. Hierarchy is based on who's the most responsible. The dog with both the brains and the brawn wins out. Regardless of your feelings, you must support their arrangement.

- ✔ **Give the royalties to the Top Dog.** As your dogs mature together, you'll notice the development of a hierarchy. You must support this hierarchy by giving all the household royalties to your Top Dog. He should be fed, greeted, pet, and allowed out first. If you pay more attention to the subordinate dog, you may cause discontent among the ranks, which can lead to fighting.

  Though young puppies are submissive, they can challenge the Top Dog status as they mature, and although it may go against every loving impulse in your body, you need to reorganize royalties based on *their* decision on who's Top Dog.

- ✔ **Remember the discipline rules.** If you don't know who did it, you can't correct either dog. That's the rule. If you find a mess after the fact, forget it. Disciplining both dogs only weakens your connection to them and strengthens their resolve to one another. For suggestions on specific problems, see Chapters 11 and 13.

- ✔ **Wrestling is OK, to a degree.** Try to teach your dogs to go to certain areas of the house or outside to play. If they're out of hand, leave their short leashes on in the house and correct them by saying "Shhh!" as you pull them apart sternly. Instruct "Sit," refocus them on a chew toy, and secure them at a station if they don't calm down.

✔ **Play the name game.** Teach your dogs two names: their personal name and a universal one that you can use when they're together, such as "Dogs," "Girls," "Boys," or "Babies" — whatever works for you. Using a single name makes calling them easier. "Girls, Come!" rolls off a little easier than "Buddy, Fi-Fi, Daisy, Marlo, Come!"

✔ **Feed your dogs separately.** Place your Top Dog's bowl down first. If you're having difficulty keeping them separate, station them apart on their Teaching Leads.

✔ **Don't start a toy war.** I know, you want them both to have a toy. But one dog keeps insisting on having both. You give it back to the other dog, and he takes it away. Give-take-give-take. Remember your Top Dog rule. If the Top Dog wants both, Top Dog has both. Period.

✔ **Dog fights — whatever you do, don't yell.** Yelling is perceived as threat barking and actually makes the problem worse as your puppy matures. If you have a dog fight, the best thing to do is walk out of the house and slam the door. No words or discipline; just leave abruptly. It's usually your presence that prompts an argument. You can also try breaking up the fight by dumping a bucket of water on their heads or turning a hose on them momentarily as you separate them quickly.

Once things are calm, review your actions. Were you supporting the Underdog? That's not good. After the fight has settled, isolate the subordinate and praise the Top Dog. I know it sounds cruel, but if the Top Dog feels supported, he won't challenge the other dogs. Additionally, if you catch a fight before it begins, shame the Underdog and reward your Top Dog with attention. I know it feels unnatural, but remember that your dogs aren't human, and they don't think you are either. If the situation repeats itself, call in a professional.

Getting Other Pets

Perhaps you want to add another species to your home. A bird, cat, reptile, rabbit, or rodent can be a real eye-opener, especially for your young dog, who may see the little addition as more of a snack than a pal.

Extra hints for two-puppy households

Left alone 24 hours a day, your puppies will form a strong bond to each other, which is good, but they also will be less attached to you, which is bad. To prevent this, separate them at least twice a day. If possible, let them sleep in separate bedrooms.

Use individual crates for housebreaking, chewing, or sleeping difficulties.

✔ Set up the cage or confinement system ahead of time. Let your puppy get accustomed to the smell of fresh bedding. Have someone play with/walk your pup while you settle your new pet.

✔ Your puppy will probably notice the smell immediately. Keeping him with you on his Teaching Lead lets him investigate the cage (remember, dogs "see" with their noses, so sniffing is a must).

✔ Discourage barking with a leash snap and the No command or by spraying the area in front of your dog's nose with Binaca mouth spray.

✔ Whatever you do, don't yell. Yelling is perceived as barking and only heightens your pup's awareness, tension, and resolve.

✔ If you're welcoming a kitten or other baby creature, keep the animals separated (by rooms or heights) until the little animal is big enough to escape and can defend itself from being snapped at or stepped on.

Introducing your new puppy to resident pets

When introducing your new puppy, don't expect your other pets to jump for joy. Talk about a corporate take-over. Puppies are chaotic, loud, persistent, annoying. Life before was predictable and calm in comparison. Don't be surprised if you catch your cat giving you the evil eye from on top of the cabinets and find your hamsters hiding in their Habitrail. Although the transition from foe to friend may take some time, here are some basics to keep in mind:

✔ Keep your new puppy in a confined area. If this area (the kitchen, for example) has been the feeding area for your other pet, think ahead. A week before your puppy comes home, change the feeding area to a quieter environment. (Do this for litter boxes and caged pets, as well: Move them well ahead of time to ensure a positive association.)

✔ Introduce the smell of the resident pet to your puppy first. Then take a blanket from the pup and place it near your resident pet.

✔ If you're introducing a cat, place the puppy in an enclosed room or crate (with a special chew for diversion) and let your cat wander around the room at its own will. Do not try to influence or interfere in your cat's reaction; if your puppy starts acting wild, however, step in to calm him.

When your cat is accustomed to the puppy's presence (it may take a while, like a week. . . .), place your puppy on a light drag lead and bring the two together in a small room. Hold your puppy's lead if he acts up and divert him with a toy.

Don't be too surprised if your cat growls or bats at the puppy. Corrections only make matters worse. Your cat is defining her space; a necessary boundary for co-existence.

✔ If the resident pet is caged, bring your puppy into its room after a meal and playtime. This restful state calms the scenario. Bring in your puppy's favorite mat and chew toy and sit near the cage, petting your puppy calmly. Repeat this exercise often.

When I was a kid, I got a French lop-eared bunny. Shadow, the bunny, grew to be a whopping 24 pounds. Unfortunately, another favorite pet, Shawbee, my Siberian Husky/Shepherd mix, decided that was big enough. The inevitable happened; she ate Shadow. It was horrible. Moral? If your dog won't give up his snack vigil, take your new pet back.

Chapter 27

Traveling with Your Puppy

- -

In This Chapter

▶ Flying the (sometimes not-so-friendly) skies

▶ Taking your pup on a train

▶ Road trip! Traveling by car

▶ Boating with Fido

- -

*E*verybody likes a vacation. The most depressing part, however, is parting with your beloved pal. His soulful stare can stay with you for hours. Why not take your puppy along? Having your pet with you can be great fun, but there are also some risks. To help you make your own decision, I go over some hard and fast traveling rules in this chapter.

Taking Your Puppy on a Plane

I myself am leery of planes, so you can imagine how neurotic I get thinking of a dog in the belly of one of those steel babies. Personally, I'd avoid taking any pet on a plane if I didn't have to. Even if only 1 dog in 90 dies, I don't want to be the one holding the empty leash. Sometimes air travel is unavoidable, however, so here are some rules that can make the plane trip go more smoothly.

Taking some preflight measures

Follow this preflight advice to make your trip as smooth as possible:

✔ The cargo areas where pets are held before and after the flight are neither heated nor cooled. Thus, you want to minimize the amount of time your puppy spends in hold. Stay with him until just before flight and pick him up directly after. Avoid all temperature extremes.

✔ Make your puppy's reservation when you make your own. Planes only accept so many four-legged passengers.

TIP

> ✔ Book a direct flight in a large plane.
>
> If you can't fly direct, book a flight with a long enough layover to reunite with your puppy. Take him out for a stretch, drink, bathroom break, and hug.
>
> ✔ If you're heading for warmer climates, book a night or early morning flight. Heat is often the culprit in airline tragedies.
>
> ✔ If you're planning to take your puppy with you overseas, check ahead of time to see what quarantine rules apply.
>
> ✔ Health certificates and proof of vaccination are required by airlines. Get them from your veterinarian and forward a copy to the airline immediately. Carry one with you the day of the flight.

Getting your puppy set to go

Follow this advice to make sure your puppy is as comfortable as possible:

> ✔ Purchase a sturdy USDA-approved travel kennel custom-fit to your puppy's size. Make sure the kennel is only large enough for your puppy to stand up and turn around in.
>
> ✔ Get your puppy comfortable with his kennel quarters a few days before departure.
>
> ✔ If you have a teenie-weenie puppy or dog who can come on board, buy a crate that fits under the seat.
>
> ✔ Write "LIVE ANIMAL" in one-inch letters on top of the crate and on each side. Tape on huge arrows to indicate the crate's upright position.
>
> ✔ On the top of the crate, in ½-inch letters, write the flight's destination, including the name, address, and phone number of the person or place you're visiting.
>
> ✔ Remove all training collars. Your pup should wear a well-fitting buckle collar with identification tags.
>
> ✔ Prep the crate for take-off with light bedding and paper (taped down) in one end to absorb mistakes. Affix two bowls inside the crate. Freeze water in one so your puppy can have a beverage while in flight.
>
> ✔ If the flight is longer than 12 hours, tape a bag of food to the outside of the crate with feeding instructions.
>
> ✔ Don't feed your puppy within six hours of the trip.
>
> ✔ The last thing you should do before loading your puppy? Let him go to the bathroom.
>
> ✔ Never padlock your crate. You don't want your pet trapped in case of an emergency.

Upon arrival, go immediately to the baggage area and insist on seeing your puppy. Kick and fuss if you must. This is another tricky time for your pet, especially if he turns out to be an escape artist. Imagine watching your puppy tearing down the runway trying to herd a leer jet. That's one time "Fido, come!" just isn't going to work.

Wanting to Go by Train? Sorry

Though I looked high and low, I couldn't find a rail service that was dog friendly. Of course, they all allow service dogs on board. My local metro north allows small well-mannered dogs on off-peak hours. Pretty limiting.

Going by Car

I've never owned a puppy or dog who didn't love a road trip. I know some dogs have less than enjoyable experiences, but even they can be transformed with some patient car conditioning (see Chapter 18 for details). Cars can be a dangerous place for dogs, however, so you must take certain precautions:

- ✔ Don't leave your puppy in the car on a warm day. Even with the windows down, your car will bake like an oven, leaving your puppy uncomfortable or dead. Nothing is worth that.

  Have an extra set of keys in the glove compartment in case of an emergency. If you must leave your puppy, keep the engine running with the air conditioning on full-blast and lock the door.

- ✔ Got a pick-up truck? Let your puppy ride up in the cab. On a leash or off, the flat bed is no place for a dog.

- ✔ Keep the windows cracked but not wide open. Some people think letting a dog hang his head out the window is cool. Actually, it's dangerous. Dogs can get hurled from the car in an accident or have debris fly into their eyes, causing permanent damage.

- ✔ Here's another crazy habit: the dog who rides in the driver's seat. Give me a break. Not only are the dog and the driver in jeopardy, but so is everyone passing them on the street. You can't drive and bond simultaneously.

Rules for the road

Your puppy must have structure in the car. If he doesn't, he'll think he owns it, which can lead to a cascade of problems, the least of which is barking at everything that moves. You have some options:

✔ **Put your pup in a crate during road trips.** Crates are cumbersome and can be a little big, but they keep your puppy still while you drive. Buy a strong, wire mesh type (for good air circulation) sized for your puppy's weight and breed. Line the bottom with something your puppy can sink his paws into.

✔ **Put up a barrier.** Barriers enclose your puppy in the back compartment of a wagon or sport utility vehicle. Aesthetically, they're not too appealing and the cheaper models collapse easily, but a good one can effectively keep your puppy safe and still.

✔ **Use a harness.** Harness gadgets secure around your puppy's body and keep him buckled in. The only drawback is that they're tough to put on, and dogs are often less than thrilled.

✔ **Use the Seat Belt Safety Lead (SBSL).** This lead, which I invented for myself out of necessity and that others have found useful, hooks into a seat belt permanently and attaches to your puppy's buckle collar while you drive. The SBSL is handy, it takes seconds to attach, and it keeps your puppy safe while you take care of the driving.

Guidelines for long trips

Are you planning a long journey? Puppies make excellent traveling companions. Following are some guidelines to ensure that you both get there safe and sound:

✔ Check your pup's buckle collar to ensure that all identification tags have been updated. If you're planning an extended stay, make a temporary tag with your temporary stats.

✔ Keep your pup's diet and feeding times consistent. A change can upset her system — one discomfort that you can easily avoid.

✔ Avoid traveling in extreme heat unless you have a good air-conditioning system. Plan to travel at night or early in the morning.

✔ Never leave your puppy unattended in an unlocked car. If the weather's extreme (either hot or freezing), make an extra set of keys so you can leave the climate control on while you lock the car and take care of your business.

✔ Keep your puppy on a leash at *every* pit stop.

✔ Give your puppy water and exercise at every rest area. Feed him before you walk him. Allow your puppy half an hour to digest.

✔ If you're planning a hotel stay, ask about the hotel's "welcome dog" policy when you make your reservations.

If you're searching for places that accept pets, you have a few resources. Many books are dedicated to just that subject. Check the pet section of your local bookstore. Guidebooks offered through AAA and Mobil Oil also list accommodations that welcome pets.

✔ Use your Teaching Lead to help your puppy adjust to his new surroundings. Station him at night on a familiar blanket with a trusty ol' bone.

Taking Your Puppy Boating

If your puppy loves the water, perhaps you should take him boating. No regulations exist, so you have to use good old-fashioned common sense:

✔ To get your dog accustomed to the boat, take him on board for short increments when you're docked. Give him his own special spot with comfortable bedding and toys.

✔ No beast, four-legged or two, can last 15 minutes in frigid waters. Do not take your dog in unstable crafts.

✔ If you're wearing a life vest, your puppy should be also. You can buy a lifejacket for your puppy in any pet specialty store. Make sure it fits right.

✔ Don't forget about dehydration. If it's hot and sunny, provide your puppy with a bucket of water from which to sip. Have fun and think safe.

Keep in mind that certain breeds, the breeds with pushed-in faces especially (Bulldog, Pug, and so on), don't swim well. If you're planning a swim, leave them out of boating situations.

Part VIII
The Part of Tens

The 5th Wave   By Rich Tennant

"I don't think teaching the puppy how to help you cheat at cards was the training and bonding experience the Vet had in mind."

In this part . . .

Top Ten lists. You can't get through a day without seeing one somewhere — whether it's on TV, at the grocery store check-out lane, or in the morning paper.

In this part, I give you my own Top Ten lists, canine-style: ten of my favorite games and ten crowd-pleasing tricks. *Enjoy.*

Chapter 28

Ten Fun Games

● ●

*P*uppies learn best through playing. How you play together, especially in those first few months, influences your relationship more than my mere words could convey. This chapter presents ten (plus a bunch) games for you to play with your puppy. Read them over, try them out, eliminate what doesn't work, and invent your own. Remember: The games you play with your pup should encourage cooperation and focus.

A Puppy's World

A puppy who plays by tugging learns to challenge.

A puppy who wrestles for freedom learns caution with people.

A puppy who hears yelling learns to tune people out.

A puppy who's disciplined by hand learns to fear hands.

A puppy who is unscheduled senses chaos.

A puppy who is pushed aside grows manic in its longing for love.

Yet a puppy who is encouraged grows confident.

A puppy who exchanges toys learns respect.

A puppy who is given exercise learns self control.

A puppy that's taught routines learns to trust.

A puppy who delights in his name enjoys togetherness.

A puppy who is forgiven learns tolerance.

And a puppy who is adored knows the gift of shared love.

—Sarah Hodgson

Cooperative Games

The games in this section are great for encouraging cooperation and focus, as well as releasing energy.

Soda Bottle Soccer

This game encourages your dog to follow you and to fetch.

Players: Any number of people and a dog of any age.

To play: Get several plastic bottles (with the cap and label removed). Place a few on the floor. Let your dog check the bottles out. When he's comfortable, start kicking. No matter how many bottles you have, your dog will want the one you've got. Kick it to him *only* if he's standing calmly (avoid challenging your dog for one bottle; it encourages confrontational play). Then go off and play with another. And so on, and so on, and so on. . . .

Rules: Play with your feet, not your hands (it's soccer, after all). Always kick the bottle your dog's *not* chasing.

The Two-Toy Toss

This game helps your dog focus on what you have, not the other way around, and reinforces the Come and Fetch commands, as well as the Show Me Your Treasure command.

Players: One dog – one person team; good for pups over ten weeks, although younger pups may show interest for a couple of tosses.

To play: Gather two or more toys or balls. Toss one toy; when your puppy races to get it, cheer her on. As she turns to you, say "Good Dog" and then produce a different toy and start playing with it. When she wants the toy you have (and she will) make sure she sits politely before you toss it.

Rule: Never chase or wrestle a toy out of your dog's mouth.

The Squeak Toy Shuffle

This game encourages following skills and can be played inside or out. This one is a great diversion for ankle happy nippers.

Players: One person with one dog; good for pups under 12 weeks.

To play: Tie a squeak or rope toy onto a 4-foot leash or line and attach the other end of the line to your shoe lace or ankle. Walk around, doing whatever you do. Puppies love to wrestle moving objects: Better the toy than you.

Rule: Don't move too quickly or snap the object out of your puppy's mouth.

Fishing for Fido

Use this game to provide an outlet for chasing instincts and divert your puppy from attacking your legs. Great for morning foot-traffic and outside runs.

Players: Good for puppies under 12 weeks and their people.

To play: Tie a squeak toy onto a 2–5-foot string and attach the other end of the string on a rod (anything can pass for a rod: a stick, an umbrella, etc.). Bounce the toy in front of your puppy.

Rules: Let your pup grab the toy often to keep her interested. Avoid tug of war. If your puppy insists on tugging, look away until she gets bored; then resume the animation.

The Extended Rope Toss

A great game for energy release. The Extended Rope Toss also helps to relieve predatory energy (better to chase a bottle in a field than a biker on a busy street).

Players: One person, one dog of any age.

To play: Tie an empty soda bottle or favorite toy onto a 20–30-foot rope. In a yard or field, swing the ball around. If there's tall grass, use it as cover.

The Treat Cup Name Game

This game encourages positive association to the Come command while teaching name identification.

Players: Start with two people; then you can add more. Any age dog can play.

To play: Fill ⅓ of a plastic cup with Cheerios or crumbled dog biscuits. Shake the cup until your dog associates the sound with a reward. Stand 6 feet from a friend and, using the other person's name (John, for example), tell your dog to "Find John!" as you point to John. When John hears his name, he shakes the cup and calls out your dog's name. When the dog's at John's side, John can send him back to you.

Rules: As your dog gets better, increase your distance, eventually moving to different rooms and playing outside. Avoid correcting your dog if she loses interest; limiting game time ensures fun.

Hide and Seek

Good finding skills lead to good walking and coming skills. You can play this game as an off-shoot of the Name Game or just use your dog's name to encourage the find.

Players: One or more persons with a dog older than 14 weeks.

To play: Leave your dog with one person or sitting quietly in a room (if playing alone). Hide (start easy) and shake your treat cup as you call out your dog's name. Praise wildly as your dog gets warmer; quiet down when she's off in the wrong direction.

Rule: Don't make finding you too difficult. If your dog takes more than 30 seconds to find you, you're hiding too well. Quick and easy finds build a dog's determination.

Give (or Drop)

Once you make Give less of a demand and more of a direction, your dog will be more likely to share her treasures.

Players: This skill can be taught from the start; it's good for puppies of all ages.

To play: When your dog is chewing on something (whether appropriate or not) approach her with a treat cup (or just a treat from your pocket) and say "Give" as you put the treat in her mouth. (If she's chewing on a dog toy, don't take it away from her.) After you say "Give" and offer the treat, go away calmly. If your dog runs off in fun, practice in a small bathroom. Leave a leash on her around the house to enable a calm catch.

Rule: If your dog is growling or clamping the object too tightly, call a professional. Aggression is no joke.

Take

If your dog loves to carry things in her mouth, you have all you need to teach this game.

Players: Practice this game one on one with a puppy who's at least 14 weeks.

To play: Start with a toy or ball and go into a small room or hallway. Wave the object in front of your pup, tempting her for a few seconds before instructing "Take." Cheer when she takes the object, letting her hold onto it for varying amounts of time. Encourage "Give" (using a treat or other toy if necessary).

Rule: Repeat this sequence no more than three times. Always quit while you're ahead.

The Four-Footed Fax

This game encourages interaction and responsibility.

Players: Two people (a sender and a receiver) and a dog over six months old, who's mastered the preceding three games.

To play: Ask your friend (John, for example) to stand 10 feet across the room. Encourage your dog to "Take" a folded newspaper and send her to John, saying "Take it to John!" Have John kneel down and call to your dog. When your dog trots over, John rewards her with a treat.

If your dog won't carry the object all the way, have John stand right next to you and slowly inch back. With encouragement and love, you dog will become everyone's favorite fax machine.

Rule: Don't discipline your dog if she won't cooperate. This game takes a lot of concentration.

Obedience Games

Who says commands can't be fun? Although you have to be mindful of your tone, mixing lessons into game time can liven both activities.

Sit, Wait, Down, or Come

This game is a fun way to work on challenging commands like Sit, Wait, Down, or Come.

Players: The person who has trained the puppy. The puppy must be older than 12 weeks and have mastered the command that's introduced.

To play: Pick one command. Race around the room or yard with your dog's favorite toy, stopping periodically to give the chosen command as you lead her into place with the toy. When your dog cooperates, let her have the toy. Get that toy back with a treat by using the Give command, or grab another toy and repeat this sequence five times.

Rules: Don't repeat your commands. If your dog doesn't listen, help her into position before releasing the toy. She'll catch on soon enough.

Musical Chairs

This game is as much for people as it is for puppies. The puppies have to concentrate on the Stay command around high-level distractions. The people have to stay cool and let go of that competitive edge, or their pup won't be able to stand the pressure.

Players: Any dog who has perfected the Stay command, with at least four dog-person teams, plus an extra person to work the music.

To play: Gather some chairs and a radio/stereo and create a circle. In the center of the circle, place one less chair than the number of people-dog teams playing. When the music starts, all teams heel around the outer circle. When the music stops, the dogs must stay as the people move to the center to assume a chair. If a dog breaks the stay, the owner must give up the chair. The person left out when the music stops is out and must remove a chair from the center. Continue until it's down to two teams and one chair — now the heat is on.

Rules: Avoid getting hyped — your dog won't be able to sit still. Line your dog up toward the middle, before instructing "Stay."

Seasonal Fun

No matter where you live, you can take advantage of the great outdoors to interact and bond with your puppy. The follow activities are some of my favorites and work great with puppies of all ages. Add to my list.

Winter (for snowbound regions)

Tunneling: Dogs love to dig; what better medium than a pile of snow? Put your mittens on and go tunneling with your dog.

Top of the Hill: After a good storm, the snow piles up. Find a drift or shoveled snow hill and race up it with your dog.

Catch the Snowball: If your dog loves to chase and catch, nothing could be cuter than playing with snow.

Spring

The Great Seed Chase: Springtime bursts with new life. To help spread it around, while amusing your dog, sit on the ground as you pull apart or blow away the seed fragments of various plant life.

Mud-Mash: April showers may bring the flowers, but if your dog's a digger, it also brings mud. Rather than getting angry at the holes in the yard, designate a time and a place for digging and take part in the fun. On go the gloves, out with the shovel, and bring some bones to bury.

Morning Dew and the Leaf Tickle: Dogs, like people, enjoy sensations. A dew-drizzled blade of grass and a budding leaf dragged across her nose are just two moments you can share.

Summer

Splash and Fun: Who says baby pools are just for human babies?

The Sprinkler Sashe: If you're a gardener, you're likely to spend a fair amount of time with the hose. While watering your flowers or lawn, you can cool off by playing some obedience games through the sprinkler. Although your dog may resist initially, the refreshing water will win her over.

The Sun Bake: This game is good for either inside or out. Find that sun spot and stretch out with your dog. Let every muscle relax, stroke your dog's ears or the warmth of her back. Ah . . . the sun can be so soothing.

Fall

The Leaf-Pile Leap: Find a pile of leaves and jump right in.

Hide behind the Leaf Bag: If your dog knows Hide and Seek, all the better. Use your own bags or ones you find in the neighborhood. Hide behind a bag when your dog's not looking and call out his name. If your dog can't find you, rustle the bag.

Pile the Sticks: If you've got a fireplace, you can actually utilize this game; otherwise, just pile some sticks on a walk. Collect sticks or carry in logs with your dog. Use commands like Carry and Give and thank your dog for helping.

Chapter 29

Ten Crowd-Pleasing Tricks

T ricks are a challenge to learn, but once learned, they're a real delight. Training doesn't have to be all work, work, work and structure, structure, structure. Once your dog knows the basic commands, covered in the Part IV, you can have some fun by teaching him tricks that will bring a smile to every face. Teaching a trick or two spices up the normal routine. This chapter gives you ten (give or take) tricks that are nonessential but fun. And you don't need to teach your puppy all the tricks in this chapter — just those your pup picks up easily. For example, if your dog's paw expressive, he'll definitely get into the Paw or Wave trick.

Never practice tricks during lesson time. Otherwise, you turn serious work into a game.

Cute Tricks That Come from Natural Acts

There are two types of tricks: ones that your dog does naturally in the course of the day, such as Bow or Wag Your Tail, and others that you direct. This section focuses on the natural kind. Encourage your young puppy to learn the words for natural acts.

Wag Your Tail

This trick is so simple and fun, you'll love teaching it. Say any phrase in a happy, delighted tone and watch your dog's tail come to life. The trick comes out of your puppy learning to wag his or her tail on command.

Here are some great phrases to use:

- Are you happy today?
- Who's the best dog in the world?
- If you're happy and you know it, wag your tail!

Kisses

If you're not into dog kisses, read no further. Your puppy picks up this trick by association: Anytime your puppy licks, you say "Kisses" and praise him calmly (too much excitement will turn a loving kiss into a playful nip).

Next, ask some friends (and kids) to help out. Rub their hands with a frozen stick of butter and say "Kisses" as you direct your puppy toward their hands. A hand lick definitely trumps a greeting jump or inappropriate sniffing.

Break Dance

If your puppy is a wiggle worm with a perpetual back itch, try this clever trick:

1. **When your dog starts to roll on his back, say "Break dance!"**

   Rolling around, stomach up, is a common ploy dogs use to escape lessons, but it can be an awfully cute trick, too.

2. **Bend over and scratch his belly as you praise him.**

Repeat this process again and again until you're able to command him to dance on cue. This trick is a real crowd-pleaser.

Bow

Does your puppy love a good stretch? Betcha didn't know you could turn this one into a trick:

1. **As your dog's stretching, bow toward him and say "Bow!"**
2. **Praise your dog like he just invented the dog biscuit.**

Repeat this each time he stretches. Soon you'll have him bowing on cue.

Cool Tricks for 'Em to Learn

Asking for a dog's paw is the most requested trick of all time, but did you know there's more to the trick than meets the eye? Once your dog has mastered Paw, you can encourage other tricks all from the same behavior. You can also teach tricks to pups who love to jump, pups who love to nudge you for attention, and so much more. So check out this section for some cool fun.

Paw, High-Five, or Wave

Is your puppy paw expressive? Does he always slap you for a pat while you're trying to read the paper or talk on the phone? You need to redirect his habits. What better way than a good old-fashioned parlor trick?

A dog can learn many tricks from one action. With pawing, for example, you can teach your dog to shake your hand, wave a big hello, or give you a high-five.

Paw

Teaching your puppy Paw is easy and fun. Start from a sitting position and follow these steps:

1. **Say "Paw" or "Shake" as you extend your hand in front of your puppy.**

2. **If he looks puzzled, press his shoulder muscle with your other hand.**

3. **Take his paw the instant he lifts it off the ground and praise him.**

   Soon he'll be reaching out for you.

Wave

All my dogs have mastered the Wave. It's a real charmer, especially for kids.

1. **Sit your puppy. Hold a treat inches from his nose and say "Wave" as you wave your hand in front of him.**

2. **Praise and treat him the instant he lifts his paw.**

3. **Encourage more enthusiastic waving as he catches on.**

High-Five

Now your dog's going to learn the high-five. Too cool. Follow these steps:

1. **Do two Paw exercises. Be enthusiastic.**

2. **Hold your hand up and out for the high-five. Say "Paw, high-five!"**

3. **Lower your hand if your dog makes an attempt.**

   Soon, he'll be bringing that paw up with gusto.

Over and Through the Hoop

Does your puppy love to jump? Believe it or not, there are appropriate outlets for that behavior. My Border Collie cross, Shayna May, epitomizes this activity. In fact, the first trick I ever taught her was Over and its many variations.

Over

Create your first jump out of a broom and two rolls of toilet paper. A low jump builds your pup's confidence and looks less scary.

Puppies younger than a year should not jump at heights above their elbows — too much development going on under the skin. Forcing high jumps could cause serious developmental damage.

1. **Place your puppy on lead for control.**

2. **Let him sniff the jump and show him a couple of times how you jump the obstacle.**

   Discourage any test chewing with a leash tug.

3. **Give your puppy at least five strides of runway space and say "Over" as you trot toward the jump; jump ahead of your puppy and cheer him for following you.**

   If your puppy refuses, stay calm. Don't pull him over. Walk over the jump several times while your dog watches; then try to walk over it together. Although it may take a few goes, your dog will soon overcome his fear and be more excited for succeeding.

4. **Once your dog takes the jump with pride, put him on a short lead. Drop the lead just before the jump and let your dog take it alone.**

   Bravo.

5. **Slowly fade off your approaching run but keep saying "Over" as you point to the jump.**

This can also be a game for the kids. Jumps placed in thresholds encourage jumping to fetch toys and balls. The kids can set up a course, inside or out, and jump with the dog.

Through the Hoop

Purchase a hula hoop at a local variety store and then follow these steps:

1. **Set up your original jumping pole across a threshold or between two pieces of furniture.**

   Put your dog on a short lead and let her sniff the hoop as you position it on the floor in the center of the jump.

2. **Ask someone to hold the hoop or prop it up securely.**

3. **Instruct your puppy "Over" as you run toward the hoop, letting go of the lead as you get close.**

4. **After your dog cooperates, combine the Through and Over commands as you start for the jump, like this: "Over-Through."**

5. **Hold the hoop higher so that it is even with the height of the jump and command "Over-Through."**

   Your dog might hesitate because the hoop looks, well, like a hoop, not like a level jump. If this happens, walk over to the hoop slowly and allow her to walk through it a couple of times; use food to encourage her.

   After she successfully completes Step 5, you're ready for the solo hoop.

6. **Prop the hoop at floor level, encourage "Through" as you trot toward the hoop, and allow your dog to go through alone.**

   Praise her and encourage her back through by running backward as you cheer.

7. **Gradually raise the level of the hoop.**

If you want to be really clever (and you have a puppy that won't grow too big!), you can practice Through the Hoop with your encircled arms. Repeat the preceding steps with the assistance of a close friend, this time using your arms in place of the hula.

Chase Your Tail or Wipe Your Feet

Take a biscuit, hold it level with your dog's nose, and command "Chase your Tail" or "Wipe your Feet" as you *slowly* rotate the treat around her body. I said *slowly.* Start slow — that's an order!

Reward half spins initially, then full spins, then two, three, four, and so on. Accentuate your hand signal, and soon you'll be sending your dog spinning on silent cues, no words needed.

When your dog comes in with muddy paws, you point to the foot mat and instruct your dog to wipe his own paws. What a classic.

Head Down

Is your dog a head knocker? Does he always nudge your arm for attention, especially when you're trying to enjoy your morning coffee? Believe it or not, you can redirect this misguided behavior. Each time your dog butts his head against you for attention, say "Head Down" and encourage him to lay his head in your lap (holding his head gently if you must).

Although he may resist in the beginning, be diligent. Pet your dog when his head rests in your lap. Soon he'll have a new and more polite way of demanding your attention, and you'll be able to enjoy your morning coffee again.

Ask Nicely

Good balance is a requirement for the Ask Nicely trick. You're asking your puppy to tilt back from a sitting position and balance on his hind paws, like the old begging routine. (Unless your dog is a natural, wait until your puppy is 9 months old before you teach this routine. You don't want to put undo pressure on developing muscles and tissues.)

1. **Break up five favorite treats.**

2. **With your pup in a sitting position, place a treat a few centimeters above his nose.**

3. **Command "Ask Nicely" as you bring the treat back toward his ears.**

   If he tilts back for a split second, treat and praise him. Encourage the slightest effort; increase your expectations slowly.

If your dog's trying but can't seem to balance himself, stand behind him with your heels together near his tail. Draw the treat back and catch his chest, leaning his body against your legs. Repeat the command, teaching him how to balance as you hold and treat him. Then praise him.

For complicated tricks like this one, praise each step toward the goal. If at first your puppy tries to lean back, praise that. Once leaning back is a snap, praise the next step your dog attempts, like lifting the paws off the ground.

Roll Over

Everybody loves the Roll Over routine. Some puppies are into it; others would rather hibernate in Alaska. Does your dog roll over on his own? Does he shift from side to side with ease? If so, he'll be into this trick. If not, find another trick to impress your friends.

1. **Get a handful of treats and encourage your puppy into a Down position.**

2. **Scratch him until he rolls to one side.**

3. **Take the treat and circle it from your dog's nose to the floor.**

4. **Say "Roll Over" as you circle the treat around his nose toward his chest.**

   It's hard to visualize, I know, but imagine a string tied from the treat to your puppy's nose; you're trying to pull his body over.

5. **If he seems to lean into it, praise him and flip his paws over.**

   Praise him wildly and encourage him to jump up.

Chill, Nap Time, or Bang

I've always thought the trick Play Dead was a little depressing. It is clever, though, so I simply switch the command, depending on the situation. This trick's easy if you have a calm puppy, and it's good practice for high-energy pups:

1. Command "Down." Encourage your puppy to rest on one side.

2. Kneel next to your pup but don't look at him; then tap the floor near his head and say "Nap Time," "Chill," or "Bang."

3. Gently apply pressure to his shoulder and help him rest his head on the floor.

4. Keep his head in place by stroking it gently while commanding "Stay."

Once your pup cooperates, take your hand off his head slowly. Eventually, stand up. Do everything gradually. Remind him "Nap Time, Stay" as needed. Soon you'll be able to drop the Stay.

Index

• Z •

Sarah
Teaches Dogs, Trains People

Sarah's PuppyPerfect® Video
Learn better by watching? PuppyPerfect is a great way to get the whole family involved.

Patented Teaching Lead

Let Sarah's methods work for you! Her Teaching Lead brings it all together. It's a humane and interactive way to train your dog. The **Teaching Lead Extension** is also available. It adds an additional six inches to your Teaching Lead, for dogs and people of all sizes.

Seat Belt Safety Lead
This easy-to-secure lead ensures your dog's safety in the car. It also doubles nicely as a short leash for quick control around the house.

- -

ORDER NOW!

Please visit and order on line at **www.dogperfect.com** or send check, money order, or credit card information to: **Simply Sarah Inc., P.O. Box 420, Bedford Village, NY, 10506.**

Sarah's Puppy Video . . . .$ 24.95
Sarah's Training Leash 19.95
The Seat Belt Safety Lead 9.95
SAVE! Order All Three for only 49.95
Lead Extension 5.00
Subtotal . . . .$____
Please Add:
    Shipping and Handling . . . .$ 4.00
    6.75% New York Sales Tax . . . .$____

My Check/Money Order for $____ is enclosed.
I would like to pay by credit card.
❑ VISA
❑ MASTERCARD
Name on Card: _____
Card #: _____
Expiration Date: _____

Your Name: _____

Your Dog's Name & Breed _____

Address: _____

City:_____ State: _____ Zip Code: _____

Email Address:_____

Visit Sarah's informative website at www.dogperfect.com

FOR DUMMIES
BOOK REGISTRATION

Register This Book and Win!

We want to hear from you!

Visit **dummies.com** to register this book and tell us how you liked it!

- Get entered in our monthly prize giveaway.

- Give us feedback about this book — tell us what you like best, what you like least, or maybe what you'd like to ask the author and us to change!

- Let us know any other *For Dummies* topics that interest you.

Your feedback helps us determine what books to publish, tells us what coverage to add as we revise our books, and lets us know whether we're meeting your needs as a *For Dummies* reader. You're our most valuable resource, and what you have to say is important to us!

Not on the Web yet? It's easy to get started with *Dummies 101®: The Internet For Windows® 98* or *The Internet For Dummies®* at local retailers everywhere.

Or let us know what you think by sending us a letter at the following address:

For Dummies Book Registration
Dummies Press
10475 Crosspoint Blvd.
Indianapolis, IN 46256

™

BESTSELLING BOOK SERIES